THE SOUND OF SUNDAYS

An Autobiography

ZUCCHERO FORNACIARI

This translated edition published in the United Kingdom in 2017 by Rocket 88, an imprint of Essential Works Limited.

First published in the Italian language, 2011 by Mondadori

This edition © Zucchero Fornaciari, 2017

Translation by John Rugman, 2016

Cover image © Gianluigi Di Napoli/Luzphoto

ISBN, paperback: 9781910978146

ISBN, hardback: 9781910978153

10 9 8 7 6 5 4 3 2 1

rocket88books.com

This book is dedicated to my father, Giuseppe 'Pino;' my mother, Rina; my grandfather, Roberto 'Cannella;' my grandmother, Diamante; my uncle, Enzo 'Guerrino;' and my aunt, Enrica.

And to Marco Figlié.

And to my children. Alice, Irene, and Blue.

To Angela and Francesca.

In memory of Lucia Lazzini Menconi.

The Dark Evil

AS I DID EVERY TIME I WROTE A SONG, I TOOK IT TO HER. SHE WOULD listen and her verdict was always the same: it sucks. I always felt like shit. I was in love.

That night in Forte dei Marmi there had been a storm, pouring rain. I had gone down to the coast from Avenza, near Carrara, where I did my songwriting in my studio at my old house. Black clouds. At home, our home—our girls' home. It wasn't only the sea that was raging. I saw her stiffen up, mistrustful. The enemy. Locked up in her own world. "Fuck you." A conflict that had lasted a lifetime. Like that crazy afternoon when I followed her and she was driving down the wrong side of the road along the coastal highway. It wasn't a movie. But no matter how much I longed to quit, I couldn't. I kept begging myself to leave her, yet I kept living with her and coming back to her. This rift, this conflict between what I wanted and what I did, seemed to be the essence of my life. The dark side of my relationship with Angela. She was my wife. Now my ex-wife. I worked tremendously hard to attain the serenity that I have today.

By 1987, after struggling for years, my album *Blue's* hit Number One on the Italian charts. It was the worst time of my life. That depression lasted three years, maybe more. I never figured I'd be talking about depression. I thought it would always remain a secret—all mine, weaknesses and cracks in my soul I would never allow anyone to get near. It was sparked by the separation. I had suffered a lot through all those years of marriage.

Angela, a girl I had loved so very much, was born in Forte dei Marmi and never left the place. We were just kids when we got married; I was 23 and she was 21. We were together for 16 years. She could never come to grips with my work, and I think subconsciously she hoped I would never make it. At the time, I was playing the dance hall circuit and I didn't have a recording contract so I got by as best I could. I knocked about and she probably thought, *let him get his kicks. Sooner or later he'll quit, come back to me, and find himself a job. A real job not as a singer.* I took on debts. For her. Around 450 million lire and not a dime to my name. I was already in the red for 40 million lire and still waiting for the royalties from *Blue's* to come in. I was in the shit. But she never involved herself in my existence, my passions. She was afraid of losing me because there was too much love between us. She always pulled the wagon in the opposite direction. It was as if our feelings—though intense and mutual—could never connect, and belonged to two different lives. It was doubly hard for me. *It's not working, Angela. I can't take it any more.* I left her in the house I'd taken out a mortgage on and split. That was the worst moment, the darkest. I lived in a shack for six months: no kitchen, no bathroom. I used the restroom at the *pension* across the way. Paradoxically, I was at the top of the charts. I was famous. The connection between my past struggles and my present, which should have been easy but instead was menacing, and the future? Everything was topsy-turvy, like a film edited upside down.

On Saturdays I would take my once-a-week shower at the *pension*—just like when I was a kid in the countryside and took a bath in the washtub every Saturday—then go pick up my girls, Alice and Irene. I never knew where to take my daughters because people would stop me on the street, and the girls would get jealous. They couldn't stand it, they pulled me away. *Blue's* was the record with 'Con le Mani,' 'Pippo,' 'Dune Mosse,' 'Bambino Io, Bambino Tu,' 'Non Ti Sopporto Più,' 'Senza Una Donna,' 'Into the Groove,' 'Hey Man,' and 'Solo Una Sana e Consapevole Libidine (Salva il Giovane dallo Stress e dall'Azione Cattolica).' They were all hits. I was the phenomenon of the year. I was a disaster. I didn't hire a babysitter or maid, because in those days (1987) that was inconceivable, at least in the farmer's mindset of the Fornaciari family—so there was no nanny to help me with my daughters and do the chores.

I even tried going back to my parents' place in Roncocesi, near Reggio Emilia, but my father didn't understand that I was living a totally different lifestyle. At seven in the morning, he'd start yelling, in dialect, *"Sa fèt a let?"* ("What are you doing in bed?") He wanted me to go out and help him in the fields. It took time, I had to take care of myself. I was on medication—Prozac—and a lot of wonderful things were happening to me that I just couldn't enjoy. All that time I felt like a stranger to myself, aching with intense pain, a dark evil.

Even by 1992, when Brian May called to invite me to sing at Wembley Stadium with Queen for the Freddie Mercury Tribute Concert, I still felt awful. I remember hanging out in the dressing rooms with people like David Bowie, Elton John, George Michael, and I was anything but psyched. I was shitting bricks. I had a panic attack. Cold sweats. My head split in two, torn between wanting to run away and doing my duty. *Let me out of here.* I must have looked like an idiot, but I was paralyzed with fear. I thought, *OK, now I'm going to die. So I'm about to die, who cares what people think!* More fear. My body was no longer mine. It didn't obey my commands. Would I be able to make it move? I just wanted to get out of there; I felt as if I was about to be put in front of a firing squad. Naked. Helpless. Stiff. Immobile. Suspended in midair. I walked onstage. The stage has a magnetic force that attracts you. Contrasting energies. I've spent a lifetime absorbing the one that gives me strength, and clashing with the other, struggling to defeat it. It consumes you. According to the set list, someone was supposed to bring me my acoustic guitar and I was supposed to start playing, then Queen would join in with me. But no one was bringing me that damned guitar. I was standing in front of 80,000 people, and being broadcast around the world via satellite, and I didn't know what to do. I was overwhelmed with anxiety, terrified. Out of the corner of my eye I saw Brian May backstage. He figured out the problem, gave me a sign,and started playing his electric guitar. It all turned out great. My fingers obeyed the commands and hit the strings, my voice boomed. Being onstage with Queen was electrifying. I played great and sang my best, my adrenaline was pumping—though I was still in pitiful shape. I was excited and burnt-out at the same time. But I still wasn't used to being alone with myself.

Solo Una Sana e Consapevole Libidine— Only a Healthy and Self-Aware Sex Drive

"KIDS, SEXUALITY SHOULD BE EXPERIENCED AS SOMETHING HEALTHY, with self-awareness." That's what my geometry teacher used to say, back at the Technical Institute of Chemistry in Carrara. He was one lazy motherfucker. Just like me. I didn't do a fucking thing, and neither did he. He'd walk into the classroom, sit down with his feet on his desk, and read *l'Unità*, the left-wing daily. "You can do whatever you want," he'd say. "Just don't make a racket and don't break my balls."

It was 1968, maybe 1969. Those years imprinted a life philosophy on me. A driving, liberating beat, like sex itself. Infernal sands. Sexual frenzy. When the moment came, I would wind up saving young people from a life of stress and Catholic Action (the Italian association that promotes Catholic values). I was the devil in the holy water. I sang 'Solo Una Sana e Consapevole Libidine' in Rimini, at a meeting of Communion and Liberation, a Catholic youth group. The groupies threw colored bras and transparent underpants at me. I've always seen black. Pussy has no other color. Or religion. But when the song was released in Spain, with the language and context changed, to salvage the pun I had to change the reference to the Spanish Inquisition. Something got lost in translation, though.

I loved the blues. I wanted to listen to that music all the time, like when I was a kid riding the chair-o-plane in front of the church in Roncocesi, enraptured by sound. I wanted to write and play the blues with the same joy. I create music that is black in color, but opens up with Mediterranean melodies. Then comes more sex. The driving, demonic beat of the blues, the ballad's soft and paradisiacal unfolding, the harmonic figure of the orgasm. I longed to play music that was alive, upbeat, bursting with energy, music that was contagious. Sex, sex, sex. You have to believe in what you do and put all the passion you've got into it.

This is my soul. This is my home. It's called Lunigiana Soul: a house in the style of the Emilian countryside, recreated in Tuscany near the Ligurian border. It's crammed with souvenirs from the blues world: New Orleans, Louisiana, and Memphis, Tennessee. My household epic embraces my blues dream. The sound of water. Incessant and reassuring. The blades of the waterwheel. Water lilies on the pond, where the real world becomes a sort of fable. Acres of olive and fruit trees, the vegetable garden, horses, cows, pigs, sheep, barley, oats, rye. Farmers. Women who work. A son—cheerful little guy, and smart, too—I see him running barefoot and carefree through the fields. The gaze in his eyes is deep, wild. His name is Blue. *"Delmo, Delmo! Vin a ca'!"* ("Delmo! Come home!") The sound of the bells at Vespers. The smell of the haylofts. The familiar voice of Grandma Diamante. Her cordial smile, the tenderness it expressed. Her azure gaze—alive, instinctive. The bigger I look, the bigger you'll be. Sunday, Sunday—it's the sound of Sunday.

It all began with my Grandma Diamante, calling me to come home for dinner one September evening. We were poor, but she was queen of that paradise of hardships. Fresh milk came from the barn, steaming like hot soup, with stale bread. A hard life. The rest of the week we worked like mules. It was late that day and she didn't know where I was. She was a good, conscientious woman.

I was in church playing the organ and had lost all sense of time. Transported by the celestial music coming out of those poor organ pipes, along with my little friend Marzia. She listened and watched me as I played. Some "little friend"—I was in love with her. Meanwhile, Grandma Diamante had begun to grow worried. I kept playing, enraptured as I was in Don Tajadela's church. A tiny world across the way from my house, near the local headquarters of the Italian Communist Party and the Roncocesi dairy cooperative. Just outside of Reggio Emilia. Instinctive knowledge of the land, nature, animals. It must be my country-boy background and crazy pursuit of soul-powered Italian music, but a healthy, authentic and laidback life in the country brings out the best in me. Like a glass of good country Lambrusco, the kind that leaves sediment in your mouth. Some people don't understand that because they're not familiar with it—they think it's no good.

I think one of Italian pop music's most mysterious fairy tales is how, coming from the world I did, I ended up playing with the likes of Eric Clapton and Queen, Miles Davis and Luciano Pavarotti. It seems absurd. My first encounter with the musical aristocracy of our times was the greatest—when I first met Miles Davis. He'd heard 'Dune Mosse'—incredible!—and wanted to play it. I went to New York, terrified because he had such an awful reputation. Starting out in the studio with him was tough. He walked in and just said, "Play!"

I began playing the piano, and he said, "What the fuck are you doing?"

I was playing the song in B minor; he said it was in B-flat minor.

"No," I said timidly. "I wrote this song, I know what key it's in."

He wound up being sweet as could be. He placed two fingers on my throat and said, "I like your voice."

Then came Slowhand: Eric Clapton. A real gentleman. He took me on tour with him. And then Sting, a prince of a guy. And all the others. The one who surprised me most on a human level, however, was Bono. After he'd written some lyrics for me, and especially after he heard me singing them, I got a deluge of love texts from him. "What is it that makes my friend Zu so special? His sexy voice, like whisky aged in an oak cask. Then his hair—a lion's mane with the soul of a poet." That portrait was a marvellous gift from my friend Bono Vox. Thanks.

It was then that this fairy tale became something more: a strange combination of the provinces and the world, of craftsmanship and show business, of the wisdom of the singer-songwriter and madcap rhythms, of lyrics in my own language mixed with blues energy. Somewhere between Reggio Emilia and the West, the music factory that would broadcast my voice worldwide was coming to life.

I'm a country boy made good. I appreciate a simple life and true friends. After a slew of events, meetings, adventures, and concerts all over the world, I return to everyday life like any regular working guy: I return to my relationships, to my work. I believe in hard work and following a routine. That's my method. I'm a cog in the machine of music. I enter the studio at 11 a.m. and stay there until dinner time. I'm not the kind of artist who falls under a spell and finds sudden inspiration in the middle of the night. I create songs the way a cabinet-maker builds a piece of furniture—I've got to get my hands inside a musical composition, and then find the words that fit the music, syllables that click with the musical phrasing. I work like a craftsman. Making records and going on tour can be a job like any other, it's the same story repeated over and over. I always tell my managers I'm a donkey who needs his carrot—I need a challenge to keep moving forward. Whenever I have a tour coming up, my panic attacks resurface. I don't sleep at night. I schedule and reschedule the dates, feeling it's impossible we'll ever get the show on the road. Then I slowly convince myself it can be done. I seek out new scenes, places in the world I've never been. But it's also nice to go back to some of the legendary places I've played already, like the Royal Albert Hall in London. The usual fierce battle between my longing to be onstage and my fear of being there. The tour kicks off, the adrenaline kicks in, and I wind up having the time of my life.

Sometimes, I must admit, I have been a bit lost. Or rather, let's say I let myself be overly influenced by outside pressures, especially from abroad. People would say to me, "You've got to duet with this French singer if you want to get airplay on French radio." You've got to do this and that. No one was forcing me, but I want to grow old with grace, musically speaking. What could happen? I sell fewer records? Who cares? The record market is going to pieces, so enough compromises. I only want to do what I feel like doing. That's the way it was with *Chocabeck* (2010). A lot of people I hadn't heard from in years suddenly turned up and said, "That record is really you." People, audiences—they can hear it. And now I'm surrounded with affection like never before.

In the Valley

THERE WAS A BIG STRETCH OF FLAT LAND AND A STREAM, THE theater of so many of my childhood adventures, a brook that seemed like an enormous river to me in the valley. That was where my family lived. In open country, just outside Roncocesi proper. A church, a square, the dairy cooperative, the bar—that was downtown. Grandpa Roberto, known to all as "Cannella" because he was long and lean like the tool his wife used to make pasta. Grandma Diamante, the blue-eyed diamond. My father, Giuseppe, known as "Pino" or "Pipinella." My mother, Rina, who hailed from San Bartolomeo. Uncle Enzo, "Guerrino"—also known as "Guerra," "Minghìn," and "Gagarèla"—with his wife, Enrica, known as "Rica," and Aunt Faustina, known as "Cèpa." All under one roof. There was a fourth son, Piero, who died on returning from the war. I never met him, and knew him only from some framed black-and-white photos at home, dressed as a soldier. He was a very unlucky man. When the war was over and he was on his way home from Calabria, the military truck he was on crashed into a ditch. He hit his head and died at the age of twenty. They said he was strong and handsome. "Uncle Piero was so strong he could hold two spooked horses still with the reins," Grandma Diamante used to say. That's the only memory I have of him, this bit of family mythology, along with his photo on the memorial to the fallen soldiers of Roncocesi, which was right across from our house.

Everyone had a nickname. My Uncle Guerra told me it was a way of desecrating and in some way removing our baptismal names, which were often the names of saints. In Roncocesi (part of the "Red Emilia" region where the Communist Party was strong) almost no one believed in God, apart from the priest and a few sanctimonious souls.

In my family, no one went to church. Though if you blasphemed, you were asking for trouble—and a few slaps. I never heard my father or grandfather take the Lord's name in vain. When they got angry, the most they would say was a euphemism, like "God sings!" Uncle Guerra would come out with "the Madonna whistles," or "God waltzes." My grandfather was very strict about this. But none of us were named after saints to avoid getting baptized. So, the nickname thing was a way of being secular. Cannella, Guerra, Diamante, Zucchero. Not one saint. Only at home did they call me by my first

9

name, Adelmo, which they shortened to Delmo. I guess that first 'A' was too much for them. In town, there were people with nicknames like *"Pela d'esen"* ("Donkey Skin"), *"Sòpa"* ("Soup"), *"Anguèla"* ("Eel"), and *"Bagai loster"* ("Shiny Thing").

The Negri family owned our place. I used to play with their son, who was my age. Grandpa Cannella worked for them as a share-cropper. The entire Fornaciari family worked for them. They were all sharecroppers under a master. We lived near the owners' house. There was a sty with lots of pigs and, later, a cheese shop, and the dairy co-operative where Parmigiano Reggiano was manufactured. Around six p.m. the farmers would haul in their tanks of milk. My father, in his rubber boots and apron, would make the cheese in big copper caul-drons. I grew up in that cheese shop. At night, I would help my father scrub the floors and check the fires under the cauldrons where the curd was made. My dad worked there with my grandfather and his brothers.

We were a beautiful family. A bit off the wall, and very tight. Like the Cervi brothers' family, who were sharecroppers from Campegine, not far from Roncocesi. They were legendary, a myth-ical fixture in our neck of the woods: anti-Fascist, part of the Resistance, the partisans, the war, heroes. My father would tell me their story on winter nights in the warmth of the barn. It was like a fairy tale. Then it was off to bed in a hurry. It was freezing. Fucking cold. But then it was warm and cozy under the covers in a bed heated by the "priest" that my grandmother had so thoughtfully placed there the structure that held up the bedsheets beneath the "nun", a bed-warming pan with hot coals inside. The Cervi brothers' story wasn't the traditional bedtime read. It was a fairy tale without a happy ending. It happened nearby, and was a very big deal around there. I love repeating their names because they evoke my country and its stories. "Tell me the story of Alcide and Genoveffa again, Papa," I would say. The parents and their children. There were seven brothers (Gelindo, Antenore, Aldo, Ferdinando, Agostino, Ovidio, Ettore) and two sisters (Diomira and Rina). Fantastic names, heroes in the wondrous epic of courage and injustice my father used to tell me, all the way to its tragic epilogue.

That was the first story I grew up with. It's a story that belongs to me. Every year I go back to that area. Whenever I need to write, I get in the car and take off for a few days. To think, to focus. "Where are you going?" Francesca asks. "I don't know," I say. Then I drive along the Po and wind up going back there. And every year I visit the Cervi Museum in Gattatico that was once their home. It's filled with historical documentation and testimony on the Resistance, on the culture of country folk. I stay there for an hour, then I hit the road again.

It's a place that conjures up memories and makes me feel at home. On the forty acres of land surrounding the house, they've built a farm and environmental park featuring elements of the native culture, typical of the agricultural landscape on the Padana Plains. In the film version of the story, *The Seven Cervi Brothers* (1968), starring Gian Maria Volontè, Don Backy and Riccardo Cucciolla, I was an extra on the embankment, dressed as a partisan. This time it was Cesare Zavattini, the author of the screenplay, who told the story of the fire in the barnyard facing the house.

I grew up in proletarian "Red Emilia" across the way from Don Giovanni Tajadela's church, where I was an altar boy, and the Communist dairy cooperative. There was an atmosphere as in the novels of Giovannino Guareschi, with a smell of milk and *sisso*, or pig manure. Important values for a poor but very united family. There was a lot of respect for the priest, Don Tajadela. No one shared his ideology, but it would have been unthinkable to challenge him. On the contrary, we helped him whenever we could. "We're not rich," my father would repeat, as long as he lived, "but our pantry is always full."

When I was a kid, I was always hungry. I longed for sweets. There was a lot of harmony in our house, but not much money. We ate bread and cheese with soup for dinner.

"What's for dessert?"

"*Ciocabèc.*"

I imagined a delicious cake, scrumptious sweets, and smelled the scent of chocolate or some other unknown aroma. But there was never any dessert. I couldn't understand why. Anxiously, I thought, *when's this ciocabèc gonna get here?* I got nothing—*ciocabèc* is the sound of a bird's beak pecking at an empty plate.

At Christmas time, crates of oranges, tangerines, lemons, and cans of tuna would show up at our house. I was amazed. My mother said they were sent from our cousins in Calabria. I heard strange names mentioned. Uncle Mercurio. It was more acceptable to mention Uncle Cesare. The biggest feast of the year, yet there was never any fucking dessert. Rarely, my mom would make *tortelli* stuffed with jam. So that gift of citrus fruit was a mouth-watering feast for me. At long last, instead of *ciocabèc*.

"*Delmo, nanoun, a ghè al ciocabèc,*" ("Delmo, little one that makes a load of noise") my father would say, to his consternation and sadness, having nothing to give to his child. Tender moments.

Ciocabèc is also the name of a kind of grass, a reed with a sweetish milky substance that makes your lips pucker when you bite into it—like a duck's beak.

There's also another version. The other day someone told me a *ciocabèc* is a windbag, someone who talks too much and doesn't mind their own business.

There's also the *ciocapiàtt* variant, the story of an untrustworthy liar making noise on his plate.

I included "*Consumomes un a la volta*" ("Let's eat it one at a time") as a line in the song 'È un Peccato Morir'—that was another of my father's favorite expressions.

How: courage and help.

WE ALWAYS WATCHED THE SANREMO FESTIVAL, BACK THEN ON A BLACK-and-white TV. My family liked the Saturday night variety shows: Abbe Lane, the Kessler twins, Lola Falana. *Studio Uno*. Like millions of other kids in Italy, I was only allowed to watch TV on Saturday nights. The other nights, it was off to bed after the Carosello commercials. I still remember the slogan: "The more you drink, the better you feel." Then my father would joke to my mother: "*Rina, l'et cumpre col caffè lè, col cas ciama piò t'in bot zo, piò nin vin so?*" ("The more you throw down, the more you throw up.")

There was this lady, a neighbor of ours, who had a big ass. He said to her, "*Oh, l'e passè al bagai loster*" ("Oh, a bright thing has just passed by"), meaning something dazzling and unreal. Almost a UFO.

At home, apart from Uncle Guerra, no one spoke Italian. They all used dialect.

We didn't even have running water in our house. There was the well where we got drinking water, and water to cook and wash with. "*Oh, Delmo, vam a tor un sec d'aqua.*" ("Hey, Delmo, go fetch me a bucket of water.") I'd hear constantly.

There was a park bench. When evening came, it was a meeting place for the village old-timers.

"*Alora at tira ancora l'usèl?*" ("Can you still get it up?")

"*Beda che la lingua e el man il gan seimper vint'ann.*" ("The tongue and the dick are perennial 20-year-olds.")

"*Me am pies i pir e am pies i pom, am pies la roba che g'a cal donn.*" ("I like apples, I like pears, I like anything a woman wears.")

I wanted to open *Shake* (2001) with that one. We recorded the voice of a farmer from Modena, Werther Dal Monte, talking about a widespread idea where I come from: "I like pears, I like apples, I like what the women wear."

"Oh, com al stal?" "La fat ceintun." ("How's he doing?" "He turned 101." In other words—he's dead.)

"Ahi ho mai vest un pret megher." ("I've never seen a skinny priest.")

There's an urban legend that's traveled up and down the Via Emilia. Back in the 1960s, Paul Anka, the Canadian star who sang 'Diana,' was on the bill at a theater in Reggio, and he was late to the show. We wanted to use this legend, which was only a joke, for the opening of the 'Vedo Nero' video. It's set in a provincial theater, and I'm the emcee and announce that Mr. Paul Anka is going to be a few minutes late. The audience begins to get restless, at which point I come out again and explain that Mr. Paul Anka's going to be a half hour late. More clamor from the audience. I ask everyone to be patient, and when once again I say, "Mr. Paul Anka…" I'm interrupted by a spectator—a dwarf in a tank top and suspenders—who reproachfully finishes the sentence for me: *"Ascolta, vecio, il signor Paul Anka pol anca ander a der via al cul."* ("Listen, old man. Mr. Paul Anka can also fuck himself.") Sadly, it is impossible to translate the pun, because as phonemes in the Reggiano dialect, the words Paul Anka sound like the words for "can also." It was all in good fun, I figured. A tribute to a great singer as the introduction to an upbeat, raucous number.

Meanwhile, I'm working like a madman on this book, wilting in the late summer heat and exhausted from the tour we're taking a break from. There's someone on the phone—he says he's Paul Anka and he's in a rotten mood. He's got a daughter in Italy who told him I have a video out that makes fun of him.

"But Paul," I explain, "it's supposed to be funny. It's a joke, a play on words in dialect. It's a nice way of remembering you."

He once again informs me that he's in a rotten mood.

"Come on, Paul. It's just a joke."

"Zucchero, I don't need your stupid joke!"

"OK, Paul. I understand. But I assure you it's nothing more than an innocent tribute. I promise you I'll cut the intro to the video."

Amusing.

Don Tajadela

IN THE SUMMER, THE ICE CREAM MAN WOULD COME BY WITH HIS CART. I couldn't afford to get ice cream every day. I got a cone once a week, on Sundays. On the other days, my father would give me ice from the cheese-shop freezer.

One very hot day, as I attempted to beat the heat sitting on the bank of the stream, sucking on a big piece of ice and thoroughly enjoying it, a boy by the name of Claudio tore it from my mouth and ran off. I was super pissed off and never forgave him for that. I, too, had discovered violence. The meanness of children.

My parents brought milk, eggs, and a bit of cheese to Don Tajadela.

"He's always there by himself," my mother said. "Invite him over on Sunday."

But my crippled uncle would say, *"Al pret al ga mai nint da fèr."* ("The priest never has anything to do.") They ended up spending entire afternoons arguing. There was a little fountain that everyone would gather around to watch them defend their ideas in endless philosophical diatribes, getting all worked up over their fiercely held opinions.

"Cul pret là al capesc gnint," ("that priest understands nothing") my uncle would say, laying it out in plain terms on the way back home.

And every Sunday: *"Ma sa fal cal pret per lò sol, al g'ha mja fameja, va' Delmo, val a ciamèr cal vegna a disner."* ("What's that priest doing there on his own, he has no family. Go Delmo, go tell him it's time for dinner.")

And I would go happily running off to church to fetch Don Tajadela. That way he'd let me play the organ for a few minutes.

For Uncle Guerra and Don Tajadela, Sunday dinners meant it was time for an ideological truce. With God and Mao on standby, we ate platefuls of *tagliatelle*, and in winter *cappelletti* in broth, homemade by my mother, and washed them down with country-style Lambrusco. The two of them became so fond of each other that a year after Don Tajadela died, my uncle died, too. True, it may have been just a coincidence, but my uncle had lost his ideological and doctrinal adversary, his only worthy opponent. It was too easy at the cooperative—they were all Communists, so there was no one he could get into a good argument with. They all agreed. He wanted someone with a different opinion, someone he could cross dialectical swords with. My uncle was a cripple and walked with a cane. He'd sit on the bench near the well where we all got our water, stretching out his lame leg, and every afternoon (he didn't work) he would argue with the priest in the shade of a great lime tree.

None of the men in our family hung out at the bar to shoot the breeze and drink coffee or a shot of liquor, or play card games like *briscola*, while foul language flew. The bar was next to the local Communist Party headquarters. It was the Communists' bar. My folks were Communists too, but they just never made a habit of spending time at the bar. They stayed home. They didn't use curse words. They told me stories. My father, and especially Uncle Guerra.

There was our house, with the well in front. There was the street, the dairy cooperative, the church, the school, the machine shop where I'd lend a hand in the summer to earn money for ice pops and, later, to rent my first portable keyboard. There was the cobbler, the tobacco shop. That was pretty much the whole world of Roncocesi, a place you passed through between Novellara and Ca' del Bosco on the way to the Via Emilia. The awareness of the land, of the countryside, of roots. A tiny place, just a speck on the map. Great civility. There was a lot of respect.

Our house had long staircases. They seemed immense to me, steep, unending. Upstairs was big. There was my grandparents' room, Uncle Guerra's room, my parents' room with their king-size bed, which looked so big to me. That was where my father set up the nativity scene at Christmas. Back then he was the family artist. He had a remarkable sense for aesthetics. He'd go looking for moss in the fields. Even though he wasn't a Catholic, creating that beautiful nativity scene every year meant a lot to him. Everyone would come by to see it. He kept all the colored statuettes in a wooden box, pieces he'd collected over a lifetime. He was a handsome man—blond hair, blue eyes. They called him the Paul Newman of Lower Reggio. He was slim, with a nice set of teeth. The women really liked him. And he liked that. He was handsome and taciturn. An anti-Fascist, during the war he had to escape from a Fascist raid. There was a manhunt for my father and Uncle Guerra. Luckily, they'd gotten wind of it—someone warned them and they hightailed it at night on foot.

After we had moved to Forte dei Marmi, my father used to say, "Let's go pay a visit to Lardeina." He was always mentioning this Lardeina, an old woman who dressed in black and lived in Udine. He had a special devotion to her, even though she wasn't a relative. I didn't understand. I never had much of a relationship with my father in terms of talking. He was closed, reserved, the silent type. There was never any intimacy between us, the way men used to be. He never touched me. Never told me anything about his life. I found out from my aunt, his sister, that he had been given refuge from the Fascists by Lardeina when he escaped. He walked all the way from Roncocesi to Udine (almost 200 miles), and this woman hid him in her house. My uncle, however, was captured and sent to

Germany. My father talked about Lardeina his whole life. I saw her only once.

Fleece

MY FATHER WOULD TAKE ME TO NURSERY SCHOOL EARLY IN THE morning, before he started work. He would set me between his legs, up front on his Vespa, and we we'd head for the school in Pieve Modolena, a nearby village, toward Reggio Emilia. The church there was a little bigger than the one in Roncocesi. There was also a beautiful athletic field and a nursery school run by nuns. First, we'd stop by the cheese shop, and my father would cut me off a nice piece of "fleece"—the cheese that oozes out of the wooden forms for the Parmigiano when it's still fresh. That thin, long strip, soft and compact, tasting wonderfully of milk. I loved it to death. He would wrap it in a piece of yellow paper and that was my snack. One day a friend of mine, who lived across the way, stole my piece of fleece and gobbled the delicacy up. He should never have done that. He was skinny and shy, but I chased after him and kicked his ass.

I attended the nuns' nursery school. They were all dressed in black, and I had my black smock and blue ribbon. I was very shy. The mother superior had an old metal box with a print on it that I liked. It probably used to hold fancy cookies, but the mother superior would shake it and pull out licorice animals for us to suck on. They cost ten lire. I loved them, and the quince jelly-candies. They came wrapped in cellophane. Delicious.

My mother, like the rest of her family, was Catholic—the only one among us. Her father was Adelmo, and that's where my name comes from. He was a farmer too, and died before the age of fifty. He worked the fields and had a nice country house, and a farm with a barn, near Pieve Modolena.

Diamante and Cannella

MY GRANDMA DIAMANTE, WITH HER BLACK KERCHIEF, USED TO TAKE ME to put the chickens to bed every evening at dusk. The chicken coop was next to the pigsty. A branch of bamboo, some feed. Cluck-cluck-cluck. Meanwhile, she would spread her legs and take a piss, standing there. She had this big skirt, but no underpants. And that black kerchief on her head. She wore it all the time, even inside. She wore all black. Always. A blue-eyed Gypsy, with a celestial gaze, sweet and deep. She talked to the chickens. She was from Cavriago. Her people had food shops. They certainly weren't well off, but they were doing better than we were. I still have a photo of her sitting on a fine chair, well dressed. She looked like a princess. Cute face, upturned nose. Her name was Diamante Arduini. Sweet, patient, affectionate.

My Grandpa Cannella was tall, thin, sinewy, with round glasses. Austere, elegant, severe, with a brown Homburg hat. The raised brim and middle pleat made it look like it was dented. He was charismatic, a man of few words. Commanding, wise. When he sat down to a meal, at the head of the table, there was always a moment of silence. His gaze filled it up, and that was all it took to keep everybody in line. I was fascinated by my grandfather. I fell in love with that hat of his, and today it's become my own trademark. Cigar in his mouth. In winter, wrapped in his cloak. When evening came, he'd take his bike and go for a nice long ride.

Once, Mr. Negri whipped Grandpa Cannella, right in front of his children. Punished him, made him kneel in front of his children and his wife, because he didn't do what the master had told him to do in the pigsty. He did it his way, and that wasn't to the master's liking.

I heard the story told many times in my family as a child. One of those epic tales that accumulates in your memory, living on through all the tales, the recollections of recollections. It became a legend for me, a cornerstone for what came later in life. I imagined Grandpa Cannella, so tall and austere, bent shirtless beneath the blows of his ungrateful master, like a slave humiliated by a slave driver.

Maybe that's where I get the blues from.

My Uncle Enzo, aka Guerrino, aka Guerra, played the harmonica and the ocarina. He knew just two songs: 'Va,' Pensiero,' and 'Bandiera Rossa.'

When Sting invited me to play Carnegie Hall in New York, for the Rainforest Foundation Benefit Concert in 1997, it was also with Elton John, Madonna and Stevie Wonder. He asked each artist to perform a song that brought back their childhood memories. I couldn't do a song like 'Bandiera Rossa'—an anthem of the Italian labor movement—so I turned 'Va', Pensiero' into a lullaby.

Pavarotti said to me, "Bravo! You sing it from your gut, from the heart. None of that waltzing around like Verdi."

On summer nights, Uncle Guerra would sit on the parapet of the little bridge over the stream and play. Girls would come, there was laughter and joking, a glass of wine, lots of fun. My father waltzed with my mother. There were other couples too, young people from the countryside. They danced and had a great time. Simple, upbeat fun. Those people worked their fingers to the bone, but they knew how to enjoy themselves, dancing on a bridge in the moonlight. Uncle Guerra kept time by clicking his tongue against the harmonica. He was ahead of his time. I liked the way he played. A good beat, very rhythmic. I still use my uncle's technique when I play the harmonica. He said he learned it in Alpini, the Italian army's mountain military corps

I would walk to elementary school by myself, from the valley to downtown Roncocesi, near the church. It wasn't far, but tough going and cold on foggy, snowy winter days. It was a fantasy land full of adventures when nature exploded with all the colors and scents of the countryside in springtime. The smells, the sounds. I'd set out with my book bag, heavy pants, wooden clogs, and my fleece cheese rolled up in a piece of paper. That was life in the valley. There was another family of farmers who lived next door. I used to play with Isanna, who was my age. There was also my friend Loris. We were very simple people—poor, but easygoing. My parents got along fine, never fought. There was a lot of family harmony, no tension. We all lived together in one big patriarchal family. My father and his brother, my uncle, got along very well. There was lots affection, solidarity, love.

Guerra

MY UNCLE ENZO WAS THE OLDEST OF THREE BROTHERS. HE WAS A DIE-hard Communist—a Marxist-Leninist, and later a Maoist. In his head he was a Communist, though not militant. He didn't marry until later in life, and his bachelor's room, with its single bed, was full of books. First and foremost, *Das Kapital* by Marx, and *The Communist Manifesto* by Marx and Engels. Then there were books by Lenin, and all the classics of socialism and communism, lots of political essays. He was knowledgeable, self-taught. He also read for pleasure, at a time of widespread illiteracy in the countryside. It was a privilege to have a library of books acquired with love and passion, amid the smells of cheese and the pigsty. He would spend his afternoon siestas reading and writing. Because of his ideas, he was persecuted by the Fascists, exiled to Germany, and imprisoned. While in prison he ate raw rats. When he got back, he showed me how to break their necks. He came home with a piece of shrapnel lodged near his heart. He was left frail and his life ruined. But not mine—since his infirmity kept him from doing any hard labor in the countryside, he ended up spending a lot of time with me. He was a kind, intelligent man. He wrote heartrending love letters to his fiancée, in handwriting that was elegant and harmonious. I was entranced just looking at those sheets of paper so neatly covered with ink from his fountain pen, singing words of love. No one else in the family could talk the way he did, because he read so much. He fascinated me with words. He built me a little airplane out of tin and sheet metal. Instead of a tricycle, I had this wonderful airplane with pedals. It was orange and had round Italian flags on its wings, and the propeller spun as I pedaled. It was marvelous, a phenomenal gift I was proud to zoom around the barnyard on.

On long summer afternoons, we'd go out looking for old discarded motorbikes to fix up. The Garelli Mosquito engine could be mounted on a regular bicycle, transforming it into a power-driven vehicle. In a shed behind the house, my uncle had his neatly kept workshop, with all kinds of wrenches and tools: a lathe, a vise, a knife grinder—truly a wonder-filled grotto. This was my world, and I spent many afternoons with my uncle there. Since he couldn't do much farm work, Uncle Guerrino, with his mighty brain and skilled hands, tinkered around all day, making things with his lathe for us to use around the house. He was an amazing mechanic. Just give him a screwdriver, he knew how to use it. I had a ball with him. Together we mounted the engine from a Vespa 50 motorbike on the frame of an old go-cart. It was simple and solid, with handlebars and little wheels. No brakes. The thing huffed and puffed. Sometimes it wouldn't start. It survived plenty of smash-ups, like a bumper car.

Uncle Guerra had a red Motom motorbike. The name alone, being a palindrome, fascinated the hell out of me. I'd climb on the back and he'd take me to visit his fiancée—he was still a fairly young man at the time. She was a farm girl from Lower Reggio, very coarse, a homemaker with big calves dotted with long black hairs. My father called her *al Gallistròn*, a polite term in dialect to indicate a strange creature that's neither hen nor rooster. Aunt Rica, she loved me dearly, but you couldn't say she was pretty.

So, my uncle would bring me to his girlfriend's house, where more marvels and enchantment awaited. There were cured pork necks hanging from the ceiling of the room she lived in. A den filled with the fragrance of sweet seasoned pork; a smell I've never come across anywhere else. That's why I went there, so that she, who would one day become my aunt, could make me a sandwich with that heavenly *coppa*.

Uncle Guerrino wound up marrying her and she came to live with us. A new addition to our family. She was no beauty, but she was the youngest woman in our rural and somewhat archaic little community. There was my Grandma Diamante, there was my mother, and now there was Rica, my uncle's young bride.

Every Saturday at five in the afternoon, Aunt Rica would take a bath in the washtub, in the warmth of the barn. I hid behind the hay bales and watched her. What a show! All those black hairs. Soapy armpits. And when she stood up, she had a hairy cunt. Women didn't shave their body hair back then—it went from between her legs all the way up to her belly button. That was my imprinting, a visual shock, the first woman I ever saw naked. Her nudity, all that hair, it drove me mad. The first shock that rocked me.

Things went well for me the first two Saturdays. I climbed over the bales of hay and spied on her, all the while prey to the fierce tension of dawning, primordial eroticism. On the third Saturday though, my uncle walked in and found me. My cheeks blushed scarlet red, inflamed with shame. He grabbed me by the ear and said, "Don't you ever do that again! If your aunt found out, there'd be trouble. Never again!"

And I never did—mostly out of respect for Uncle Guerra, whom I loved so dearly.

He worshipped Mao to such a degree, and was so infatuated with Chinese communism, that he ate white rice every night. Since he couldn't work, my aunt would go out and work while he made dinner. And every night it was white rice. Chinese, yes. Communist, too. But Emilia-style. Oozing with melted butter and covered with plenty of grated Parmigiano. One day he had a heart attack while he was cooking his rice and we found him on the floor.

On Christmas Eve, we took the train from Reggio to Milano, to visit Aunt Wanda, my mother's sister. She'd married a fellow from Reggio, who had a good job in a paint factory. Uncle Enrico. My cousin's name is Alfonso. They lived near the Ghisolfa Bridge. The train ride with my parents, in the winter with the snow, just before Christmas, was a fascinating adventure—as was our arrival at the train station in Milano. Who had ever seen such a big building? I couldn't wait to get to there. There was a stand in the station that sold delicious sandwiches loaded with baked ham. I was crazy about them. Then there was my aunt's pasta with tomato sauce made with lard. Christmas Mass. Holiday warmth, warm family bonds.

Aunt Wanda was fundamental in my life. She let me sleep in Alfonso's room when I began going to Milano in search of recording contracts, and couldn't afford a hotel.

In summer my parents couldn't afford to go on vacation. They sent me off to Corniglio, to Camp Roversi. There was a chestnut copse and a beautiful hillside. We would walk to the river, to the Roman bridge. They were wonderful summers. On Sundays, parents came to visit. A fateful place, it lay behind the Pontremoli mountains. I often go back, but it's a nasty sight today. They built apartment houses where the camp used to be, but to me it's still a magica place where I spent five happy summers.

In My Town

AT A CERTAIN POINT, AND AFTER MUCH EFFORT, CANNELLA MAN-AGED to set aside a little money and bought himself a house in downtown

Roncocesi. A metropolis of seven hundred inhabitants. He left the valley and moved there. The place was tall and narrow, three floors. He rented out the ground floor to an old guy, a cobbler bent from a life of resoling shoes. Gold-rimmed glasses, leather apron. It was across from the fallen veterans' monument with Uncle Piero's photo, to the left of the church. Two hundred meters beyond that, the dairy cooperative and the Communist Party headquarters, then the school.

After that move, my father found work at the local Parmigiano warehouse as a cheese-turner. He wrapped and rewrapped wheels of Parmigiano to make sure they aged properly. He was an expert. Local gold, truly. He would climb up the racks and turn the wheels of cheese, using cloths. The cheese was very greasy, so it was a dangerous job. My uncle found work there as well. My mom stayed home. My grandparents were ancient by then.

To make room for his children, Grandpa Cannella had his room on the ground floor. He had a stove, a table, his wicker chair. Grandma Diamante's room was on the floor above. Behind her room was another tiny room, which was where I slept. To get to my bed I had to pass through my grandmother's room. My room was also used to cure pork, so I slept with hams and salamis hanging over my bed. When they oozed, I would wake up covered in grease. But what delicious smells! It was a small rectangular room with a little window facing our neighbors' house. They had a daughter, Vittorina.

Uncle Guerra also wanted a room for all his books, that library where he spent hours. On the top floor was my parents' bedroom. Down below, the kitchen, living room, pantry. Out back was a beautiful courtyard, and a ladder against the wall that led to the attic, where I'd sneak off by myself. The typical farmhouse rafters were visible. In the courtyard there were chickens and rabbits, with the chicken coop next to the woodshed, which I took over for a while when I wanted to be a painter. I filled it with easels, canvases, and paints. That was the setting of my childhood.

Before going to school in the morning I would run to the church very early before any parishioners or nuns showed up. There was an old pipe organ with a bellows. It's still there. Don Tajadela taught me the ABCs, a few basics, even a little Bach. *Toccata and Fugue*. Then it was time to hurry off to school, right next door. That church was where I learned my first moves on the organ, by ear. In exchange, I served Mass—I was an altar boy. A bit more Bach, then at last I learned to play 'Senza Luce,' the Italian cover of the beautiful Procol Harum song 'A Whiter Shade of Pale.' It sounded great on that old organ, and it's still my favorite song, the miller telling his tale, and the young woman's already ghostly face turning a whiter shade of pale. The priest let me play. "But you've also got to learn to play church music, so on Sundays you can play at Mass." So that I did. Later my technique improved, but I learned the basic chords there. I served Mass and played the organ on Sundays. And a half hour before school on weekdays.

I was also the bell ringer. The previous bell ringer was an old lady who hardly came anymore. The priest said to me, "Delmo, learn how to ring the bells." So the old lady taught me how to ring the bells, the sound of Sunday. I worked both the big ropes and the little ones. I was quite proud of myself.

The teacher liked me because I was polite, a product of Grandpa Cannella's strictness. He was a stickler for decorum, and I was a very well-behaved boy, bashful and reserved. Red cheeks and loads of shyness. "*Buongiorno, signora maestra,*" I would tell the teacher. When she asked me a question I would reply shyly, but I was always precise and prepared. I was a skinny little thing. I sat in the last row, never bothered anyone, wasn't rowdy like the others. I just minded my own business. Since I was so sweet and introverted, my elementary school teacher, Nada Cosmi, started calling me "*Zuccherino*" ("Little Sugar"), or worse, "*il mio Zuccherino*" ("My Little Sugar"). Imagine the other kids, the bastards, teasing and making fun of me! Outside school they'd laugh and say, "Ha! Zuccherino!" "She called you Zuccherino!" "He's her little sugar." Lots of teasing for that one. The teacher asked me, "Do you like jam on your bread? Do you put sugar on it?" Things were getting worse. Now everyone started calling me "Sugar-and-Jam." It went on like this, and soon even my mother started calling me "Zuccherino." Thus, the nickname Zucchero was born. I never liked my real name, Adelmo, much anyway, even though it was also my grandfather's name. So, when I was twelve and we moved to Versilia, I told everyone to call me Zucchero Fornaciari. The teacher there trusted me and used me as a messenger to take notes to the fifth-grade teacher, a guy by the name of Rinaldi. She wound up marrying him—I was carrying love notes. I was good in Italian and art. I still have two drawings I did. One is of the church in Roncocesi, with the priest, Don Tajadela, on the parvis reading from the Mass book, and electric wires with swallows perched on them in the background. Very romantic. The other drawing is of me, my father, and my little brother, Lauro, who's seven years younger than me. We were picking dandelion greens, also known as piss-a-bed. When they're young and fresh, they go great in salad. A slightly bitter taste. My father loved them and ate huge salads with them and a hardboiled egg. On Sunday morning, we'd go to the fields to pick dandelion greens.

When Christmas approached, I'd join my friends Marco and Marzia—he was my best buddy and she was my first great love (although she didn't know it at the time)—and we'd have fun putting on little shows on Sundays. I'd draw posters with a magic marker and we'd make a tour of the nearby churches. Villa Cella, Ca' del Bosco, Pieve Modolena. "Today at three p.m. Show in the church featuring the Lord's Flowers"—our name was a tribute to the spirit of the times, the spirit of the flower children and the hippies. With two guitars, Marco and I did covers of songs by the Nomads and Equipe 84. We were a "beat" group. I did an imitation of Ruggero Orlando and his famous, "From New York, this is the voice of Ruggero Orlando." I was

27

super skinny and played Stan Laurel, while my friend Marco, on the chubby side, played Oliver Hardy. Marzia did Scaramacai, the clown who was all the rage on Italian TV, a creation of Guglielmo Zucconi from Modena. That clown was another example of our expressive Italian dialect: "You're a *scaramacai*, a *pajàz*, a clown." After our performances, someone would go around with a hat. Three old ladies and a few mothers gave us fifty lire. But most of all there was already a longing in me to perform, to have a group. Myself, Marco, Marzia, and Ricky, our factotum.

On summer afternoons my father took naps, and he made me take them too—our siesta. We'd finish lunch at one o'clock, then go to bed. I'd sleep in the big double bed with him for at least an hour. It was the warmest bed. This gave my mother a chance to wash the dishes in peace and straighten out the kitchen. I hated those naps. While the other kids were swimming in the stream, my father made me take those naps. They were torture. As soon as he fell asleep and started snoring, I'd sneak out of the room and catch up with my pals at the stream. We would float along on big black tractor inner tubes. Each of us had our own tube to swim with. We'd jump into the clear, freezing water in groups. It was pretty dangerous since the current was so strong. Sometimes we went fishing with our hands in the mud. We would go looking for chubs in their dens. Sometimes we caught sunnies. The Modolena Creek was shallow. One of us would stand on one side with a *sburlone*, a half-moon-shaped net, while the others on the opposite side made noise with their legs to drive the fish toward the net. Once I caught two tenches at the same time. I felt the smooth skin of a fish, grabbed at it, and came up with two. One was on top of the other. Next to them was a broken bottle bottom that sliced my finger. A deep cut. I still have the scar.

Every evening my uncle returned home from Reggio on his motorbike, the red Motom. One day he got hit by a car that practically sliced off his leg. It was just hanging by the skin from the knee down. He was rushed to the hospital, and they somehow reattached it. Only they didn't do such a great job. He came home all bandaged up and the wound festered. The house became unbearable. The pus had a nauseating odor that went everywhere when he changed the dressing. The poor guy, he already had a piece of shrapnel lodged near his heart from the war, now this disaster left him a cripple for life. He didn't curse, but he became ornery. The poor soul suffered atrocious pain. He was jinxed, and how. But his misfortune was my own good luck, because now that he couldn't work at all anymore, I had Uncle Guerra to hang out with. His skilled hand and sharp brain at my disposal. He was all mine.

Soon after that, he built me my first guitar. I drew a picture for him that looked like a medieval mandola, pear-shaped. Made of chipboard. Heavy fishing line for the strings. When I was five or six I was crazy about that instrument. Just its sinuous, erotic, feminine shape was enough. Of course, that guitar with fishing line strings didn't really play. It just made twangy sounds. But I was happy all the same. It was the first instrument that was all my own.

On Sundays, my mother would bring me to her brother Marino's house, and together we'd go to the cemetery to visit their parents' graves. There was a soccer field near the cemetery, so I often stayed outside the gate. It was sad inside, and I preferred the soccer field. I acted as ball boy, bringing the ball back to the goalkeeper when it got kicked out of bounds. I was always drawn to goalkeepers. Uncle Marino was a heavy smoker and he died rather young.

In the afternoon, my schoolmates and I would play soccer. There were three of us: Riccardo, Marco, and me. We're still friends. We played in the churchyard. I was a reckless goalie. I would go for the opponents' feet. My idol was Yashin, the great goalkeeper for the glorious Soviet national team. Then a guy who'd started a team called *Il Risorgimento* rode up on his Vespa one day to talk to my mother. His team had blue uniforms, with Ca' del Bosco written on them. Two

29

of us tried out for the same spot. The other guy was Balù—Balugani. I was torn. I went to the games, but I skipped practice. I had to rehearse with the band. I wanted to play music.

The priest gave us a practice room behind the church. I brought my portable keyboard and a guitar, Marco had another guitar, plus there was a drum kit. In exchange for the room, we cleaned out the church basement, which was full of bird shit and dead birds. Don Tajadela was a devil of a fellow in his own right. He had a tough role in that land of Communists who preferred Lenin to God, and Togliatti to De Gasperi. He used to walk back and forth in the churchyard all day with his Bible, his black tunic outlining his large belly.

"I could do his job all right, but let him try to work the fields!" Don Giovanni Tajadela was still alive when I first hit it big with *Blue's*. He was very proud of me, of having taught me to play the organ in the church in Roncocesi.

Chair-o-Plane

SEPTEMBER 3 WAS A BIG DAY FOR THE FEAST OF SAN BIAGIO. A CHAIR-O-plane ride was set up, along with three stands selling cotton candy, almond brittle, and licorice in front of the dairy cooperative.

The chairs swung around and round. There were no bumper cars yet, just the chair-o-plane in the little amusement park that had come to Roncocesi. I adored the chair-o-plane, and being launched as we tried to grab the prized tail. They also had a sound system playing the latest hits. That was where I heard 'Lady Jane' by the Rolling Stones for the first time. Also 'Uno in Più' by Riki Maiocchi, and 'Dio è Morto.' I heard them all for the first time thanks to that turntable with the awful speakers on the poetic chair-o-plane ride in Roncocesi. I also heard records by bands like the Nomads from Novellara ('Noi non ci Saremo'), Equipe 84 from Modena ('Un Angelo Blu'), the Crows from

Parma—stars of the Italian beat scene who ushered in modern music along the Via Emilia, from Modena to Reggio. There was also 'Hey Jude' by the Beatles and Caterina Caselli from Sassuolo. As I sang on 'Chocabeck,' in 2010, to memorialize those times: "*Ecco io, laggiù laggiù, da ragazzino ne sapevo di più. Di più di più l'amore fu. Un calcinculo e tante stelle lassù.*" ("I knew more when I was little. There was so much more love. A chair-o-plane and a starry sky above.")

The ride stayed for a whole week. Enough time for a kid to become a devoted fan of the Nomads, Equipe 84, and the Crows, who sang: "*Io sono un poco di buono, lasciami stare perché sono un ragazzo di strada.*" ("I'm no good, leave me be, 'cause I'm a boy from the streets.") All the greatest hits of the day. I didn't really like the Beatles back then. They seemed so candy-coated. I preferred the Rolling Stones, with their grungy sound and aggressive guitars. At that time, I wasn't even into Battisti, who sang 'Balla Linda,' and only came to appreciate him later. Flying around in a circle on those woven red plastic seats, I liked listening to 'Sei Rimasta Sola' by Adriano Celentano. Moving, a bit hypnotic, just right for that ride with the fantastic and evocative name ("kick-in-the-ass," as it was called in Italian) that swung us round and round.

I felt so good when I heard that music on that flying jukebox—it was true ecstasy. Freedom, fantasy, listening as I flew through the air. European and American music, as well as the Italian music that in part tried to imitate, in part tried to translate, and in part tried to rework the stuff that was coming out in the developed world. From the chair-o-plane in Roncocesi to the clubs in London, the Scottish and Irish pubs, the city squares of America. The world was changing thanks to music.

Even today, I can't listen to music just sitting in front of a stereo. I'll get in the car and cruise the winding roads in the hills of the Apennine. I put on music I've written. I listen. I escape. Traveling, in motion, on the road.

I rode the chair-o-plane every time there was a fair in the neighboring towns, too.

The first pop song I learned to play was 'California Dreamin',' by the Mamas & the Papas.

After elementary school, I enrolled in sixth grade at Enrico Fermi Middle School in Reggio Emilia, near the church of Santo Stefano. The city, at last. I broadened my horizons, made new friends. Along the Via Emilia there were record and musical instrument stores. Delrio. Domeniconi's. Round trip from Roncocesi was ten kilometers by bike. That was in the summer. In the winter, I rode the blue bus that stopped at the well in Roncocesi and picked us all up. We'd take the Via Emilia at Pieve di Modolena, then change buses to get to Reggio. Sometimes I'd miss the bus and wind up chasing after it on my bike, pedaling like a madman as far as Pieve.

I had an Italian teacher who was very good, and pretty, too. She was married, dark and curvaceous. Another woman in my imaginary erotic gallery. Dark, Mediterranean, radiant hues.

I hung out in the attic of a painter, Fontanesi. I really liked to draw and was fascinated by all the canvases, easels, and oil paint splattered everywhere. And the models. I'd go watch him paint. I liked Ligabue, Van Gogh—paintings with lots of substance.

Near the Church of the Blessed Virgin of Ghiara I'd go listen to a group called the Apostles rehearse. There were also the Savages and the Strays. They were popular groups in Reggio. It was the same neighborhood where the priest had given me permission to use a hole in the wall so at last I could practice with a friend who had an electric guitar.

In summer, my father would bring me to Reggio and we would drink barley water in the cathedral square. It wasn't made with orgeat syrup, but was dark and tasted like licorice with ice water. We loved it. It cooled us off in the hellish heat. I remember La Standa department store, and the market with its wrought-iron Art Deco design where I'd go shopping with my mother. Along with beat music, La Standa was a sign of modernity, a veritable paradise of shopping desire. I had never seen so much stuff. The overflowing toy department, the clothes, the escalator.

There was a legend that went around among the boys in Reggio. The Reggiana goalkeeper was Lamberto Boranga, famous for his saves, and even more famous for being well hung. According to the story, he'd fucked a clerk from La Standa up the ass. La Standa clerks were another distinctive feature of the economic boom's new mythology. Apparently, the unlucky lady had to go to the hospital to get sewn back together. It was a game for us boys to stalk the aisles of the store and try to guess which clerk it was.

"You think it was the brunette?"

"No, the blonde."

"But what about the redhead?"

"I think that's the one."

I began eyeing instruments in the shop windows. But I didn't have any money.

That first summer I worked in a lathe shop next to our house. I was friends with the owner's son, Marco Panciroli. Sometimes we'd play doctor together, and his sister was my beloved Marzia, the cutest girl in town. I wiped the shavings off the lathes with a steel brush. I saved up a little money.

The year after that, I went to work at the famed Montanari bakery in Piazza San Prospero, in Reggio Emilia—the oldest and most prestigious bakery in town, near boxing champion Gino Bondavalli's appliance store. I'd deliver supplies on one of those big, bulky bikes with two baskets, one up front, the other in back. From seven in the morning until two in the afternoon, then another shift from five o'clock to eight. I'd even have to ride up the hill toward Rivalta—I really busted my ass. They finally took pity on me and gave me a Trotter motorbike. Hauling supplies on that was a breeze. Some afternoons they had me making pizzas and savory *erbazzone* vegetable pies. So, I became a baker.

The last summer, when I was eleven, Montanari sold the bakery to a man by the name of Melli. He had a gorgeous eighteen-year-old daughter who would go take showers in the workshop behind the oven, in the dressing rooms where we washed up. This was still a world where you bathed only on Saturdays. I made a hole in the door. She was beautiful, all hairy, with stupendous tits. I had the hots for her. I spied on her three or four Saturdays. Then unfortunately I moved away.

Working summers, I managed to save up a little money to buy instruments. I rented a microphone and stand, plus a hard Bakelite plastic portable keyboard with a fan from Domeniconi's which blew when you pressed the keys, emitting sounds. My father had given me a five-speed green Legnano bicycle, and I triumphantly rode home on it, bearing my musical loot, all the way from Reggio to Roncocesi, with the microphone resting on the bar and the keyboard under one arm. I couldn't afford to rent an amplifier, so my Uncle Guerra, genius that he was, found an old wooden Minerva radio and hooked that up to the keyboard and microphone. I felt like a king. I could at last sing and play with amplification.

Roncocesi, Suburb of Memphis

SOMETIMES A BLACK GUY FROM MEMPHIS, WHO WAS STUDYING AGRON-omy at the University of Bologna, would come to Roncocesi. I don't remember why. Maybe he had a relative who lived there, or friends. But he had all these 45s by Wilson Pickett, Aretha Franklin, Sam and Dave, Ray Charles. I had never even heard of them. He played an Otis Redding record for me. I was floored. I'd never heard music like that in my life, that way of singing. So rhythmic. And the sounds, the way they were broken down, the vocals. I wanted to sing like that. 'Sittin' on the Dock of the Bay' was a beautiful song. I strummed a little guitar. I had never studied it, though I had taken a few lessons at school with Mr. Miselli, the music teacher. He played the accordion in small orchestras. He began with *solfeggio*. I never went back. That heaven-sent fellow from Memphis, a black angel brought by fate to Roncocesi, taught me the chords on a six-string Eko. My first blues chords. I'd sit beneath the lime trees at home, trying to imitate Otis Redding and that way of singing, bent on improving. Every two or three months, when he finished with his classes, the man from Memphis would come to town and we'd go to the church where Don Tajadela had let me set up a rickety old drum kit. There was also a big guitar we used as a bass, since we didn't have the money to buy an electric bass.

It was listening to those records that hooked me on soul, blues, and rhythm & blues.

With all the stories my Memphis friend told me, I spent the whole summer dreaming of America. Tales of Mississippi, Louisiana, the Delta blues. He was the one who encouraged me to love the blues. He fired up the devil in me.

His name was James. Everyone in town called him *Yames*.

I listened to those records over, and over again, until I wore them out. I figured out the chords and tried to play the music too. The first song I played on the keyboard was 'Hold On, I'm Comin',' by Sam and Dave.

This wasn't the sound you heard on the chair-o-plane. That's where I'd heard Procol Harum and the Moody Blues, who wrote 'Nights in White Satin,' which the Nomads covered as 'Ho Difeso il mio Amore.'

It was a very formative period. I still go back to those days when I'm looking for sounds. I loved the Italian groups along the Via Emilia. I'd go listen to the Apostles, local heroes who played at the Rosa d'Oro dance hall in Upper Ca' del Bosco. Alberto Mazzuccato and His Disciples, who played a good version of the Turtles' 'Happy Together.' Dear Edmondo Berselli, who showed up in my dressing room many years later and had me play that song for a TV program about the Po River Valley. We played it together and he demanded I sing the countermelody.

Vittorina

VITTORINA LIVED NEAR US, ACROSS FROM THE CHURCH. DARK COMPLEX-ion, she wore her hair in a teased wedge cut—that was the fashion in the 1960s. Fleshy lips, short miniskirt, barely covering her groin. Amazing hips. High heels. She was beautiful, the prettiest girl in town. She must have been eighteen years old. She worked in Reggio, in the city—maybe the only girl in town who did at the time. She was the most modern, ahead of all the others. Less of a country girl. She worked as a clerk in a clothing store. She already had a boyfriend, who every now and then brought her home in his Fiat 500. These were all reasons why word went around in town that she was easy. Everyone took notice and would remark, "*Chissà sla valà pò a fèr a Rez.*" ("Who knows what she does in Reggio anyway"). Even the priest would say things like, "Don't follow her example." She was gorgeous, exuberant, beaming—and that was enough for the old sanctimonious townsfolk to brand her as no good.

I watched her, spied on her, jerked myself off over her. Vittorina was the representation of desire—she was sex. Imaginary, fantasy, agonized over. She was the triple somersault to the sexual experience I had not yet encountered.

On Saturdays, the town's women took their baths, cleansing, and ablutions in the barns, in their washtubs. Saturday was now Vittorina Day. We'd climb one on top of the other to see her naked—her out-rageous curves, that triangle of fur. Black. So enticing. We'd climb up to look through a window in her barn and watch Vittorina bathe in all her striking beauty. *"Tàca a me, at tlè bèla vesta."* ("It's my turn, you've already seen her.") We'd slap one another to reach the top of that human ladder leading to paradise.

There was that atmosphere of strong and naïve eroticism. We were still kids, but when Vittorina sauntered by, our tongues would all be hanging out, our heads in the clouds and our dicks hard.

One torrid summer afternoon, I managed to extract myself from the clutches of naptime and took off while my father was still asleep. I went outside, rubbing my eyes, assailed by the shower of light, heat, sun, in that suspended, immobile summertime of long ago. I walked over to the shade of the lime trees in the yard, and began strumming my guitar while sitting on a bench. That was a fateful and fortunate flight on my part, because soon Vittorina came up and said, "Delmo, Delmo, give me a hand."

"What's the matter, Vittorina?"

"I have to go to work, but my bike has a flat tire. Do you have a pump? Hurry, Delmo. Help me. I'm late."

I ran out back to Uncle Guerra's workshop and returned triumphantly, pump in hand.

When Vittorina bent down to take off the tire, that miniskirt of hers rode up, and I got a peek of the hairs sticking out of her white underpants. I almost fainted. I was shocked by those hairs. This was ecstasy. I began to believe that God exists. From that point on, I've always seen black, and continue to do so to this day. It was there that I contracted the hairy cunt syndrome.

I may never have experienced such a strong emotion in all my life. I ran home and wrote my first song and recorded it on a tape recorder with two tracks, guitar and vocals. A ballad in dialect in which I stuck up for her against everyone who said she was no good. It was called, 'La Vittorina:' "Near Masensatico there was a village whose name I do not know... 'What's the meaning of this?' said the priest, scandalized. 'How can that cow Vittoria go around with her ass sticking out like that?'"

She later got married and I lost track of her. I used to go back to Roncocesi after I moved away, and one time I ran into her and told her I had just talked about her in an interview. She hugged me and asked, "Adelmo, what were you saying?"

Bull, Maino and the Calves

AS SOON AS THE SEASON GREW WARM, MARCO, RICCARDO, ANOTHER boy nicknamed Bull, and I started skipping school to go swimming in the creek. First, we'd stop by the tobacco shop to buy cigarettes: one Macedonia, one non-filter National, one Gala, one Sachs. They still sold them individually in those days. Then one by one we would go and smoke them under the Autostrada bridge, or we'd go fishing and build Sioux and Cheyenne huts along the banks, pretending to be Black Boulder and Captain Miki. We'd catch chubs, and use the pan and the seed oil we kept in one of the huts to fry them up. We felt free, independent, and, when we smoked, transgressive. Then came the jerk-off contests in the sorghum fields to see who had the biggest hard-on. That was Bull's big moment.

"Look, I've got the biggest one of all!" he cried with satisfaction. We'd make a hut in the sorghum and compare our dicks. We were still little and never came. But that's how we spent our days: carefree, naïve, happy.

There was an arbor at the dairy cooperative where the adults would play cards in summer. The kids used to hang out there too. It was our meeting place, and someone would always wind up treating us to a Popsicle or some candy. One day, Maino, the village greengrocer, came driving up to the cooperative on his Ape three-wheeler. He was a weird guy, a bachelor. Something of a cherub, with no identifiable

38

sexual identity. He might've been gay. He was an odd sort, a bit mad. He'd call us kids over and tell us about his adventures, said he went to whores in Reggio. He waved a 500-lire bill in front of us and made obscene gestures with his tongue. The adults made fun of him: "Maino, what are you up to?"

"I've got a dick as big as this," he'd say, gesturing indecently with his arm. "Twice the size of yours."

The other grown-ups just went on teasing him.

He would tell terribly vulgar stories: "Last night I found one in Reggio, and fucked her till she couldn't take it anymore, front and back."

The amusement park was in town, but we didn't have any money for the chair-o-plane. We were curious and didn't quite understand what he wanted to do with that 500 lire and those nasty tongue gestures of his. So, we decided to go with him. All four of us. He took us to his house. There he lined us up, pulled down our pants and underwear, and touched My us. One after the other. "How pretty, let me give you a kiss." Then he pulled our pants back up and gave us the 500 lire. We took the money, laughed, and raced to the amusement park and the chair-o-plane. We were light, happy, naïve.

Even if it was objectively disturbing, I wasn't shaken up by the episode, and neither were my friends. I don't think Maino was a pedophile. Maybe he wasn't even gay. He was just a poor devil, a character, a part of village life, with all its primitive eccentricities, animal instincts, and brutal violence. A rural farming community. A world that can be cruel, if still genuine.

Our gang consisted Riccardo, Bull, and a certain Giuseppe Tagliavini, who was a bit on the pudgy side. Little brats, all of us. I was in love with my neighbor Marzia. She was really cute, and we'd go walking in the afternoon, study together—or pretend to study—and the whole time I'd be blissfully sneaking glances at her, especially when we watched *The Black Pirate's Grandmother* on TV. She watched the television out of the corner of her right eye, sideways. Soon I was doing it too. Marzia was on the ball, quick and lively. I really believed in her. I trusted her. I was infatuated. "She must see better that way," I thought. When her mother got back she'd see us sitting there sideways, watching Grandma Sprint and Nicolino in that strange, unlikely crosswise position. Her mother was a beautiful brunette with hairy legs and armpits. She was buxom, with big, fleshy red lips. She'd give me a kiss on the mouth when she came home, an affectionate, truly innocent kiss, chastely maternal. Nothing improper about it. But at my house that would never have happened. I felt a strong urge run down my back, the bewilderment of an unknown pleasure when she kissed me. It was my first encounter with something so strong. A shock, a storm.

I did my homework with Marzia and had a terrible crush on her. She was so sweet, so cute. A year later we began exchanging little kisses on the cheek. I thought she was my girlfriend. At a certain point she said to me, "I don't want you anymore. I like Tagliavini."

It was an awful disappointment. Damn it! What do you mean, Tagliavini? He was fat, ugly, and had zits. I was flabbergasted. I didn't know what to say.

"No. I don't want you anymore. I want Tagliavini."

The gloomy judgment had been handed down.

Now she went to Tagliavini's place to do her homework. So I convinced my crew we should go do our homework at the despised fat slob's too. It was nice and warm inside the barn where we went to do our homework, with the hay and the cows and their calves. But that day Marzia didn't come.

What with all the warmth, our hormones were pumping, on the loose. We lined up, all five of us. The calves were there, they didn't have teeth yet, and we burst out laughing. There was nothing mean about it, those early rumblings. We had a contest to see who had the biggest hard-on. We wanted to see what it felt like. All lined up, we took those calves by the ears in Tagliavini's barn.

"Mine's awesome, and sucks great!"

Marzia wasn't there. She was at home, doing her homework.

The Dukes

WORD GOT AROUND THAT I COULD PLAY THE ORGAN, AND, MORE importantly, that I had a keyboard and a microphone. A long-haired bass player with a cool Elvis Presley hairdo showed up at my house. He had a Fender electric bass and a Vox amplifier, professional gear that would have been unthinkable for the rest of us. He was way ahead. He even rode a red Motom like Uncle Guerra's. His parents were farmers, but they were fairly well-off. He wore dark sunglasses and a black leather jacket.

"You have a portable keyboard?"

"Yeah."

I showed it to him.

"Look, I'm putting together a band I want to call the Dukes. We start rehearsing next week at the drummer's house. Wanna come?" He didn't beat around the bush.

The place where we rehearsed was past the Crostolo Creek bridge on the way to Upper Ca' del Bosco. A country house. I showed up and we started playing with him on the bass, me on the keyboard, another guy on guitar. A beat group on the other side of the Costolo, the creek that marked the boundary of our territory. It seemed like the other end of the world to me. We'd play almost every night, chasing our dreams of breaking out, of glory. My parents had so much trust in me, and realized how much I longed to go, that they let me do it even though I was still just a kid. They'd understood how serious my passion for music was. We practiced from eight o'clock to eleven. I'd carry my keyboard under one arm and take off on my Mosquito. Off to band practice, on the other side of the Crostolo Creek, in another world. I'd get back home at midnight. When it came down to it, I was a good kid, and very responsible. I simply had a longing to play music.

One night on my way home after practice, I crashed into a mile marker at a curve in the road. I dropped my keyboard and it broke. The motorbike was thoroughly trashed, and I had a very swollen foot.

The next day the Dukes were supposed to play at the dairy cooperative in Roncocesi, our debut performance. Even with my mangled, huffing and puffing keyboard and broken foot, I still played. I didn't care about the pain. I was in my village and I could play at the local cooperative, in the town square. In Roncocesi. That's like saying in Red Square, in front of the Kremlin. For the first time, I felt the warmth of an audience. Our set list included a few songs by the Rolling Stones. The first time I sang as a soloist. I did 'Senti l'Estate che Torna delle Orme,' the song that kicked off my career. The Dukes didn't find any more gigs after that and we broke up without regret. I was eleven years old.

In the summer my father took me on his Vespa to go swimming in the Enza Creek, or at the Lido in Boretto, with the bridge on the barges, where I heard local groups play—bands with the coolest, evocative names, like the Apostles and the Strays. There was a different group playing at the Lido every night in summer. On the Vespa, the route was Roncocesi, Ca' del Bosco, Lower Castelnuovo, where we stopped at an epic Texas-style bar called the Saloon with classic Western-style swinging doors. We'd walk in, and order an ice pop. Then we'd ride straight to Boretto, where we'd take a swim and at last hear the bands rehearsing.

I was no angel back then. Sometimes I'd steal fifty or a hundred lire from the priest's alms—I was an altar boy, so I knew where he hid the little velvet bag with the brown handle. I took just enough to buy myself a *prosciutto* sandwich at the grocery store across from the church. I've never tasted anything like it since: the savory fat of the ham and the crunchy fragrance of that bread baked with olive oil.

Meanwhile, my Aunt Faustina had married and lived with Uncle Arto, who had a great passion for fishing. He had a closet where he kept his poles and tackle, and the half-moon-shaped nets used for fishing in the streams.

"Delmo, come with me."

We went to Casina, a town in the hills nearby. While he was busy fishing, I would swim with my aunt. We set out early in the morning on a beautiful sunlit day. He started fishing, my aunt was sunbathing on the cobblestones. I was hot and went for a dip in the stream. I could hear the water rippling, clean and cold. I took a step, there was a deep hole in the bottom and I didn't know how to swim yet. I went under, pushing myself with my feet. I took a mouthful of water and couldn't yell. I shook my arms, waved my hands. Up and down I went, four times. Finally, my uncle realized what was happening and jumped in after me. I'd swallowed a lot of water and seriously risked drowning. Ever since, I've had a terrible relationship with water. Even so, the call of the stream, more than the sea, has remained strong. Sometimes I go swimming with my son in the Verde, the stream that flows through Pontremoli and into the Magra Creek. The water's still fine. I watch it flow, as cold and clean as the streams of my childhood. Now I bring my adult thoughts with me and watch my son, Blue, happily splashing about. In him I see myself as a child.

Then there was the parish cinema, where on Sunday afternoons I'd go watch my favorite movie, *Merveilleuse Angélique*. I was crazy about Angélique, with her petticoat and bare shoulders, getting a peek now and then. Or the legendary, titanic feats of Hercules when he challenged Samson, or the adventures of the Man in the Iron Mask. The parish youth club was the center of our world. Admission to Sunday movies was 150 lire, in exchange for all that fantasy and so much to learn. Eros, myth, adventure. Better than school.

One day in Reggio, my father, standing in front of the shop window at Delrio, a musical instrument store, gave in to my pleas and bought me that much longed-for guitar. Every day after school I would walk by that window just to look at it. I was always afraid someone else would buy it. It was a cheap brand, an awful ocher starburst.

"Papa, Papa, that's what I want."

It cost too much. A heap of money.

Please, *papà*.

He got it for me. I was in love. I thought it was beautiful. I even brought it to bed with me. All the guitars I play today have the same sunburst design—only today my favorite is a vintage 1955 Gibson. My father's salary was 120,000 lire a month, and that wonderful guitar, not even a name brand, cost 10,000 lire.

Uprooted

ONE NIGHT MY FATHER CAME BACK HOME WITH HIS HEAD BANDAGED. He had blood dripping from his temple. I fainted seeing him in such bad shape. I also fainted another time, one morning before school. I'd gone to the church to play the organ, and inside it was freezing. I had just drunk warm milk, fresh from the barn. I was hit with such congestion that I passed out right on that poor pipe organ.

"I'm not working there anymore, I don't like it," said my father. "I'm always up high. I'm afraid I might fall."

And fall he had. A wheel of cheese slipped, and he fell and hit his head. My mother was very worried. "What are we going to do if you don't work anymore?"

A friend of my father, a former coworker, also a cheese turner, by the name of Gianni Riquadri, had opened a grocery store in Massa, where he sold locally made cheese and hams.

"You should come here, Pino," he told my father.

My father fell under this friend's influence, and my mother didn't like it. Riquadri eventually convinced him to try his luck in that neck of the woods.

"Come over and make your fortune. I've found you a place to rent in downtown Forte dei Marmi. You can come here and open a little store."

Despite my mother's objections and my crying at the thought of leaving Grandma Diamante, my father decided we would move to Forte dei Marmi.

That's the way the world was. We did it and that was it. We moved. A rented flatbed truck, and some shabby furniture tied down with ropes: a little Formica table, our red chairs, a caved-in, fake-leather couch, and three bed frames. Very sad. My father drove along the Cisa Road, there was no Autostrada back then. We passed through Quattro Castella, Castelnuovone' Monti, Il Cerreto. My mother and my little brother Lauro up front, me in the back, sitting on the couch and making sure the ropes held. I had fun, I enjoyed the responsibility. Most of all, it was an adventure. It was September and still warm. With a great deal of commotion, we set out. When we got there after the long journey, my father's friend said to him he hadn't received the permit to open the store. It was a nice location, near Parmigiani's, a delicatessen that had been in Forte dei Marmi since World War I, where they sold cheeses and hams from Parma. My father should have thought about getting that permit first. He was totally unprepared, but that's the way he was. He had trusted his fast-talking friend. Now we were in the street. No home, no store, no place to sleep.

"Tonight, you can come sleep at my house, and tomorrow we'll sort things out."

The next day they found a little shop that was for sale, near the market square. It was for sale because business was so bad—it was a store with no future—summer was over and winters in Versilia are infinitely sad. So as not to return home in defeat, my father made a deal that was bound to be a bad one. He took inventory: rusty cans of tuna, dusty flasks of wine. He also found a cottage to rent, towards Querceta, in the middle of the fields north of Forte dei Marmi. The place wasn't bad, near a go-cart track that later became a skating rink. In the summer, local bands played there. Or someone would play records, like on the chair-o-plane. There, for the first time, I got to hear Creedence Clearwater Revival's 'Proud Mary' and 'Hey, Tonight.' I discovered the Bee Gees' 'Massachusetts,' the first bars of 'Let It Be' by the Beatles, some early Led Zeppelin. The effect of those sounds was immediate. I'd never heard music like that before. It was all new. And nothing would ever be the same again.

Winter was awful. The store wasn't working out, we had no money left. We couldn't even turn on the heat. After school, I'd go scrounging around for empty fruit crates to light the stove with, which barely kept us warm. Luckily, winters in Forte dei Marmi aren't that cold, so we managed to get by. I remember once I opened the cash box and saw that the day's take was a mere 14,000 lire. Before going to school each morning, my job was to cut the first slice of all the cold cuts—the black, deteriorated one, to show that there was turnover. If my father was worried, my mother was desperate.

We gave people credit to entice customers who couldn't pay right away, and many of them never paid up. Still, it didn't stop them from being demanding. Forte dei Marmi is a strange place. One that I, at least back then, didn't understand. Instead of good, honest table wine that didn't cost much, the customers who paid on credit would want Gallo Nero Chianti, all the best products. "Mark it down!" they'd say. One day I got pissed off at a couple of snooty teachers, a husband and wife, who left a hefty bill unpaid. I went to their house to ask for the money. They treated me as if I were nothing but a brat. Arrogant slobs. Insults and swear words flew. It was thanks to similar litanies that I became famous one night at Cala di Volpe, in Porto Cervo. One thing's for sure, and that is that since I was a boy (I was only twelve when the incident with the teachers took place) I've had a hard time holding back in the face of injustice and arrogance. Those two cheapskates didn't want to give me the money. But I insisted and got it. They never set foot in my father's store again. For the sake of keeping the peace, he would have forgotten about their debt. But we were in the shit.

Summer returned at last and with it came salvation. Back then, in those parts, everyone worked during the summer. In the morning, I would hop on my bike with two baskets and go deliver the shopping for breakfast, and get focacce. Later, ham and cheese for lunch. Then I made another round for dinner, from four o'clock to eight.

All the while I missed my friends back in Reggio, and had fits of nostalgia for my faraway grandmother, who'd stayed in Roncocesi. I didn't fit in in Forte dei Marmi. I'd brought a tender little jar of soil from our old vegetable garden with me. I carried it in my pocket, and every now and then I'd take a whiff of it, with a bit of pathetic romanticism. Once my math teacher, a rotten Tuscan from Pietrasanta, saw me and asked what I was doing.

"I'm smelling the smell of my yard back home," I said.

He blasted me in front of the whole class. They laughed and teased me. The bastards. I suffered, humiliated in front of everyone. I felt homeless, friendless, uprooted, alone. With my frustrations in a hostile place, trapped by the claustrophobia of that mean little town, so petty and unwelcoming.

My only real friend was Giampiero, or Gary, as he was called. He played the drums and was a true phenomenon, a child prodigy with a tiger-striped Hollywood drum kit, which he played in a local band, the Chessmen. I kept playing my keyboard, and sometimes we'd play together at the students' Carnival and New Year's Eve parties.

Winters dragged on. Everything stopped. Nothing happened. People stayed inside, waiting for the return of summer. Forte dei Marmi is a strange place for an Emilian farmer. A non-place. Lots of rich people flocked there in summer, to their exclusive beaches and millionaires' mansions. In the shadow of all that luxury, the inhabitants, the natives, would sit around the whole rest of the year, waiting for the elite of Milano to come oozing back. Everything was backwards. We'd work like crazy all summer and do nothing in the winter. At some point during the summer we would go visit my grandparents, where we slept crammed into a shack behind the garden, with the corrugated asbestos roof, and rent our house in Forte dei Marmi to rich folks. It was a nonstop playground. A playground of the soul and desires. Nasty, rife with envy and rancor, mean. Full of gossip. Living in Forte dei Marmi after summer ends is like staying in a dance hall after everyone leaves: the music's over, the lights are off, and all that's left is sadness, anguish, solitude. A sense of being estranged from the world around you.

I was sad, but bursting with energy. My never-ending contradiction of identical opposing forces. I spent all summer working. In September, I'd hang out at an arcade called Las Vegas, with its pool tables, pinball machines, and foosball tables. It was at the shore, and for me, with my imagination, it could easily have been the coast of California. I went because they had a jukebox. I didn't have money to play anything, but all day long I'd listen to the records the other kids put on. I discovered the folk rock of Simon & Garfunkel's 'The Sound of Silence,' against the backing of Paul Simon's guitar, one of the best songs ever written, and 'Mrs. Robinson' and 'Scarborough Fair.'

The jukebox also pumped out the energy of black music, the rhythm & blues of James Brown, Otis Redding, Aretha Franklin, Wilson Pickett. There was a local group, the New Lights, that played rhythm & blues while wearing matching jackets and doing synchronized choreographed numbers. They had a horn section with a trumpet, a trombone, and two saxes. The singer was mulatto, Duilio from Viareggio. He had a black voice, kind of like James Brown's. They were popular around Forte dei Marmi.

The scene was hopping everywhere you went, bands sprung up like mushrooms. That was 1967. Italian beat was all the rage, as was pop. Some people were even playing rhythm & blues.

I had my band, too. A classic lineup featuring Gary on drums; Beppe, aka Steel, on bass; Marco on guitar; and me playing the organ. The Dukes. It was the same name I'd used for my first band on the other side of the Apennine. We played contests for Italian beat groups, at Cinema Principe in Forte dei Marmi. We played that ludicrous number 'Simon Says.' I also sang a song nobody knew yet by the Moody Blues, the progressive British rock band with roots in rhythm & blues, 'Ride My See-Saw,' which I really enjoyed. We played at a bubbly New Year's Eve bash at the Bernina del Cinquale Pensione, after which the Dukes died a second and final death, due to a chronic and sad lack of gigs.

I wonder what would have become of me and my musical experience if I'd stayed in Reggio Emilia and hadn't moved to Forte dei Marmi. The Via Emilia, from Modena to Reggio Emilia, was mostly a hard-rock kind of scene, along with the protest music of singer-songwriters in Bologna, due to the more educated crowd that gravitated to the university there. In Versilia, the mood was more West Coast, influenced by the San Francisco scene, the hippies and the flower children. It was all about sandals, flower-print shirts, patchouli, and smoking dope. We listened to Simon & Garfunkel, but rhythm & blues as well. Musically speaking, the climate was mellower. Who knows what would have become of me if I'd stayed in Emilia?

A Sax and a Whipping

THE CANAPONI WERE FROM PIETRASANTA; THE IMPERIALS, WITH THEIR flashy, charismatic bass player, were from Vallecchia, near Forte dei Marmi; Nouvelle Vague, with their horn section, were from

Viareggio; Massa had Daniel and His Disciples. Every town had its band. Those sounds were formative, I understood that what I was listening to meant a lot to me. I wasn't able to analyze it, I still didn't know what harmonic scales were, but in the mean time they germinated, produced skills, patterns, ideas. I was so psyched, willing to play any instrument just to be in a band. If they already had an organist but needed a drummer, I'd play drums. I wasn't just winging it—my friend Gary had taught me the basics, and soon I was ready to play drums in a group called the Black Devils. I also played sax, since another group was missing a tenor sax. I went to a flute player by the name of Martino and asked him to teach me the scale, which is the same on sax as on flute. I learned to play two songs in a week. I auditioned and they took me. Only I didn't have a saxophone and they wouldn't let me in the band unless I had one. Every Sunday my father would put my weekly allowance of 100 lire in a Galbani cheese box with a slot he'd cut in it, like a piggy bank. I managed to scrape together 5,000 lire. Not a bad little sum. So, I went to see Paolo, who studied piano at the conservatory in Lucca, and asked him where I could find a tenor sax. "Super used," I told him. "I don't have much money." He told me there was a store in La Spezia called Resta's. We took the bus there. They had a marching band saxophone that was steel-colored, not even brass—a crummy Orsi with a torn, ugly, dark green case. It cost 55,000 lire. I only had 5,000. New ones cost 150,000.

The instrument dealer saw me there with my 5,000 lire, feeling dismayed but still motivated, and decided to let me pay in eleven installments, even though I was hardly more than a child. While he was putting the sax inside that hideous tattered case, Paolo, who'd come with me, spotted a friend of his walking by. It was the flute player, Martino, his classmate at the conservatory. Martino took him back to Forte dei Marmi on his Vespa, leaving me stranded. By now it was dark and I was in totally unfamiliar surroundings. *Where the fuck was La Spezia?* Infinitely far away from everything I knew. I had no idea where it was, with respect to Forte dei Marmi. I was happy I had the sax to keep me company, but I'd been abandoned like a dog. Alone. Forlorn. In the dark. In La Spezia with a half-broken saxophone inside a rotten case. I was lost in the world. My father expected me home at seven. I'd be in trouble if I didn't make it back. I couldn't take the bus because I didn't have any money left. I tried hitchhiking. *Which way was Forte dei Marmi?* I got a ride to the Carrara interchange. From there, one road went toward the mountains, another to the sea. An hour later I got a ride to Forte dei Marmi. When we reached the square, I got on my bike and pedaled furiously homeward. Steering with one hand only, carrying the sax with the other. By then it must have been nine o'clock, or later. I didn't see my father. He was hiding behind the door with his belt in hand. I got the whipping of my life, which I remember to this day.

Finally, though, I began playing the sax. And with ten lire here, twenty there, I managed to pay off the installments.

Massimo, the singer of the group I was in, had red hair. He was missing two phalanges on one of his fingers that he'd lost in an explosion. He had a hollowed, mean face like Jean-Paul Belmondo, and ruled the neighborhood. A local bully. Violent. Arrogant. Brutal.

Before going to play, I still helped my parents with deliveries, and sometimes I'd stop to get something to drink at the bar where the town's most deranged and outrageous kids hung out. The Crazies' Bar, they called it. It had a phone booth with a pile of phone books from all the cities in Italy. And a jukebox.

"Where do you think you're going with all that stuff, boy?"

"I have to deliver it to a customer."

"In your dreams. That stuff is ours."

Then they had their snack. Wine and *prosciutto*. Once again, my father tore my ass up.

Massimo, the redhead, used to hide nitroglycerine in the phone books. He committed robberies around town. Raised hell at the

Mugello racetrack. Finally, he killed four *carabinieri* in Pietrasanta. He'd been in jail for burglary, but escaped and hid out in a dilapidated house in the poplar woods in Forte dei Marmi, where he was supposed to meet up with his girlfriend. The cops surrounded the house, and he came out blasting a submachine gun. Killed four of them. The news rocked the town. We all went to the funerals. He got life in prison.

The band I played sax in was left without a singer, and we broke up. After that, the guys from Pietrasanta came to recruit me. Good musicians, good players. Semiprofessionals. They got people dancing. Pippo sang, I played sax. We were supposed to play at the Alhambra in Sarzana, one of the two most popular dance halls in the area. The show was scheduled for Sunday, with an afternoon and an evening set. Our bass player and leader, known as Gi, told me our singer Pippo couldn't come. He'd had a fight with his girlfriend. They'd come to blows, a messy situation. So who was going to sing? The only one who knew the words to all our songs was me. I was very diligent, even if I'd never sung in public before, except for a few little tunes back at the church in Roncocesi. We managed to salvage the evening and our contract. Who cares about sax? You sing! I got through that Sunday pretty well. I sang, and during the breaks I played sax. Lee Hazelwood's 'Some Velvet Morning' as recorded by Vanilla Fudge. Procol Harum, the Moody Blues. At the time, 'Save Me' by Brian Auger and the Trinity was all the rage. It was a pretty heady set list. I also sang 'Fire' by Arthur Brown, who was known for lighting himself on fire while singing it.

I went to see Genesis play at the Piper in Viareggio, where they had the New Trends Festival. I saw Ivano Fossati's Delirium, Joe Vescovi's Trip from Genoa, the Other Side of the Coin, the Bronze Ballet, Mia Martini and the Machine. It was the era of groups like PFM and Banco del Mutuo Soccorso, of the 'Beat Mass,' rock gigs inspired by Marcello Giombi's *Mass of the Young* of 1966.

I found myself back in church, jamming with Gary, my old drummer friend, even playing some songs we'd written ourselves. We started playing around a bit. Parties, a few pensiones, New Year's Eve gigs.

Emilio Tarabella, from Forte dei Marmi, had a passion for recording equipment, and owned a four-track recorder. He made a record for us, my first 45, 'Vorrei Volare' ('I Wanna Fly'). The group's name was Piano Verticale, and the song was written by Paolo, our piano player, who studied at the Boccherini Conservatory in Lucca. Tarabella printed a thousand copies, which we distributed among the faithful at the beat masses.

We mostly hung out at two places, either the Las Vegas Arcade or the Green Cross. We'd spend entire days there, playing soccer, cards, and music. The older guys couldn't wait till payday at the end of the month. The first thing they did was go to the whores. One night they brought me along as their mascot. We went to a house near the Cinquale, where one by one they entered a room. When my turn came...she was fat, falling apart, red lipstick smeared all over her lips. I hightailed it.

It was April, and though the water was cold, we went swimming in the sea. I had always gone swimming in creeks, and had been to the pool in Reggio twice, but I had never swum in the sea. The others were old hands. They leaped in near the Forte dei Marmi Pier, swam out to the famed structure, and climbed up the ladder. They teased the shit out of me. For my heavy Emilian accent. And my politeness. My good manners. "*Fornacino*," they called me: "little Fornaciari." I was skinny, courteous, with red cheeks and a heavy accent.

"Go on, jump in, Fornacino."

To show them I was up to snuff, I accepted their challenge and threw myself in. The water was freezing, the sea was rough. I floundered, salt water came rushing down my throat, I couldn't take much more. But I was still only halfway to the pier. Someone saw I was having trouble, and sadistically cried out, "Go to the buoys and hang on." When I finally reached them, I hung on for dear life, but they were covered with mussels, so by the time I came out of the water I was bleeding and cut all over. They could barely hold back their mocking laughter. I walked away, feeling their gazes searing into my back. Where was I? What was I doing? The sea, blood, mussels? What was I going to tell my mother when she saw me?

Once again, I felt lost in the world. Like in La Spezia. A hostile world. If only I had stayed in my beloved Roncocesi, this would never have happened.

The Lavorini Syndrome

WE WOULD HAVE PARTIES WITH GIRLS, AND IT WAS MY JOB TO PUT on records while everybody else smooched. Slow dances. Some of the kids would go upstairs. Maybe they fucked. Then came the year of the Lavorini murder, in the pine woods of Viareggio (1969). The fall-out was enormous. The victim was my age—twelve. It was one of the most scandalous cases in post-war Italy. The disappearance of Ermanno Lavorini, the sweeping searches, and the recovery of his lifeless body were in the news for months, sparking horror, scandal, and debate. The homosexual community was targeted when investigators labeled the case a sex crime, which later turned out to be baseless. In Italy back then, homosexuals weren't called gay, they were called *finocchi*—"fennels," like the vegetable. All anyone talked about was "green dances," meaning sex between men and underage boys. The epicenter was Viareggio and the area around Reggio. The two worlds of my geography. Irrational, morbid, persecutory paranoia spread.

"Watch out, Fornacino, or you'll wind up like Lavorini."

Wretched, macabre jokes. The Lavorini syndrome. People began eyeing one another suspiciously, the gossip flew out of control, accusations of pedophilia and perversion.

"Watch out for that guy. He likes little boys."

People would arbitrarily accuse anyone.

I went to a little party at Paolo's house one afternoon. Paolo was older than the rest of us. At around seven, most of the guests headed out. Then Paolo and his crew started taunting me.

"Fornacino's a fag. Fornacino's a piece of ass."

They tied me to a bed by my wrists and feet. They whipped out their dicks. One guy tried to put his in my mouth, but I clenched my teeth tight. Another hit me on the head with his. Another guy started jerking off. I don't think they really wanted to rape me, but the sexual abuse was still real and gratuitous. Senseless. Brutal. They ganged up on me. I started screaming. They got scared and let me go. I tore off home on my bike. I was in shock. I didn't know whether, or not, to tell my parents. The Lavorini episode was still in the air—that polluted and poisoned air. And it had happened so close to us. To make matters worse, at a time when things were rough going for us, uprooted and living in such a hostile place, my father tended to blame me and say everyone else was right. That's how he was, and I decided to shut up about it.

I could forge my father's signature to perfection, and that helped me skip school more than once. I wrote a letter in his handwriting, threatening to press charges with the *carabinieri* if his son ever got molested again.

Signed: Giuseppe Fornaciari.

Before school, I went to Paolo's house and slipped it in his mailbox. From that day on, they left me in peace.

Another time, I was attacked by a group of boys who hit me with rolled-up newspapers and magazines while I was playing cards at Pierino's bar. It hurt, they were violent. I had to defend myself. I slammed one guy in the face. Later I made him a featured character in one of my songs: *"Pippo, che cazzo fai?"* ("Pippo, what the fuck are you doing?") At any rate, they wanted nothing to do with me. It was a very hard, sad time in my life.

I continued to deliver groceries to the tourists. But I didn't go to the beach and sit under an umbrella. Who could afford that? I had to work in my father's store. I didn't integrate with the locals. To them I was a foreigner who spoke Emilian.

Dance Halls

ACROSS FROM OUR STORE, ON THE WATERFRONT, STOOD THE CARAVELLA, a renowned dance hall. Further on was the Capannina. Then there was the Bussola in Focette, the Pirata and Mecca in Marina di Massa. This was the geography of the music clubs where I went to listen to bands rehearse. Outside the Caravella, which was covered but had an open-air dance floor, I would hide behind a laurel hedge. I got to hear soundchecks by the Motowns, and the Primitives featuring M. One day Lucio Dalla, who had just written '4 Marzo 1943,' (1971) caught me behind the hedge.

"Hey, what are you doing? Who are you?"

I told him I was listening to the rehearsal, and that I was a musician. He didn't seem impressed.

"Tell me something, then. Is there any sweeping going on here?" he asked.

Naïve as I was, I didn't get it. *Any sweeping going on?*

"Yes," I told him. "The sidewalks are clean."

He thought I was trying to be a smart ass. But I didn't know that "sweep" was slang for "fuck."

"Look, kid, don't get smart with me. At least tell me where I can find a newsstand."

I told him I'd go downtown with him, and got in his Jaguar.

Gorgeous, dark red, with chrome spoke rims. I got out and bought him a newspaper, feeling like I was someone important. Then Dalla took me home.

"*Ciao.*"

"*Ciao.*"

The next day, he was playing at the same place. I had an idea. I went to my father's store and made him a magnificent sandwich with *prosciutto crudo* from Parma. The sweetest and most exquisite. I cut open a roll and carefully filled it with slices of that pink marvel with the heavenly scent of pork. I ran with it to Dalla and gave it to him. It was the only thing I had to give.

Then Pooh played the Caravella. In those days, Valerio Negrini still played drums for them. Once again, I got caught listening behind that hedge.

"You from here? You know a cheap pensione?"

"Yes, a friend of mine has one. It's called the Campagnola. It's a bit out of the way. Shouldn't cost too much. It's small."

I hopped in their van and rode with them there. In exchange, they gave me a bright red jacket with fringe and a hippie medallion. A musician's outfit. Very fashionable. I was in seventh heaven.

Back then, all the cafés in Forte dei Marmi hosted shows with small orchestras, so my pals from the Dukes and I went to the notorious Crazies' Bar to ask the owner if we could play there, in that den of stoners and madmen. It was downtown, but there was a pine copse nearby.

"Set up tables," we told him. "People will eat and drink and have a good time while we play."

He was perplexed. To him, it sounded like a lot of unnecessary fuss.

"Come on. We'll play the first show for free."

We convinced him. He built a basic little stage for us with four planks. I wore the red jacket I got from the guys in Pooh, and my gold-colored medallion. Wearing that gear got me really psyched. I overcame my shyness and tasted glory. I sang 'Georgia on My Mind'—written by Hoagy Carmichael and Stuart Gorrell, but of course made famous by Ray Charles—which had become a standard in my repertoire. I'd got the group back together in a hurry, so we didn't have that many songs. I sang 'Georgia on My Mind' again. And again. Four, five, maybe even ten times. At which point the owner came storming over, snorting and cursing.

"What the fuck are you doing with this Georgia?! No way, no more Georgia! You and Georgia can get the fuck out of here!"

Yet another attempt had failed. But soon I met Enrico, who had a green Mini Minor. He said he knew a group looking for a keyboard player.

The Corpse Collectors

"THEY'RE A LITTLE OUT OF THE WAY, ON THE 115, WHERE THE NEW GOLF course is. They play pretty bad, but they're really great guys."

At last I could hook up with people I liked, on the same wavelength. They were from the countryside.

Forte dei Marmi has always survived by catering to rich folks, while at the same time despising them because the locals wanted to be like them. In the winter, they may have been poor, but they still wore their blue Oxford shirts to ape the rich folks from Milano. I had red pants, a worn-out orange sweater, any old shoes. I wore whatever I happened to have, and that was certainly nothing fashionable. No one in my family ever had the time or the taste to coordinate colors much. Back in the countryside, we'd wear anything without pretense, but here the locals strutted around like the Milanese as they took their Sunday stroll, elegant as could be. In those days I had long hair, and technically I was the hippie type: poor, uncouth, shabbily dressed.

My father summed it up this way: "They may have nice shirts, but their fridges are empty."

At my house, it was just the opposite. The content of your fridge was more important than the brand of your shirt.

Going out toward Querceta and the hills, the demography changed. Out there, people worked the land. Sure, they may have gone to the seashore in summer—two or three times, tops—but they were more genuine. We had lots in common.

Two guitarists, Salvatore and Domenico; a bass player, Aldo; drummer Angelo, a helluva nice guy; me on the keyboard; and Giuliano on sax, who literally had to come down off the mountain to join us. There wasn't even a road—he had to walk down the old mule track to catch the bus to come to rehearsals. Two hours here, and two to get back in the middle of the night.

Our fortuitous name referenced Manzoni: The Corpse Collectors. We practiced at Salvatore the guitarist's garage, from eight o'clock to midnight. He was also a damn good hairstylist, by the way. Then we'd feast on green onions and tuna fish, and flasks of wine, which was good in that part of the country. They even had their own vegetable garden. It was the first time I'd found friends after moving to Forte dei Marmi. I meant a lot to them. I was younger, their mascot of sorts, but respected because (objectively speaking and without bragging) I played better than they did. They gave me lots of support, protected me. For once I felt like I was wanted and cared for, out of friendship and the warmth of simple people, which meant a lot because otherwise those were very tough years.

Even my mother encouraged me: "You're good, Delmo, you're good."

My father was busy grappling with the difficulty of supporting us all. He was totally absorbed by his problems, and they wore him down. On the outside, he appeared uninterested in my struggle to start a band. He'd been uprooted too, and was far from what he considered home. He had few friends, maybe none. He didn't smoke, didn't drink, didn't hang out at the bar. The only time he ever went out was to go to the movies. He was alone and tormented by his problems. Very sensitive and introverted. Taciturn. He had no time for my music.

There'd be long silences at the table. If I didn't feel like eating, he'd utter an essential and pragmatic: "*Magna.*" ("Eat.")

"I don't feel like it."

"*Magna.*"

And that was it.

My mother later told me that when he saw me on TV for the first time, at my first Sanremo Festival, he cried in silence. Almost as if to make up for so many years of emotional distance between us. Back then, it was hard for men to express their feelings or show any kind of affection. My father considered hugs and kisses a useless exercise in exhibitionism. The absence of intimacy marked the normal virility of people who had lived through two wars, Fascism, the partisan revolt, bombing, dead friends and siblings. People had become toughened, put off by emotions, overburdened with sacrifice, just to survive. My father never integrated in Forte dei Marmi, consumed by constant tension, by his business that never took off, by an environment so hostile to our simple and deep-rooted farm culture. He never showed true joy. I think he had enough of his balls being busted. He probably figured music, with its cheerful energy, was something frivolous, and totally outside his realm, apart from waltzes and mazurkas. As were my dreams of glory. But the Corpse Collectors appreciated me, and it was the first time in a long time that I felt appreciated. I clearly perceived that someone had recognized my talent. They believed in me. I felt wanted. It was a beautiful feeling.

We performed at the Veliero, in Cinquale, near the airport. I played organ and sang. It was an old-time dance hall—discotheques hadn't arrived on the scene yet. There was a coal-burning stove propped against a pole in the middle of the hall. Straw-woven chairs. Ladies on one side, men on the other. The men would get up and proposition the seated ladies to dance: "Oh, do you dance?" Then await the verdict. The answer was almost always no.

We had a truly awesome set list. Lots of songs by Creedence Clearwater Revival. From 'Have You Ever Seen the Rain?' to 'Bad Moon Rising' and 'Proud Mary.' I sang with a gritty voice. I was skinny and performed shirtless, with an unlikely rabbit fur jacket, open down the front, and a live mouse on my shoulder. I had seen the Crows perform with a crow perched on their shoulders, so I showed up with that mouse and that hapless hippie fur jacket I was so proud of. I'd become something of a character in part thanks to this absurd look. There, at last I began to meet chicks, all older than me. There was one, she must have been eighteen, with long hair and a flower-print hippie dress. She looked like Native American and was always waiting for me in front of the stage. She had a red Ciao moped. I was still a virgin. My mind was still mostly on music; I wasn't ready. An innocence you possess only once. She was already a woman, mature. An expert.

One April night, she invited me for pizza with her sister and her sister's boyfriend. I accepted. We decided to go down to the beach. The two of us went inside a changing room, where she pushed her hand down my pants and started working on me. That was a whole new experience. She pulled down my pants and started sucking. Another first. Outrageous. I exploded right away. But there was more where that came from—eight times, I think. She kept going. Over-the-top eroticism. In the end, I couldn't come anymore. I went out with her for a while, and was really into it—it was new, that desire—but I wasn't in love with her.

The owner of the Veliero, who was a big drinker, had a load on that night we performed there and said he didn't want to pay us. An argument arose. Angelo, our drummer, was a big guy. He grabbed him and hung him up on the front gate. The owner paid, nut he didn't hire us for any more gigs.

The same guy had another dance hall in Pietrasanta. One Sunday, Dik Dik played there. As soon as they started singing, '*Guardo te e vedo mio figlioooo*' ('I look at you and see my son'), the electricity went out. Someone said, "Sorry, guys. Technical problem." Then it happened again. Three times. The band got mad. It turned out it was that fool owner who was cutting the juice on purpose because he thought they were playing too loud. That's how that world was. The dance hall owners were all weirdos, full of obsessions, whims, fixations, fancies. They were all crazy, in a small world. Pietrasanta, Forte dei Marmi, Cinquale, Massa—that was their whole world.

Once a month I'd scrounge a ride back to Reggio. I wanted to see my grandmother and not lose contact with my friends. My real friends.

Meanwhile I had become leader of the Corpse Collectors. I arranged the songs and had got it into my head to make a record. One day, I read that much longed-for ad in a magazine: "A well-known record company is currently seeking artists for recording opportunities." Tokens, phone booth—I called.

"This is Zucchero Fornaciari, from the Corpse Collectors. We want to make a record."

An appointment was made for two days later in Milano. Incredible, super easy.

"Guys, the day after tomorrow we're recording!"

Aldo didn't give a fuck about it. Angelo mumbled, "OK, but what songs are we gonna do?"

"What do you think, Angelo? The ones we have."

They were titled 'May Song' and 'Autumn Afternoon.'

"No, Salvatore," howled our guitarist's fiancé, who was very pretty. "Don't go to Milano. If it works out and you get famous, I know you won't come back." Typical small-town view of the big city, success, the sparkling world of entertainment, all sex-drugs-and-rock'n'roll.

"My girl doesn't want me to go," griped Salvatore, sadly shrugging his shoulders. "Sooner or later you guys'll be in the same boat."

But Aldo the bass player—only five feet tall, with long hair and always played the same note—was psyched.

Eventually we managed to get it together and set out for Milano. We had a van that we called Bubba and filled it with mattresses. We rolled into town the night before the recording session and slept in the van, parked on the street. The next day, we went straight to a barber shop to get spiffed up and clean-shaven. Hair done and smelling of cologne, we showed up at the record company.

"Welcome!" said the man. "You're the Corpse Collectors? Ah, what a pleasure!"

He took us into a well equipped and comfortable studio on Via Berchet. We were psyched to make a record. Giuliano's sax had a broken pad cup, which he tried to fix with a rubber band. He couldn't even play the three notes he was supposed to. I had to play them on the organ. We brought the recording home with us. At the door, as we were leaving, the guy told us to wait and invited us to a party that evening. He said people from the press and TV would be there. We certainly weren't expecting that. "But you need costumes. You can't show up like this." Of course, we had no money for costumes, so we decided to head back home.

Meanwhile, Salvatore kept babbling like a broken record, "My girlfriend, my girlfriend!" He wanted to get back to his girl. The Corpse Collectors made their exit. And happily, too, because surprisingly the guy kept complimenting us.

"You kids were great! Fantastic songs! I'll take care of the rest."

Just as we were about to leave, though, he had us sign a piece of paper.

Twenty days later, we got a letter saying we owed him three million lire for the recording, the costumes (which we never wore), and the photo session (which never took place).

"They're gonna throw us in jail," moaned Salvatore.

Luckily, a friend of ours had a brother who was a lawyer, and he saved us from a heap of trouble.

Eighth Grade

IN 1968 I WAS IN EIGHTH GRADE AND LIKED TO GO ON THE ROOF TO protest, just as the kids do today. More than revolution though, I enjoyed being the head honcho and every time there was a protest, I'd take the whole class with me. I played my keyboard at student parties and got to know lots of people.

There was Nocker, a nerdy blond-haired kid from Alto Adige—reminded us of a German. He always sat in the front row like a dweeb. For the other kids, though, I was the real foreigner. When I'd walk by he'd whisper, "Bastard!" After hearing him call me that so often, one fine day I gave Nocker such a smack I knocked him off his seat. The teacher sent me out of the classroom and the principal gave me a good scolding.

"I know you're a musician, and playing music is fine. But it's also nice to know what happens in the world. Do you read the papers? Are you informed?" she asked me, cool as a cucumber after scolding the shit out of me.

"No, I could care less, ma'am. I'm into playing my music, that's all I really care about. I want to become a band leader."

"Ah, you've got a so-what attitude. Noncommittal. Whatever happens is fine with you." The principal was a left-winger.

Why did she say that? Noncommittal? I was committed to my music. I didn't give a shit about anything else, but I did take part in the protest movement, the student occupations. The general mood was very politicized in those days.

I wound up flunking eighth grade, along with everyone else in the class. I had a crush on a girl named Ivana. I was thunderstruck. She was gorgeous, and I've always had a thing for chicks with long hair and dark complexions, like hers. She was shy. Dazzling smile, fleshy lips, skinny legs. I'd walk her home. Her parents considered me a hippie and didn't want her hanging out with me. I suffered because of that. Ivana's folks were from Chiusi, and she spent a month there every summer. I missed her and so one morning decided to take the train to Chiusi. I got to the station and knew nothing more than the girl's last name.

"Excuse me, sir. Do you know the Nasorri family?"

"They might live in Upper Chiusi. They certainly don't live in Lower Chiusi."

"And where might Upper Chiusi be?"

"Up that way."

I set out on foot. By the time I got there, it was already four o'clock and I was completely out of breath.

"Excuse me, sir. Do you know where the Nasorri family lives?" I asked someone.

"There are lots of Nasorris up here."

"But a girl with long black hair. Ivana's her name."

Come on, she's gorgeous, I thought. There's no way you haven't seen her. I was starting to lose my cool.

"Oh, sure. She's the one staying in that house in the country."

In the country. Another three kilometers on foot. By the time I reached the house I was exhausted.

I knock on the door and she answered. She turned red, those inflamed cheeks contrasting with her black hair.

"Are you crazy? What if my parents find out you're here?"

She looked great, all red like that. Robust sensuality. Terrified at the idea of her parents seeing her with me, she took me to the playground. It had a swing and a slide. I got an ice cream that day, but not a single kiss. We rode the swing for an hour, then I beat it and went back the way I came. I got home at three o'clock the next morning, feeling wretched and in love.

Augusto and Beppe

I LIKED HIM AND HIS VOICE. WITH THAT BEARD OF HIS AND HIS GLASSES, he was very charismatic. I lived in Forte dei Marmi and saw a poster for the Nomads concert at a dance hall in Sarzana.

I rode there alone on my bike. I don't remember how I managed to get in. I wasn't even fourteen years old, and what's more, didn't have a dime to my name. They still played with the original lineup: Manfredini on drums, Campari on bass, Augusto sang, Beppe played keyboards. After the show was over, while the band broke down the gear, I went over to Augusto. He smoked Murattis, one after another.

"Can I bum a cigarette?" I asked him boldly.

He gave me the butt he was smoking. I didn't have the guts to ask for anything else, so I hightailed it.

One day, my parents and I rode the Vespa to the fair in Scandiano. We really liked that fair, but the actual, unspoken reason for our little journey was that the Nomads were playing. My father drove, my mother sat behind him, and I crouched up front, in between my father's legs. A black-and-white snapshot of the 1960s. That night they played 'Noi Non ci Saremo,' which I already knew, and the just released 'Dio è Morto.' Two beautiful songs written by Francesco Guccini, who was a thousand years ahead of everybody else. I was enchanted, bewitched by Augusto's voice. I was in ecstasy. The Nomads didn't have a road crew, just a guy who worked the mixing board. The band still broke down their gear themselves.

I went up to the stage. Beppe Carletti was tinkering with the cables around his organ.

66

"Hi, Beppe. I'm Zucchero, and I'm a musician," I said. "Tell me, how does one go about making a record?"

I must have had the most tender and naïve look on my face.

So, he says: "Eh, you've got to make a demo tape of your songs. Even just guitar and vocals. Then you bring it to a record company."

"I've got a demo tape, but I don't know anybody. Can you help me?"

Please, please, please.

"Well, if you want, I can get you an appointment with our record company."

He smiled, but he was serious!

"You have to talk to a gentleman by the name of Bruno Tibaldi."

I liked that name.

"Give me your phone number. I'll let you know."

I was in disbelief. And as incredible as it might sound, a week later he called to say he'd talked to the artistic director, and had set up an appointment for me at EMI in Rome, on Viale dell'Oceano Pacifico.

Fuck. I didn't have a demo tape.

I summoned Gary, called Paolino the piano player, and Marco the guitarist, and we went to a studio. We recorded ten or so songs. They sounded a little like Jethro Tull, with a syncopated piano. It was a weird blend of Guccini and progressive rock. There was a tambourine, an Ian Anderson–style flute. The songs were all long—endless—like Francesco's. Back then, that was in fashion. 'La Morte di Irene,' 'Il Bosco.' Even 'Il Dubbio'! ('The Death of Irene,' 'The Woods,' 'Doubt.') What song titles! A presumptuous concept album! Every one of the songs lasted at least as long as, 'La Locomotiva.' Oh, and I almost forgot: 'Il Paese di Ken.' ('Ken's Town.') Echoes of PFM, the best progressive rock group in Italy at the time. It worked though, and was musically akin to bands like Genesis, Pink Floyd, early King Crimson.

My old pal Marco—together we used to steal cigarettes and money from pinball machines, and later I put him in my song 'Pippo, che cazzo fai?'—came to Rome with me. We walked from the train station to Viale dell'Oceano Pacifico. Who had cab fare? That day I found out that Viale dell'Oceano Pacifico is in the EUR section of Rome. I thought Rome was going to be like Carrara. But after three hours on foot, we still hadn't made it there. It was July, our feet were boiling and blistered.

When I first saw Mr. Bruno Tibaldi, I thought it was a mirage. But Beppe had provided an introduction, and I started to believe it was happening. I stepped into the dream of his world. A hallucination from the Far East. There were two huge wicker chairs with big round backs from Thailand in Tibaldi's studio. The East was very trendy in those days: the sitar, mystic trips, *Emmanuelle*. I walk in and sit down, wrapped in this exotic wicker chair. He's got his back turned to me, on the phone. Guy stays on the telephone for a good hour. Then turns to me and, without even a hello, he says, "Ah, yes. You. So, you're Beppe's cousin, eh? Let's see..."

Beppe's cousin? Wow! Nice going, Carletti.

"Man, this is dragging on. How long is this single?" he huffed, after putting on the tape.

Help.

"But," I started muttering, "look, Mr. Tibaldi, this is an album. Actually, it's a concept album."

That was suicide.

"Ah," he said, brushing me off. "Let me listen to the whole thing then, at my leisure. We'll get back to you."

"I just have one favor to ask," I dared. "If you aren't interested, could you please send it back to me? It's the only copy I've got."

It wasn't true, but it was expensive to make copies back then.

I never saw the tape again.

Angela

MY FATHER'S STORE CONTINUED TO DO POORLY. THEN HE GOT IT INTO his head to go work as a clerk at a deli in Avenzaa town near Carrara. Once again, working for the man.

He said to me: "The rest of you stay here. You'll continue with school, and in the afternoon help your mother in the store. I'm going there."

In the industrial zone of Carrara they worked year-round, not just in summer, like in Forte dei Marmi. We hadn't been making ends meet, and this way he could bring in a paycheck.

My father had a light blue Fiat 1100 that never started. To save money, he'd converted it to methane. On winter mornings before going to school, my brother and I had to push it to get it to go.

My mother and I managed to eke out a living without him, though. The summer was good in the tourists' paradise. Winter was hell. No, a desert.

Meanwhile I kept playing with the Corpse Collectors.

One day, the owner of the store where my father worked as a clerk offered to sell him the shop. My dad was a hard worker and the owner liked him, so he gave him a good price and let him pay in installments. My father sold everything in the Forte dei Marmi store and we moved to Avenza, some twenty kilometers away.

Uprooted yet again—only this time it was worse, because now I had a band, and the Corpse Collectors had good vibes, a good atmosphere. I had to leave the few friends I'd only recently made: Gary and all the people I hung out with at the Green Cross. But most of all, Marco, a guitarist of exceptional talent. He was eccentric and kept to himself. Plus, he had a sister: Angela. She was fifteen, I was seventeen. They lived in a little house with a yard, and like a lot of families in Forte dei Marmi, they had a bungalow out back they lived in during the summer, when they rented their regular house to tourists.

It was winter. We decided to rehearse in the bungalow, which was empty. Then in comes this gorgeous young chick. Almond eyes, sad look on her face. Brown hair, very long. Red and black Scottish kilt, big pin, black stockings. Elegant to a T. Like a little girl who wanted to look grown-up.

"This is my sister, Angela."

A vision. I couldn't sleep at night.

Marco was going out with a girl named Carla, who had a green Prinz.

"Hey, Marco," I said. "Let's go to the movies in Viareggio! You and Carla, and me and your sister."

I confessed I was crazy about her. He told me to forget it, she already had a boyfriend. "You're definitely not her type." He felt that was important for me to know. He protected her. The next day he told me he'd talked to his sister and she said, "That guy? He makes me sick."

Bummer. I didn't say anything more to him about her.

It was Carnival season in Viareggio, and Marco called to say, "Tonight we're going to the Carnival in Viareggio. My sister's coming, too."

We piled into the Prinz and set out. Me and Angela in back, the other two up front. I felt spastic, intimidated. She didn't speak the whole time. Didn't even look at me.

It was a big Carnival celebration. People laughing, joking around, it was lots of fun. But Angela was cold, tight-lipped, in her own world.

I thought, *she's not even fucking paying attention to me. No, she doesn't like me at all.*

On the return journey in the car that frustrating evening, about midway home she suddenly looked at me and, without saying anything, put her hand on my pants. On my crotch. I was still naïve. I could hardly believe it was happening. Who was this girl? She kept on not saying anything. Just awkward glances in an unbearable silence.

70

Then she gave me a little kiss. "When will we see each other again? Are we going out?" My anxiety-riddled, stupid, petulant questions. I hardly managed to utter them. She still said nothing, confident in our tacit agreement. A silent, fleeting promise for the future. Nothing. That night I couldn't sleep. I was so happily dazed by a girl who drove me crazy.

Our move to Avenza, was another torment for me. Homeless once again.

"Just for a month," he said.

We took temporary shelter in a house that was under construction. Still in rough shape: no windows or doors, no bathroom, no kitchen. Four cots with mattresses, that's it. Plastic hanging down in place of doors. No electricity. We used flashlights and candles and the store toilet. No shower. Just the can and a sink. We lived like that for a month.

Yet my mother managed to send me and my brother to school clean every morning. Then at last we moved into a nice house, just like my father had always promised. It was even too big for the four of us—it had six rooms. But it was a home, at last—with a yard, too.

The only problem was that Angela lived in Forte dei Marmi, and I went to school in Carrara. I was always in the wrong place at the wrong time. As soon as classes finished, I'd eat and hurry to her. Then I had rehearsals with my group. Every day I had to figure out how I was going to get to Forte dei Marmi and back to Carrara. It was a nightmare hitchhiking. I always got there late. I didn't have money for the bus. The Vespina 50 wouldn't start. To this day, I'm haunted by a nightmare that wakes me up in the middle of the night—I can't find a ride home. My whole story has always been lived somewhere else. I've never been where I wanted to be.

La Topolino, the Fiat 500

I WENT TO THE TECHNICAL INSTITUTE OF CHEMISTRY IN CARRARA, where I never learned a fucking thing because the students were always on strike. Art school was more prestigious, but they were always on strike too. Capovani from Sarzana, with his classic Eskimo jacket, was leader of the student movement. They occupied the school every morning, yelling "Scab!" at anyone who tried to get in, and would even resort to force to keep people from entering. When I saw there was trouble, I took shelter in an old wine tavern. The place was filthy, dilapidated. It didn't even have a proper floor, just dirt. It was run by Ponsacchino, who was an alcoholic and always drunk, with a nose like Mastro Ciliegia, the red-nosed carpenter in Carlo Collodi's *The Adventures of Pinocchio*. There was no heat. He had a greasy, grimy old meat slicer he used to cut his fantastic cured meats. The pickled onions and peppers he served them with were awesome too, which we ate inside *focacce* and bread from Altopascio. We'd spend all morning there, eating and drinking wine, shooting the breeze. I preferred the cured Tuscan meats, salty and full of pepper, to the excessive politics of the student movement and the dismal ideology of the assemblies They had little allure for me.

I still lived in Forte dei Marmi during my first two years studying chemistry in high school. I convinced Stefano, a friend of mine who already had his driver's license, to come to Reggio Emilia with me. By train. I told him to bring along his license. We went to my Uncle Guerra's and I begged him to find me a Topolino, or "Mickey Mouse," as the Fiat 500 was affectionately called.

"But you don't have even your license yet."

"Just find me one, don't worry."

The next day: "Delmo, I found a guy with a Topolino. It's in his barn, but it hasn't been driven in a long time."

We went to have a look. The paint was all chipped, and contained just about every color imaginable. Mustard brown, blue, yellow. It was strewn with straw. Hens laid their eggs in it, and it was covered with chicken shit. We had a hard time convincing the farmer to take it out of the barn. We cleaned it off. Vroom, vroom. It started on the third try. My legendary uncle gave the guy 25,000 lire for it, without the registration. We drove off down the Cisa, the road that runs from Parma to Massa-Carrara, and arrived happily on the coast.

I made a deal with Stefano: "The car is mine, but since you've got your license, you keep it, and drive me to school in Carrara."

Now I had my own road manager. He would pick up me and two other friends in Forte dei Marmi and drive us to school in Carrara, and we paid for the gas. Life improved. I had new friends, my band, a Topolino. And I had Angela.

Stefano was a lifeguard at one of the beach clubs in Forte dei Marmi, which was famous because it was frequented by a lady from Milano, who was supposedly a nymphomaniac—an urban legend that fired our imaginations. Rumor had it that she especially liked younger guys. And now we had a car. One night we invited her to go for a ride and she said yes right away. We climbed in the Topolinio with the top down and headed for the mountains, to an abandoned house where couples went to neck. We brought a few bottles of wine with us, imagining we would seduce her, all kinds of X-rated scenes racing through our heads. It was a dream, and we were kids with a lot of imagination. As we sat looking out the window of that ramshackle house, she told us her life story. She was a gorgeous redhead from Milano, the kind whose husband came down to the shore on weekends. Now, we were good kids, and the whole thing was kind of a prank—but we thought we were going to have a threesome. Instead, we got her life story. We pretended to be interested and understanding, but what a pain in the ass. Nothing happened.

My encounter with the people of Carrara made a strong but good impression on me—the cutting way they pronounced their z's, the harshness in their way of speaking. I certainly liked it better there. They had their history, their cathedral, their royal palace. It was home to anarchists, an excellent and centuries-old fine arts academy, the white marble of the Apuan Alps, sculpture. And besides, it was still 1968 and the student movement was going strong. Nothing like those losers in Forte dei Marmi with their preppy light-blue oxford shirts.

The times were vibrant, there was lots of creativity. When we skipped school, we'd meet up at Padula Park with our guitars and sing 'Bella Ciao' and 'Addio Lugano Bella.' Our idol of course was Francesco Guccini. His first record (*Folk Beat No. 1*) had just come out, with songs like 'Noi non ci saremo,' 'Auschwitz,' 'Il sociale e l'antisociale,' 'In morte di S.F.' Songs that talked about us, songs we could identify with. Guccio's lyrics were poetry. What envy I felt.

At school, our hero was the geometry teacher. A big guy from Forte dei Marmi, who looked like the actor Alberto Sordi. One day, he asked me, "Hey, Fornaciari, what do you play? The *zinzone?*" That's the double bass. Then, kicking back with his feet on his desk and his newspaper, *L'Unità*, folded up in his lap—he made the whole class keep quiet while he read it every morning. He said to me, "Fornaciari, sexuality should be experienced as something healthy, with self-awareness." I added that this would "save young people from stress and Catholic Action," and together the teacher and I had created a motto for our class, which then became the whole school's motto. Little did either of us know that one day we'd turn out to be true wordsmiths.

Of course, Catholic Action had plenty to say when the song came out years later, on *Blue's*, but what can you do? It's the kind of slogan that runs through pretty much every young person's mind, and some of the older ones as well.

Later I got an unexpected call from someone at Communion and Liberation, the Roman Catholic lay movement. They wanted me to play at one of their rallies. I warned the guy I'd be playing that song. It was the hit of the year in Italy. No problem, he assured me.

We were on live TV, on RAI 1. While we were rehearsing, a cluster of fellows in ties and blue jackets approached and looked around. Without mincing words, they said it would be better if I didn't play that song. I told them that I'd explained on the phone that I was going to do the song, that it was my big hit, they'd been playing it on all the radio stations in Italy, that *Blue's* had sold 1.4 million copies and everyone was singing the song. They walked off, looking confident and convinced that the band and I had got their message.

I sent someone to fetch some cassocks and the whole band dressed as monks. With no underwear underneath, of course. I warned the guys: "We'll take the song off the set list, then play it for the first encore."

When it came time for the first encore, I started in: "Sexuality should be experienced as something healthy, with self-awareness…" The TV cameras starting swinging around chaotically as the cameramen were badgered with cries from the people who didn't want us to play the song because they considered it blasphemous. When we got to the last notes, the whole band turned around, lifted our cassocks, and shined our lovely asses at the audience. Then we made a dash to the camper and took off in high gear, chased by a herd of Communion and Liberation supporters who wanted to beat us up. A big hit.

But let's get back to Carrara and Forte dei Marmi in the late 1960s. Where Marco, Angela's brother, played the magically electric songs of Santana and Jimi Hendrix on his Gibson SG. He was a whiz on that thing, and taught me all kinds of unimaginable guitar secrets. We'd spend entire afternoons at the Green Cross playing Jethro Tull and writing our own songs. Once we went to Milano to see Santana, six of us piled in my used blue VW Beetle (which I'd bought with the earnings from our first shows, and which triumphantly replaced the Topolino once I got my license). After the concert we all got drunk. While the others slept inside the car, I slipped underneath and lay down, where I snored peacefully until the next morning. On the way back, with the joy of Santana's magical solos and the sweet notes of 'Samba Pa Ti' still ringing in my ears, we stopped off at Portovenere to take a marvelous swim that refreshed and regenerated us after a night of carousing. Other times we'd go to Maldacco and jump under the waterfall—freezing, super clean, wonderful. Then we'd go to Fregio's deli and feast like princes, starving after our swim. I felt great those days. I was happy because I had friends, a blue Beetle, and a girl—even if she did piss me off. Since the beginning, we had a lot of conflict. Somehow it always made her more attractive to me. Anyhow, I spent a lot of time with her and her brother. We'd go to Punta Corvo, where there are 360 steps down to the sea. It was a wonderful little lagoon, much loved by nudists. Bonfires, guitars, and singing all night long under the stars.

My First Fuck

IN SUMMER, BUSINESS AT THE DELICATESSEN IN AVENZA PICKED UP, AND since things were going so well, my father had me deboning hams. I'd do as many as eight or ten a day. I worked, waiting for her—Angela— as the days grew long. We'd been going out since the previous winter. My memories are filled with horrible winters, because business would be so bad at the deli. Anyway, she'd already given me a taste of her temper, and I should have understood then and there that we weren't made for each other. Right off the bat we had a turbulent relationship, combining passion, novelty, and desire with incompatibility. We had a lot in common, but there was also a lot of misunderstanding. We waged a subtle and muted war of love, and it burned with all the desire I had for her.

She hung out a lot with her brother, and we'd go to the Unità celebrations, where we all sang together.

Angela was beautiful. But hardened, closed, ideological. She accused me of being a wannabe and egocentric when I told her I wanted to become a musician. She didn't even come to our shows when we played. Maybe it bothered her that other people could be interested in me and what I did. She had a sort of silent empathy with her brother, Marco. They never really talked to each other, but you could tell that deep down their bonds were strong. They were always together. He was good-looking too, just like her. When we went to the beach, he could climb up the vertical pole with one hand, and even walk on one hand in the sand. He was handsome and strong, besides being an excellent musician and talented guitar player. And he was also terribly unlucky. Early on he was struck with multiple sclerosis.

She hoped—no, she wanted—the two of us to be like her brother and his girlfriend. They'd moved into a tumbledown house and had these incredibly boring dinners full of doctrinal delirium and unending babble about the sex of the angels, which at that time was a very hot topic. Marco had a party trick that became a true fixation: lighting farts. He had his girlfriend squat doggy-style and show us the gaseous state of her farts by lighting them up. Angela, my beloved little girl, said, "Come on, let's try it." How romantic. We hadn't had sex yet, at most a little necking. She was so beautiful it drove me crazy, but she was stubborn. I loved her, and she made me play the light-the-fart game.

Before I started going out with Angela, I had another band called the New Lights, and one night we played at a swimming pool in Arezzo in the summer. The week before, Equipe 84 had played, so we were psyched. Down in front of the stage there was this hippie chick with blond hair. Splendid. The whole show, she distinctly gazed at me with a pair of languid eyes. I gazed back.

She came up to me afterward and said, with a heavy British accent, "*Ciao*, I'm Bunny."

"Are you English?"

"Yeah, my father's a diplomat."

We went out for a while. I still have the pendant she gave me. On one side it says "Bunny," and on the other side, "Sugar." We lost track of each other. It was one of those kinds of romances. Then one day she called me up.

"I'd like to come see you again," she said.

"OK. For Avenza you have to change trains at Carrara."

I went to pick her up. It was about three in the afternoon. When I got to the station, on platform one I was overcome by the heavy, acrid smell of patchouli. That couldn't be anyone but her. She was on the other side of the tracks, yet the whole station was wrapped in that cloud of perfume I always found so nauseating. I brought her home and we had dinner with my folks. We were all embarrassed, no one said a word. Then I took her to the movies. It was a terrible film, I remember. Then I brought her back to my house. She was older than me—I was fifteen or sixteen and she must have been around twenty. We went into the living room, where I usually did my recording, and pulled out the sofa bed for her. She wanted to have sex. So we went for it. My first fuck. Things started out all right, but they didn't end up as planned. At a certain point, the door opened. It was my father, coming home early from the movies. He too had seen a lousy film. He saw us while we were doing it. Talk about your awkward situations!

"Sorry, Mr. Fornaciari," she said, utterly embarrassed.

"Delmo, get in your own bed, now!" yelled my father, totally pissed off. "We'll deal with this later."

Mortadella and Lasagna

I WASN'T MUCH INTERESTED IN THE STUDENT MOVEMENT OR POLITICS. I lived for my music, and my world consisted of my girl, my band, and not much else. I had joined the New Lights when their old singer quit. We played almost every night, locally and out of town. We were seriously committed. We followed all the latest styles, played covers of lots of great songs, the big summer hits, like all the groups did. With Marco on guitar and me singing, we weren't bad at all, and gave the band its own style and identity.

Those days were great. Intense, productive, formative. I saw Ray Charles play at Franceschi's Capannina Club. The place was legendary and still exists. It was the backdrop for electrifying summers at the shore in Forte dei Marmi back in the 1960s. There was a bar where they served cocktails, four tables where people played cards. Young people danced, courted, and seduced one another on the dance floor. A storied summer haven for music. High-class all the way. Edith Piaf, Paul Anka, the Platters. Even Montale, Ungaretti, JFK and Jackie came to sip the Negronis that the creative bartender concocted. I was there that evening when Ray Charles played. As always, outside—who had the money for admission? Inside, everyone was rich. Luckily, at that time, the dance halls on the shore were all open-air affairs. It was the most seminal and fortifying time of my growth as a musician. The Capannina opened at around six p.m., when people were starting to leave the beach. After a swim, they'd stop by for a drink at the open-air bar, then have dinner and watch the show. I watched Ray Charles from outside. He was young and had a big orchestra with a conductor. I had never seen or heard anything like it. The pioneer genius of soul music. He played 'Georgia on My Mind,' of course.

I spent entire afternoons parked in my Beetle in the pine woods with Angela. A cloud of smoke—I didn't smoke, but she lit up one after another. Marco and our other friends teased us. Did you lay that egg? You spent all day inside that egg? It was a weird relationship. I was head over heels in love, and she talked about philosophy, politics, the student movement. Fucking boring. She smoked, talked, and I sat there listening. Never a kiss, not even a caress or a hug. She just talked. Talked and smoked. I didn't dare ask for anything more. I just suffered. She even criticized my passion for music. "You want to play? You're a wannabe. You want to show off? You're a piece of shit."

I wanted to become a musician, and that hurt. I didn't understand. I put all my heart into it, all my commitment. Maybe I even had talent enough to justify my musical ambitions. So why was I a wannabe?

Angela's mother, Adele, ruled the roost at their house. An authoritarian woman. Her husband was a merchant seaman, always out to sea. He counted about as much as the deuce of spades in that family. Angela's mother was very pretty, she had a stupendous face. Plenty of men courted her. She'd hoped for something better than the life a merchant seaman could offer. She may have regretted not making a better investment of her beauty. She was frustrated. Bitter and resentful. She also had to take care of her husband's father, Angela's grandfather, who really liked me. He made these great model boats and gave me one. A good guy, and a bond of affection arose between us.

As soon as her mother found out I was going out with Angela, she hit the roof. One afternoon, we were sitting on a bench and turned around to find her spying on us. At which point, she started hurling insults at me.

"Go back to the countryside, *mortadella*, and leave my daughter alone! You big lasagna! She's not for you. She's an angel. You're phlegm."

I was humiliated, offended, mortified. For a long time, I carried around those insults, so biting and mean, inside me. Later I freed myself of them in a song I wrote. "I like lasagna. I like you. A little marijuana. Beneath the sky of blue. I like bologna. Cuba libre, too."

The New Lights began to be a semiserious group. I was nineteen. We had deals with a couple local clubs where we played regularly. The first money started coming in. It was a very creative period. Our drummer and his brother Giulio, whose family was better off than ours, had money and bought tons of records. We would spend all day

80

long listening to them. While studying the masters, we began to write our own songs. This was the time when I really learned a lot about music, and to this day I go back to the reflections and ideas from that period when I need inspiration. Carlos Santana, Jimi Hendrix, and Jethro Tull were Marco's favorites, while our drummer was into Three Dog Night, Iron Butterfly, Chicago, Blood, Sweat & Tears, James Taylor, and various niche groups. They had different tastes, and my own musical culture began slowly to evolve.

Dante, our bass player, was a real lone wolf. He spent winters in the attic, bent over his guitar, chain-smoking, with a little wine, listening to all these American groups that back then were unknown in Italy. He learned their songs and was a skilled player, very creative. I owe a lot to him, too, for the development of my sensibility and musical training. We hit it off, we understood each other musically and especially as friends. He was from Castelvetro, outside Modena, so we could kid around and tell each other to fuck off in our own dialect. Our own language, which smacks of the flavors of fatty foods and a land where everybody sings—the land of romance and song, the land of the Communist song 'Bandiera Rossa' ('Red Flag').

Once he put on some music by this extraordinary group I had never heard of. Same sound as Santana, but with a horn section. They called themselves Malo and were Mexican. Our drummer was a pastry chef by trade. He got up at three in the morning to bake bread and sweets, finished at three in the afternoon, then we'd meet at four o'clock at his house, in an isolated section of town, and practice until night, in between songs eating the sandwiches, sweets, and Chinotto soda he'd bring along. More than weed, peyote, or acid—all of which were all in fashion those days—we scarfed snacks, and drank wine and beer. Those were our drugs.

Back then, the only time I ever smoked weed was in London. I was already fairly drunk, and when we got back to the hotel I had a nasty panic attack. I wanted to throw myself out the window. Awful experience. Many years later in Amsterdam, after a concert a gorgeous chick asked me to have a drink with her. She passed me a joint. That time everything went OK. We spent a great night together. I like drinking and hanging out with friends, transgression and all that, but I can't stand the thought of losing control.

Angela worked in a photography shop in Forte dei Marmi, and every day I walked her home. I was head over heels in love. She kept to herself and continued to treat me rather coldly. With her brother, the New Lights and I broke out and played in towns like Sarzana, Carrara, Pietrasanta. We wanted to play at the Sanremo Music Festival, in the Young Artists competition. Our drummer and leader of the group, Aldo, said he knew a songwriter who was friends with someone important at Sanremo. But that "someone important" said he had no idea how he could help us, especially since we didn't have a record out. We signed up all the same, but nothing happened. At any rate, I had already begun to make the rounds in Galleria del Corso in Milano, where all the record companies had their offices. I had Gary, who could really draw and studied at the Fine Arts Academy in Carrara, make me up a sort of business card. With that and a cassette tape, I wondered aimlessly from record company to record company.

As usual, Uncle Guerra came to the rescue and gave me my first two-track Sony recorder. On one track I recorded the guitar, on the other my voice with guitar.

City Records was tiny, but had extensive distribution in Italy thanks to two bands that were hits: Nico and the Seagulls, and Bruno Castiglia and the Bisons, who sang 'Occhi di sole.' I sent them two songs: 'Canto di Maggio' and 'Juanita.' They wrote back to Aldo, our drummer, and his brother Giulio, who played the organ (and years later committed suicide). City Records liked our songs, especially the second, so we recorded a 45, our first record. Aldo designed the cover by hand, with our faces glued on underneath. It was horrible. They printed a thousand copies. There was no promotion, and the record went nowhere. But thanks to my fans, 'Juanita' resurfaced some many years later and became a cult hit.

Around that time, we piled in the Beetle and went to see Joe Cocker in Milano. I had seen the film *Woodstock* and was shocked by the way he looked like he was having an epileptic seizure onstage, and sang like a black guy—like Ray Charles. When he did 'With a Little Help from My Friends,' the whole place lit up. A light turned on in my head—that's what I want to do, too. Of course, I didn't know how to go about doing that. This was rock, but he was singing black. A white guy, singing black. Artistically speaking, I fell in love with that style.

And this was the season of the anarchists, Lotta Continua, Feste dell'Unità and Potere Operaio—all kinds of left-wing movements. I was still too young to get seriously into it, but the older kids were swept away by that political wave. We sang at lots of Unità celebrations, along with featured acts like Guccini, Gaber, and De Gregori, all of them leftist singer-songwriters. The whole atmosphere infected me as well.

I discovered that Angela was a great singer, always able to harmonize on the first shot. In her own way, she too was an artist.

Veterinary School, the Bestiary

THERE WERE NO MAJOR ISSUES THAT LED TO THE BREAKUP OF THE NEW Lights. We gradually drifted apart, without much ado. We played our last gig at Sassalbo, a small town near Cerreto with no chimneys because they get so much snow in winter it would knock them down. One of the main reasons we broke up was the advent of the discotheque, which took work away from people who played live music. For the groups, it was genocide. Lots of talented kids lost all hope. Besides that, we couldn't update our gear because we didn't have the money. Meanwhile in came the first synthesizers, keyboards that sounded like string sections.

The New Lights was my first serious, professional band. We were disciplined, we all worked on the material and showed up well prepared. Our drummer was the best musician in the group. He had a background in jazz and had played on cruise ships. The van was his, and he took good care of it—he even painted our name on it. He had a gorgeous girlfriend, who dressed like a flower child and played percussion. After they married, they had a beautiful baby girl and I became Uncle Zu. Even though I lived in Carrara, I was always with them in Forte dei Marmi.

Sometimes my father would grumble and complain that I wasn't spending time in the store to help him anymore. He realized music was my passion, and though I didn't know if I could ever make a living off it, he never stood in my way. At any rate, I did have a Plan B in case the music didn't work, and enrolled in veterinary school at the University of Pisa. At first I attended classes regularly, but the commute was long. Every day I had to take the train from Carrara to Pisa, then walk two kilometers to campus. It soon became a struggle to reconcile my studies with my music. I'd get home late at night, and classes began early the next morning. More than anything, I had no doubt as to the road I wanted to take. I managed to complete thirty-five out of fifty-three exams, and I still have my course registration booklet from the University of Pisa. The exam I'm proudest of was in animal anatomy. I scored thirty out of thirty, with honors. I enjoyed veterinary science, especially parasitology, biology, and anatomy, whereas I didn't give a shit about physics and chemistry. I'd discovered a way of studying that was different from what they taught you at school, much more engrossing, and I made it to the third year. But there was nothing I could do about it—my true passion won out, I left veterinary school, and abandoned any ambitions I might have had of treating domestic animals.

Instead, I created my own bestiary and made them characters in my songs. My funky rooster lived to a ripe old age in comfort, well fed and lavished with affection by a clutch of hens at his disposal down at the enchanting world of the old mill in Pontremoli—unlike his friends, who wound up in the pot. There was Tobia, my beloved Bernese Mountain Dog. The only dog I ever really felt was my own, I'd had him since I was a kid. We got along great, and I was very fond of him. "Hey, something's wrong with Tobia," said Fra one day. "He can't go poop. Let's bring him to Luciano." That was a veterinarian friend of ours who lived in Avenza. We got there, left Tobia in Luciano's yard, then went to eat a pizza. When we got back, Tobia was nowhere in sight. I thought he was probably sleeping somewhere. I didn't realize the front gate took a while to close. Tobia had run away. The next morning a fellow gave us the description of a dog that sounded a lot like ours. He said he'd seen him roaming around at about six a.m. I ran into the yard. "Tobia, Tobia!" Then into the street. "Tobia!" No sign of him. We got in the car and spent the whole day driving around looking for him.

"Let's make some posters and hang them up. We can put my phone number on them," said Fra.

Every now and then someone would call saying they'd seen the dog. He seemed to be further and further away each time. The night he'd run away it rained, and he lost the familiar smell of his surroundings. He must have been looking to get back to Pontremoli, but got lost. I never saw him again. My first ever barking song was dedicated to him. Actually, it was written from his point of view, after getting lost and trying to find his way back to me: "I'm goin' home, but I ain't got no home. I'm goin' home, but where's that? Oh, no. I'm sniffing and searching. Where could you be? I'm lost, lost in the wind." Then there was 'Donkey Tonkey,' dedicated to my donkey, Camillo—the one who had hard time getting laid.

Sugar

AFTER THE NEW LIGHTS BROKE UP, I GOT AN OFFER TO PLAY WITH A group from Massa at the Vela d'Oro Festival, organized by Gianni Ravera, a sort of "disco for the summer," held in September. The singer's name was Daniel. His folks had an appliance store, which at the time sold records, too. They were well off. Daniel had bought himself a long car and cruised around town in it. He was a local hero, without a doubt the coolest guy around. He'd already made a record and sung at the International Festival of Contemporary Music in Venice. His group was called Daniel and the Disciples.

They hooked up with me because they wanted to put together something like Sam and Dave, that extraordinary duo of American soul singers who inspired Dan Aykroyd and John Belushi's Blues Brothers. This was the late 1960s, a time when Aretha Franklin was the only one who could top their hits on the rhythm & blues charts. Our idea was to have two singers who would sing alternating parts and harmonize—an innovative project in Italy in those days. He had a nice falsetto and sang the high notes. My voice was gritty, and the two melded together perfectly.

The group transformed into Sugar and Daniel, marking my official christening as "Sugar." We bought avant-garde equipment: a Fender piano, Gibson guitars, Marshall amps, remote control lights, a twelve-channel mixer, and a red Ford van—the real star treatment. We also had the best sound system you could get back then: Altec. What a luxury. We were equipped like a real band. We contacted the Santini theater agency in Viareggio, which managed dance hall singers. They worked as far afield as Sarzana, Santa Margherita Ligure, Montecatini, and Chianciano. I was a nobody, whereas Daniel was a local star and had already been on TV. The two-singer thing went over big. Santini got us gigs as a professional group. Things were starting to look good again.

In winter, we played the Kursaal in Montecatini and the Bussolina in Chianciano, which were major venues. All summer long, from June to September, we played every night at the bigger dance halls and discos. The Capannina, the Bussola, the Sporting Club in Bologna, the Casa del Popolo in San Miniato. We were especially hot in Tuscany, Liguria, and Emilia. We'd set out Friday evening and play till Sunday night. We slept in fleabag hotels. Got paid well enough. Sunday dances, a matinée show, then another that night. They gave us one free drink each, the rest we had to pay for ourselves. Club owners, and oftentimes their wives, could be super strict. During our break, from five to six o'clock, we sucked up our free drinks and went on the hunt for chicks. Just one more reason for taking up this trade—picking up chicks becomes a snap! You also pursue it because you love music, of course.

We were at the same level as the Mingardi Orchestra. We played the Italian hits, from the 1970s to the early 1980s, as well as the big disco hits by Chic, Kool & the Gang, and Barry White. We also managed to sneak in songs that we liked by groups like Pink Floyd, Chicago, Three Dog Night. When *The Dark Side of the Moon* came out we learned all the songs on it. We began composing our own, too. I proposed a few songs I had written myself.

One day, a big date came in. They asked us to play the Forte Village in Santa Margherita di Pula, in Sardinia. It was run by a half-Italian, half-English guy by the name of Mr. Pecorelli. His artistic director, Ivo, played in Wallace's Collection, a band that had its moment. We were paid to play for three months at the Forte Village. It was the first time I had ever been across the sea. My first plane ride, too.

The Evil Eye

LET ME TAKE A STEP BACK IN TIME HERE, THOUGH. MY PRIVATE LIFE was going down the tubes. I felt jinxed. My bands had broken up. I didn't know what depression was, but I was always down, melancholy, sad. I saw black.

"You've got the evil eye, come with me!" an old lady said to me. A shrewd Gypsy I met on the street one day when I was really depressed. "Come with me and I'll remove it!"

Couldn't hurt.

I wound up going all the way to Genova with this lady, who promised she'd help me get rid of my evil eye.

"You're going to be successful, but first you must cross a great stretch of water," she said as she performed her ritual with divining rods. I was in the remote alleyways of Genova, with an old woman sprinkling oils, who wanted me to cross some obscure stretch of water to reach the height of my career. I began to feel uncomfortable. It's true, when I got home, I learned that the gig at Forte Village had come through. But there was little rejoicing, because once again, Angela spoiled everything for me.

She didn't like the fact that I was going to be away for three months, so to make me suffer, she decided to leave me.

"I don't love you anymore. Don't call me."

I was stunned. "Are we crazy here, or what?"

"*Ciao.*"

And the funny thing was, she took off on her red Ciao moped.

Desperation set in. I got in my Beetle, but I couldn't move. I didn't want to go anywhere. I couldn't. Not home, no way. I cried like a cut grapevine.

Meanwhile Marco came riding by on his bike.

"Why are you crying?"

"Your sister left me."

I really started bawling then.

"She says she doesn't love me anymore."

I was weeping like a baby.

"Forget about it," he said. "She's half crazy. You knew that already."

After torrential fits of tears, I finally regained my composure. Where to now? Straight to Forte Village.

As soon as we got there, they gave us these traditional Sardinian costumes. Picturesque. Busloads of German, English, and Dutch tourists showed up. Our noble task was to greet them with accordion and tambourines when they arrived, playing Sardinian folk songs and stuff like 'Una Paloma Blanca'—it would be noon, one o'clock, with unbearable heat, and the waiters serving up rivers of Mirto, the famous herbal liqueur of Sardinia. Devastating. We thought we were going to play Pink Floyd. Instead we were dressed as Sardinians. We were frustrated out of our minds. We played either on the beach or in the arena, depending on the whim of the hotel director. The heat was stifling, and every day we had to move all the equipment to satisfy his fancy. We weren't allowed to talk to guests, especially not the girls. We didn't sleep at the resort, but down the road, in a dilapidated bare-cement building. We slept on bunk beds with the waitstaff. I wrote 'Auschwitz' on the wall. I felt like shit. There was only one pay phone, and by the time you managed to scrounge up the tokens you needed to use it, there were always long lines.

I was tormented by the thought of Angela. I was sure she had someone else, that's why she'd left me. I called the store where she worked. She never came to the phone. I was crazy jealous. Once, the store's owner told me some guy had come to pick her up on his motorcycle. No! I was fucked. She went dancing she, of all people, who hated discos. I flipped. I couldn't talk to her. After a month of reclusion in Sardinia, I worked out a plan to escape from Forte Village. I wanted to go see her. I found a guy with an inflatable boat who took me and our drummer to the airport in Cagliari. The hotel director followed us in a motorboat, like in a James Bond film.

"Where the fuck are you going? You're under contract. I'll press charges."

He escorted us back to the camp.

Another month went by. Our drummer found a very sweet Japanese girl, and they had a little romance outside the resort. We made friends with the farmers in the hills nearby. After we finished playing, they would feed us. *Pecorino sardo* cheese and *pane carasau*, the bread nicknamed "sheet music" because it's wafer-thin. Maggie, an English girl, started making eyes at me at Forte Village, but I couldn't talk to her because she was a guest. That was asking for trouble. She bribed a night watchman at the reception desk, and he let me in after our show. I slipped into her bungalow.

Finally, this shitty time came to an end. Dressing up as a Sardinian folk clown in the morning, then playing every night—and they didn't even feed us. Home, at last. I went looking for Angela, shattered. My Beetle wouldn't start, so I took my father's Fiat 128 without even asking permission. She had relatives in Genova, and had gone there to spend the summer with them. I drove there. She took me to Righi, in the hills, with its beautiful view of the gulf. Bathed in light and romantic. The moon lit up the sea. That was the first time we made love. When I got back home she called me, and for the first time in history, she was nice to me.

"Guess what? I saw blood."

She was happy and so was I. A touching moment, a fateful flash. Rife with passion. Our daughter, Irene, happens to live in Righi today, with a musician from Genova. I like that, it moves me. Because that's the place where her mother and I first united. I brought Angela back to my empty house my folks were at the deli—and we went to my room. She sat on the edge of my bed.

"Will you marry me? Angela, I want to marry you."

She wanted to leave home and escape her harassing, despotic mother. I didn't know what I was saying. In love and irresponsible. She said yes. We kissed. We made love with our clothes on (which is to say I came in my pants). Fifteen days later, we got married. It was 1978 and I was twenty-two. Beside myself with glee. We had our wedding in a pretty little church scented with fresh flowers, with the mid-morning sun filtering in through the windows in a little town with a fateful name: Poveromo ("Poor Man").

I was happy and nervous, wearing the white tuxedo I played in. She was gorgeous in a white bridal gown. Her parents, mean and spiteful; mine, happy. Even the guys from the band were in top form.

Chewing Gum

TO EARN A LITTLE EXTRA CASH, I TRIED WORKING AS A PRODUCER. In Milano, the producer Romolo Ferri informed me that Durium Records was looking for a group of young, fresh black singers and dancers for a program on RAI hosted by Giancarlo Nicotra. I went straight to work, looked around, and found two gorgeous Filipinas in Marina di Massa, and Fiorenzo, a black kid from Eritrea who sang.

I put them together, called the group Chewing Gum, and wrote a couple of upbeat little beach tune for them: 'Tangolé' and 'Co Co Co.' Exotic 1980s dance stuff. I tinkered with their voices, their look, even choreographed their routine. I brought them with us on our honeymoon, in my father's light blue Mirafiori. My wife was already fuming.

We got to Rome, but we didn't have a hotel. I had to pay for Chewing Gum, too—they were my investment. We found a cheap, run-down pensione. What a dive. Plaster peeling off the walls. Musty stench. It was the first night of our honeymoon.

"Where have you brought me? This place is crawling with roaches! I'm not staying here!"

It was late—one in the morning. Desperate, I called Romolo Ferri, who had tipped me off. He'd come down to Rome for the audition with Nicotra. He saved my neck—and my marriage. I left the poor kids in that hovel and took Angela to spend our wedding night at

Hotel Leonardo da Vinci, at Ferri's expense. A nice room at last. The alluring alcove of our love. As soon as we got there, Ferri called. It was two o'clock in the morning and we'd just started making love, the moment I had longed for. He told me the next day's appointment was moved to nine o'clock, which meant I had to get up early and go pick up the group. The romantic atmosphere was ruined. Angela was furious.

"You promised we were going to see the Vatican Museum and the Catacombs of Callixtus."

"Come on, just wait for me at the hotel. I'll go to the audition, and then I promise we'll go be tourists and have fun."

She was pissed off.

I went to the audition with Chewing Gum. Their performance was terrible. Nicotra didn't want them. I was mortified, crestfallen, bewildered by the rejection. I felt powerless, and what's more, I'd ruined our wedding night. Plus, I still had to deal with Chewing Gum, who were heartbroken. I put them on a train and sent them back to Versilia.

The Catacombs of Callixtus, the Trevi Fountain in a horse-drawn carriage. But it was too late. The atmosphere was gone. The first *fuck you*'s flew, and we started screaming at each other.

Wuthering Heights

I NEVER HEARD MY PARENTS ARGUE, SO I WAS TRAUMATIZED BY THE verbal violence between Angela's parents. The vibes there were horrible; constant wall-to-wall tension, poised to flare up at the slightest pretext. Still, every Sunday Angela insisted on going to lunch at their house. Luckily Marco was there, an extraordinary person, very sensitive. He was my friend, and suffered like a dog because of the poisoned atmosphere in that family.

Angela and I had gone to live in Avenza, where we had a room in my parents' house. We couldn't afford anything else. Business finally picked up at my father's store, money started coming in, and the time came to expand operations and maybe even hire some staff. One day my father gave me an ultimatum: "I don't want outsiders. Either you and your brother come and give me a hand, or I'm going back to Reggio."

I was attending the University of Pisa and I had a new band, Sugar & Candies. I couldn't upend my life again and go to work as a deli clerk. My brother was still in high school and his mind was elsewhere—mostly on his first girlfriend.

My dad wound up selling the store and moved back to Reggio Emilia with my mother and my brother. He worked as a swineherd for one hundred fifty pigs in Bagnolo. He'd had enough of Versilia and Forte dei Marmi and Carrara. It wasn't his world. He had to go home—his roots were calling him. What could he do but heed the call?

My mother was heartbroken. "Delmo, we're leaving Delmo all alone." She was very worried.

I kept living with Angela in our rented house in Avenza. I bought a chipboard wardrobe—we didn't even have that. I was assailed by the landlady, an old bag as sour as yogurt gone bad and as mean as poison.

"Fornaciari," she told me, "there's no use in buying furniture, because you're not staying here."

Blind with rage, I began spewing my usual array of insults and swears. It was a rehearsal for my show at Cala di Volpe years later.

The hag left us in peace for six months. Then we moved to a lowly section of town, the Bronx of Avenza. We found a little white house with the rooms in line, one after the other, like train cars. It was down a cobblestone alley, just wide enough for a team of oxen to pass. I was very familiar with that unit of measurement. It meant you had to leave the car in the adjacent street and lug whatever there was to lug up to the house. Very inconvenient. Out back was a little yard with a prefab bungalow that had a corrugated asbestos roof. Angela was already pregnant with Alice. The landlord, a retired tax police officer who was kind and generous in his own way, asked us if we wanted to buy the place for 45 million lire. Who had that kind of money? But he was moved by our youth and Angela's growing belly, so he said we could pay in installments: five million every six months. I went to Uncle Guerra, who had a pension. He was so good and had always helped me solve my problems.

"Don't say anything to your father," he warned.

I tore a page from a notebook and wrote on it: "Dear Uncle, I owe you five million. Thanks. I'll never forget it." I gave him the note. I managed to pay him back before he died of a heart attack—thank God.

I made the first payment. Then I hunkered down and did what I had to do. Times were tough. Angela, being pregnant, had stopped working. Just to survive, I gave guitar lessons to a few knuckleheads. Angela never wanted to come when I performed on weekends. Instead she would go to her parents' house in Forte dei Marmi, so she wouldn't have to spend the night alone. When I got back, there would always be squabbling, accusations, fights.

"You walk out on me."

"But, love, I have to work."

I did the household chores. We had a coal stove. They delivered the coal to the corner of the alley, and I had to carry it home slung over my shoulder—breaking my back! I did the shopping, went to the bank to pay the bills. I even put together a vegetable garden, with tomatoes, lettuce, onions. A little pond with three Chinese ducks.

I turned the bungalow into my studio, and soundproofed it with Styrofoam and chipboard. I had my piano and a telephone line, and I would coop myself up in there from nine in the morning until sundown. I had to write, I had to find the right song, the one that would turn things around. That was my world. Angela couldn't stand it. When I came home for dinner, she was nasty and unhappy. She felt alone, abandoned. I was away all day writing songs, and tired. I felt misunderstood and ignored.

I've still got lots of that material from back then on tape. I wrote a lot, furiously. There was a song called 'Anni Sessanta' that went on to become 'Chocabeck.' It was an intensely creative time, and a desperate one as well. , I couldn't find the song I was looking for. Then, of course, there were Angela's furious outbursts.

I fixed up the house. I bought a nice bed and replaced the coal stove with a kerosene that caught fire one night while I was playing in Recco. Angela was alone at home with our newborn Alice. Panic. Two neighbors managed to haul out the stove before the whole house went up in flames. Things got worse. I'd either be out playing or holed up in my studio writing songs, while Angela became more and more unhappy. She even had it in for my piano. She broke off a key and wrote "asshole" on it. I'd go to Milano to try and sell my songs, then come home at nine in the evening. She and Alice had already had dinner. I should have got back earlier. I'd spend all day getting doors slammed in my face. She wouldn't speak to me for days at a time. I was constantly stressed out. What saved me from becoming disheartened was Angela's pregnancy. She was more cheerful then, and glad about becoming a mother. She was gratified. That summer of great expectations in Finale Ligure. She adored Kate Bush. Filled with hope for what was to come, we listened to 'Wuthering Heights' over, and over again.

At one point, I had a Citroen Dyane, a secondhand wreck. I drove it to Milano on December 23 one year. It was cold, there was snow. As usual, I was trying to sell my songs. While everyone else was busy with Christmas Eve preparations, I was out there alone, getting a nonstop whipping. I didn't even have the money to eat in a trattoria.

95

I ate salami sandwiches, like the ones from my father's deli. I headed back in dejection at around seven, hoping to be home by nine at the latest. But before Piacenza, the car stopped. It was dark. Cold. The tractor-trailer trucks whizzed by in a spray of sleet. I turned the key. The battery finally clicked. The car sputtered and lurched to the toll booth. I managed to find a garage, but it was already closed, so I left my car in front of the gate and went to seek shelter. I found a room in a pensione. I didn't have a dime to my name. Christmas Eve in Piacenza—talk about shitty.

Free Love

ANGELA'S FLOWER-PRINT DRESSES AND THE BRIGHT COLORS OF HER hippie tunics. The counterculture, the Beat Generation, the sexual revolution, psychedelic rock. There was lots of ferment in those days. It was an exciting world for young people, there was a current that electrified us, even as we grew dismayed over the war in Vietnam. The mandate was "make love, not war." Free love has fascinated me ever since. I adore how the hippie spirit blends the sacred and the profane when it comes to love, and how they meet and meld to the point where you can't tell them apart. Often, when I write, I seek inspiration in that culture, and try to translate it into erotic tension that's conveyed through my music.

I was already married to Angela, but the idea of free love didn't stop tempting me. We used to go out a lot with our drummer and his wife. We were friends, we got along great. I had a feeling the drummer's wife had her eye on me, especially after I became a little famous. I don't deny that I would have liked to get it on with her, or even all of us together. One night we went swimming, then the couples went off for a bit of intimacy. But there was this longing in the air—for togetherness, maybe even a foursome. Maybe get other friends involved, too. But suddenly a car shined its headlights on us. Cops. Fuck. We got dressed and that was that. We kissed those fantasies of making love like flower children goodbye.

Deep down, I don't think Angela really shared much of that spirit. She wanted to appear fast and loose, show everybody that she was ahead of the game, she was uninhibited. But she was faking it. She had always been jealous. That night, though, she didn't show it. Although, there were times when she would just stand there, looking to see what was going to happen. Once, we went to the movies with 'Pippo che cazzo fai?' and his wife. On the way back, I turned down a quiet little road and started saying how great it would be if we could all make love together. We were really into each other, we were a group, we had a mutual understanding, freedom, like the Beatniks, like Ginsberg and Ferlinghetti and Corso... *The Divided Self*, anti-psychiatry, counter-culture, and all the other battle cries of the day. The topics of all our endless discussions. The ones punctuated with infinite swarms of "like," remember? The long and short of it was, that night I was fed up. I wanted to convince them, once and for all, to transform our spirit into practice. We started playing a fun little game.

"I don't like this game. Not a bit. Enough. Stop it!"

Pippo's wife—what a ballbreaker. Game over. But I sensed that Angela wasn't averse. Maybe because she was interested in 'Pippo che cazzo fai?'

Mecca Goes Up in Flames

ON NEW YEAR'S EVE, WE PLAYED A CLUB CALLED MECCA, IN MARINA DI Massa. It was owned by a guy named James Zerbini, originally from Guastalla. He was a big fan of the cha-cha. He had a rockabilly haircut and was constantly yelling, "Hey, minstrels!" He had a curly-haired wife who was very hot, a real prima donna.

There was an understanding that, for the New Year's Eve show, since the band had to play until four or five in the morning, the musicians' girlfriends could get in for free. We got to Mecca. My wife Angela was pregnant with Alice, we had my brother Lauro in tow. I was sure it would be no problem. But the bouncer, known as 'Punch,' because he was such a brawler, stood blocking the door, alongside him the notorious *signora*, with her curls. I asked her whether or not, my brother could get in for free.

"No way! You're here to work!" she squawked. "What the fuck do you want? It isn't enough that your wife is getting in free to keep you company? You want your little brother, too? How about your aunt? Your grandma?"

I had enough of this already. One of my moments ensued. One of those when I can't hold back and there are no brakes on my tongue. "Listen, quit giving us a hard time!"

She started screaming and walked off. All that was missing was Punch, but then he came over and blocked my way.

"No. You're not coming in. What did you say to her?"

Get lost, Punch.

"Go ask her what I said, if you want to know."

He went over to her, which meant the coast was clear. I managed to get Angela in, as well as poor Lauro, who had unjustly been barred.

It was in this friendly spirit that we managed to get through that tremendous evening. My wife and my brother had to stay backstage and weren't allowed access to the club. The band was treated like shit. Back in those days, there was an unspoken rule that if business in a club was bad, it was the fault of the waitstaff and the band. At five in the morning, after we'd finished playing and all the toasts had been drunk, Zerbini came over to me.

"They told me you were rude to my wife." He talked like Yogi Bear. "You know, Zucchero, you may not be all wrong on that score. Come on, play one last song for me: a cha-cha-cha."

And Yogi Bear kicked up his heels to his favorite triple step with glee, along with one of the waitresses.

We went back to Mecca to play the whole month of July. The neighborhood was rife with drugs and prostitutes, all run by one Musumeci, from Calabria, who kept a puma chained up in his house and had already done time. Late one night, one of his thugs showed up at Mecca. Good ol' Punch, instead of treating him with caution, was faithful to his nickname and gave the guy a nice little beating. He tossed him out into the street in bad shape, and the guy stumbled off. We finished playing and went to the pizzeria across from Mecca, where we generally wound up after our work nights. We had just bought brand-new instruments, high-quality gear. On the installment plan for the next decade. When at last our *Napoli* and *margherita* pizzas arrived, we heard someone yell: "Fire! Mecca's burning!" I walked outside and I'll be damned if the whole place wasn't going up in smoke! All our instruments inside, burning. Afterward, the only things I found intact were a lousy bell and the cymbals. Arson. We didn't get a dime in damages. We cried like babies, right there in front of the club. Our shows had been getting better and better, and we were about to be rewarded for our efforts by debuting at La Bussola, the area's top club. It was a great opportunity we couldn't let slip away. We had no money, and couldn't buy any more instruments on credit. A truly generous gentleman saved the day. He had a musical instrument store in Viareggio. We were steady customers. He believed in us. He didn't have instruments as awesome as the ones that had burned, but he was able to provide us with everything we needed to play that gig. He took us at our word.

A Rotunda on the Seashore

LA BUSSOLA IS A NIGHTCLUB ALONG THE BEACH IN MARINA DI Pietrasanta, in the Focette district. Along with Franceschi's La

Capannina, in the 1970s it was one of the most popular clubs in Versilia. Musicians dreamed of playing there, it was almost a holy place, with owner Sergio Bernardini its high priest. He was a great manager, with an international outlook. He wanted Juliette Gréco, Ella Fitzgerald, Ginger Rogers, Louis Armstrong, Marlene Dietrich, Josephine Baker, Frank Sinatra, Tom Jones. And he got them. He made Mina the Queen of La Bussola. She gave a series of memorable shows there that established her as a legend, along with the club.

We opened for the featured acts. People like Fred Bongusto, Peppino di Capri, Bruno Martino took turns livening up the summer nights. A fifteen-night stint for each. It was pretty much the nightclub scene, which I've never really been a part of. I loved the blues, I loved rock. But Bernardini gave me work.

La Bussola had its own private beach, with Plexiglas barriers, and an open-air dance hall. Carletto Pirovano, the chef, would make a superfine fillet for dinner. Bernardini would hang around through the wee hours in his linen shirt, open at the neck; charismatic, magnetic, elegant to a T. The best time to talk to him was at around three in the morning, when he would sit down to a very peculiar snack: a large bowl of coffee, into which he dunked dry bread. It showed an austerity that contrasted with the outrageous habits of many of his customers, not to mention the eccentricities and caprices of the stars—Italian and foreign—who graced the stage, which he referred to simply as "the old bitch." His first guest was Peter Van Wood, who drove the audience wild with 'Butta la Chiave.' Everyone played on that stage: Renato Carosone, Marino Marini, Celentano, Frankie Lane, Johnny Ray, the Platters, Domenico Modugno, Fred Buscaglione, Chet Baker. In the audience: Angelo Moratti, Felice Riva, and sometimes even Gianni Agnelli, who preferred dining in a private room off to the side, known as the Bussolotto, for those who wanted to keep their distance from the mayhem.

Bernardini's true passion, however, was Mina. When he

discovered her, she still went by the name of Baby Gate. "A marvelous woman," he said, "who knows how to love without tricks or rhetoric. She doesn't care about power and money. King Farouk of Egypt filled her dressing room with roses and she never once accepted a glass of Champagne in his company."

Other big stars on the scene who played La Bussola included Vanoni and Patty Pravo. They put up a circus tent in the huge lot next door, called Bussoladomani ("Bussola Tomorrow"), and lots of top artists played there: Renato Zero, Iglesias, Aznavour. The tent held something like five thousand people. The artists who played La Bussola, which inside seated five hundred tops, would play to much bigger crowds in the tent. It was here, in the summer of 1978, that Mina bid farewell to the music scene with a series of live shows, all of them packed.

Urban legend has it that Bernardini lost the club playing poker.

He had everything under control. The band had to wear costumes. Light blue. Only one drink on the house each, in compliance with the strict nightclub code of conduct. We didn't enjoy that drink at the bar in La Bussola, but tucked away backstage. People gambled at green tables, others danced. We did a cavalcade of contemporary international hits: 'Cheek to Cheek,' cha-chas, sambas, waltzes. It wasn't the kind of scene for Pink Floyd or Chicago, the kind of music I liked. I had to sing 'My Funny Valentine,' which I hated with all my heart. But it was a great school. The piano player, the only one of us who'd studied music, gave us the keys. I couldn't memorize all those songs by heart, and had to find the chords on my guitar and sing, winging it. There were scores on the music stand, with lyrics in English. I could play a repertoire of worldwide hits, from Nat King Cole to Frank Sinatra.

I had become a professional musician, good enough to play any style requested. A little disco, break time, that was the last frontier in live music. We had rehearsals in the afternoon, where we would work out a new song for each gig. On stage from ten o'clock until midnight, followed by a break, then the main attraction. Fred Bongusto was doing a fifteen-night stand at the time on a revolving stage. The instruments for his band took up most of the space, with little left over for our gear.

"Roll the stage," ordered the head of operations one night.

Fred's about to come on! The band was all set.

Then I saw Fred duking it out with Bernardini. Most likely over terms of payment and such. With Fred indisposed, the head of operations mouths to me to whip up something on the spot. I figured I'd play something of a tribute to Fred, and did 'Una Rotonda sul Mare'—a perfect imitation! The crowd thought I was him. They applauded and screamed. Then Fred comes on. From behind I hear: "Asshole! Now what am I supposed to sing?" We became great friends. He was famous at the Rotunda, yet he came to my more than humble home in Avenza to hear my songs. I told him I was a songwriter. He recorded 'Tutto di Te' for Warner Brothers—music and lyrics by yours truly. That was my songwriting debut.

Fred's wife was an avid card player, and loved to play poker and bridge until the club closed at dawn.

Then it was Peppino di Capri's turn—he alternated with Fred. A real worker, he set up and broke down the mixer, and when necessary soldered the cables underneath the piano. And he was already famous, but had his own way with the band, his own personal style and approach.

It was the birthday of one of Bernardini's fiends. Sergio asked him to sing 'Champagne.' Then he ordered forty bottles of Champagne to be brought out, and popped open each one in honor of his friend.

One night, there a show featuring French dancers. Outrageous—they were half naked. Guys with tiny loincloths, chicks bare-breasted. One guy must have been out of his mind on drugs—he whipped out his dick and started shaking it in this lady's face. A lady bedecked in jewels, mind you. He insulted her, slapped his dick on the table. Cursed out capitalism. Bernardini came over, totally pissed off, and started pounding the shit out of him. Tables and chairs flew.

Those were the days when we could entice a bunch of hot chicks and lure them into our web of seduction. After we finished playing rounds of sambas and congas, at four in the morning Pirovano would whip up a batch of spaghetti and fillets for us. Then we'd hit the beach or go skating. Lots of guys got laid in the changing cabins. Music, nights, the seaside, summer. It would never ever be the same. I'd get home at six or seven in the morning. Angela certainly never thought our life together would end up like this. She met me back when I was playing with her brother.

She might have guessed it would be like this, but she always figured I'd quit and get a serious job, a real job that had nothing to do with singing. She never came to my shows, even though I begged her. She never gave a hoot about hearing me play. Yet I was still crazy about her. I would have had her every night. It's only now that we've been separated for so long that she comes to my shows. She's a fan.

Paolino

DANIEL LEFT, BUT THE GROUP STAYED TOGETHER AND CHANGED NAMES. The Decals were born. We played all of December, including New Year's Eve, at the P4 club in Recco. They really liked us there. It was an enormous dance hall, packed with people. Then our bass player split. Emergency. I called an old friend from back in the days of the Green Cross: Beppe, aka Accio. He'd played in my earliest bands. We were like brothers. I was counting on him. "Do me this favor. We've got a nice contract. I'll give you our set list and the keys the songs are in. You've got a week to learn them. I'm begging you." He played the first two songs all right, but then he started to make mistakes.

"Didn't you learn the songs?"

"Yes. No. Maybe. My record player's broken."

I didn't expect this. I was hurt. "What do you mean? We've been friends all our lives, and I can't trust you?"

We managed to get through the evening. People danced without even listening to the music. When I see Accio today, we still hug—the two of us share so many memories. But he could have at least asked to borrow my record player to avoid putting the band in such a tough spot.

I called up our old bass player, and he played New Year's Eve with us. We played until six in the morning. It was pouring rain. We were tired and decided to sleep in Recco. Everyone but Paolino, our piano player, who promised he'd come back home after the gig. We had a Fiat 850 van, with the engine in the rear and a flat front nose. He set out. Rounding the big turn in Massa, where the hospital is, just five hundred meters from his house, a drunk driver came barreling into him head-on. It was cold and rainy. He opened the window for air. They found him soaking wet, in a coma and with a broken sternum, at seven in the morning. Besides knowing music, and the songs, Paolino was also an excellent student at medical school. A smart kid, very resourceful, and a great guy. He died a month later.

We'd lost him, our friend, our piano player, our partner on the streets and stages, in music and life. I sank into despair. We'd lost a dear friend. After the disaster of losing our instruments in a fire, this was a tremendous blow, both emotionally and professionally. But I refused to give up. I heard about a keyboard player who was talented but had a reputation as a real madcap. An instigator, a troublemaker. I remembered him because he took part in the student protests back in high school. We found a gig at La Casina Rossa in Lucca, afternoon and evening, and if things went well, we'd have a two-month stint there. We were back on the circuit, trying to re-emerge from a spate of rotten luck. *Guys, let's give it all we've got. We've got to give 110 percent.* Things went fine at rehearsals. Everything seemed to be going smoothly the night we played, until the piano player went up to the bar to ask for a second drink during the break. He was a big drinker. As usual, we were each entitled to one drink on the house. The hag behind the cash register was your typical club owner's wife and demanded he pay for the second drink. A quarrel broke out, the piano player took it too far, and they kicked us out. That event marked the end of the Decals. Who ever thought up that horrible name? We had recorded a single, though: 'Un'Ora.' It was our only original song, and on the b-side was an instrumental version.

Sugar & Candies

THEY WERE LEAN TIMES, AND NOT ONLY IN TERMS OF SONGS. THERE was a lot of pain and rotten luck. I was still attending university, and though everything seemed to be working against me, I refused to give up on any front, and stood my ground. Even though Paolino was dead and we'd lost our instruments, and the band broke up, Giancarlo Santini, the local manager, believed in and encouraged me. We'd been his top group and meant a lot to him. He wanted to give it another try, so he put me in touch with a band of guys who were older than I was, in their mid-thirties. Seasoned session men who'd spent a lifetime playing nightclubs and cruise ships, they knew their chops and were respected because they'd been around so long. They called themselves the Saints and there were three of them. Their leader was pianist Bruno Mosti, who also sang. Then there was Fabrizio, a drummer from Prato who was a swell guy, and the bass player.

We formed a super group, with me on vocals and electric guitar, along with my old guitar player, Alfonso, an excellent musician from Carrara, and of course my bosom buddy Gary on drums. We played with two drummers so we wouldn't have to kick either one out—that was something people had never seen before, a group with two drummers. It worked out well. However, we didn't have a name yet. Mosti, who was the oldest member of the band, wanted to crown his long career with a record, and would have done anything to record one. He was a sly old fox and figured the presence of a young singer like me in the band would help things. And once again, Romolo Ferri, the guy who saved my wedding night, came to the rescue. He was becoming a successful producer in Milano for Swiss-owned Saar Records. Even Vasco Rossi recorded for them back then. Ferri gave us a song he, himself, had written. Mosti and I did the vocals. It was some hideous disco music, 'Voulez Vous Danser,' backed with 'My Woman,' a pretty ballad, on the B-side. I would later rearrange the tune and put it on my album *Blue's* as 'Bambino Io, Bambino Tu,' with beautiful new lyrics by Gino Paoli; it was real poetry.

For the single launch, Ferri came up with a name for the band: Sugar & Candies. Another stupid name. They invented a look for us, did a photo shoot of the six of us in white tuxedoes that Ferri had managed to get for free from Pierre Cardin. We were proud of those suits and the white ankle boots that went with them—a very elegant detail. Who knows where they found them? We played dressed in those costumes. The record went absolutely nowhere. We appeared on TV in our white tuxes, but still nothing happened. There wasn't much cohesion among us; the group didn't gel. Actually, we remained two separate groups. We worked together, but energy and warmth were lacking. We played some of the bigger venues, including La Bussola again. Mosti had an unbelievably vast international repertoire. He sang the songs of Julio Iglesias—which he really had a knack for—and we played a cavalcade of the latest hits.

We also got an engagement to play a two-month stint at the Nautilus in Varazze, a renowned dance hall with a round terrace on the shore, run by a guy called Toni, who belonged in the sun-tanned-open-shirt-gaudy-gold-medallion-on-the-chest category. Always sweaty.

Wore a toupee and walked around with two ferocious Dobermans. We stayed in a run-down pensione with no phone or air-conditioning, not even a fan. It was deathly hot. We'd rehearse in the afternoon, do shows at night for a somewhat older crowd: lonely ladies waiting for their husbands to come down to the shore on weekends, a smattering of couples, and a few pretty girls. While Mosti delighted the old bags with Iglesias and his mawkish nightclub Casanova routine, the bass player, a really nice guy, would be chatting up the ladies at the tables on the side of the stage. He was laying the groundwork. And I'll be damned if every night he didn't hook up with one of them! One night, he sank his hooks into a blond from Milano, a pretty 40-year-old. He proposed going to eat spaghetti at a friend's house and invited her along. This friend was a waiter at the club, who'd picked up another couple of chicks. After we had our spaghetti, they told me to put on some records. My cursed fate, as usual. "We're going upstairs. You come up later." A half hour later, I started hearing all this sighing and moaning, but nobody called me. I put on one last record and quietly snuck upstairs, where I entered the room and saw them fucking, and jumped in bed with them. I figured she was already nice and hot, and would fuck me, too. But as soon as she touched my hair and realized there was someone else in bed with them, she started howling like a maniac. They turned on the light and kicked me out. The bass player was super pissed off. "I told you I'd call you when the time was right," he snapped. "You just ruined everything!" Then they went back to their business. She was a real fury, tireless.

Another 15 minutes went by, but apparently, the time still wasn't right. I wasn't about to give up, though, so I went back upstairs, and she finally agreed to take me on. She was burning hot, and we wound up having a generous threesome.

As for Mosti, our piano player, he was a careful chap. We took turns using our cars to save money, and whenever it was his turn, he'd put everything on the bill: gas, oil, even wear and tear on the battery. He would always say he wasn't hungry so he wouldn't have to pay when we went to a trattoria, but then he would pick at our plates. He never paid. To get back at him, we'd play totally cruel pranks. Fabrizio, the drummer, shit on a sheet of newspaper and smeared it on his car door handle. Once, late at night, after the show, we took the wheels off his Alfa Romeo. See you tomorrow. He started up the car, but it wouldn't budge. Another time he had finally managed to pick up a woman, and we all came into his room naked, with hard-ons, while he was fucking away. When he slept, he snored, so we built this little coffin-type thing out of chipboard to cover his head. He woke up screaming in the middle of the night with his head inside the box.

These freewheeling shenanigans did nothing, however, to bring the group together. While I was still working in Varazze, a guy from Warner Brothers called to tell me that a song I'd written, which without too much imagination was titled 'Din Don Dan,' had a nice melody and that Michele Pecora, who the year before (1979) had a summer hit with 'Era Lei,' liked it. He wanted to use my song for his next single. Great, I thought. At last some royalties coming in. He wants to do the lyrics? Fine, that means less work for me, and I get to sell my music. I was hoping it would be a hit. Psyched by the news, I went to see my friends from the band to tell them. Total ice. The old goats were envious.

One afternoon in Varazze, we went to the beach for a swim. I'm not much for the shore myself. I can't take the heat and stickiness, and I'm not big on swimming, as I've said. By the time evening rolled around, I was exhausted. I sang 'Rock 'n' Roll Robot,' that summer's big hit by Alberto Camerini—I had to, it was Number One—but I was in a cold sweat. I felt a stabbing pain deep in my chest, and my heart was racing, but my hands and feet were cold. Frozen. I put down my guitar. I was afraid I was going to die. I had my mates take me back to the pensione and I went to bed. My body kept going from hot to cold and back again. I tossed and turned all night; it felt like I couldn't breathe. I thought I was going to suffocate or have a heart attack. My head was spinning. By the time the sun came up, my condition still hadn't changed. I felt like I was losing my mind, which kept wandering over all the shit that had happened. My wife, alone and terminally pissed off. The band—no good vibes there either. I was playing just to eke out a living. No passion. Not to mention the stifling heat. This was the debut. Some malevolent god had ushered me into the marvel-filled, brightly tinted world of the panic attack. My first time.

I got in my super-used, smoke-spewing gold Opel with the gear shift on the steering wheel and drove back to Carrara at 20 kilometers an hour with the window open, gasping for air. I made it home and told Angela I wasn't feeling well, and asked her to call a doctor.

"Who knows what you've been up to now?!" she said, attacking me.

The doctor confirmed I'd had a breakdown and prescribed 15 days' rest. But the owner of the club was furious. The guys in the band, who were envious, told him I'd left not because I was sick, but because I was making a solo record.

"Nobody here believes you're sick. If you're not back by tomorrow, I won't even give you last month's pay. For me, you're history."

One of the worst effects of a panic attack is the fear of the next attack, so I got Angela to go with me. She didn't want to stay with the band, of course, so I rented a little place for us. More money spent. Thanks to her though, I managed to get through the season, and we went home. I was in the middle of a big-time crisis. Depressed and frightened. The band had fallen apart; my career was going nowhere. "With that face and that voice, where do you expect to go?" they said. As a songwriter, I'd only sold one other song, 'Te Ne Vai,' and I had no idea where the fuck to turn. I saw black alright—and this time it was really black.

Zucchero Who?

AFTER THE PANIC ATTACK, I WENT THROUGH A TRYING BOUT OF DE-
pression. I had a daughter and a family to provide for, so I couldn't
stop playing with the band.

One day, an impresario from Pistoia by the name of Capecchi came
to see me: Nando Capecchi was a legend in Tuscany. He launched the
careers of people like Pieraccioni, Panariello, Ceccherini, and Conti.

"Zucchero, you've got to go to Castrocaro!" he said. "To Castrocaro!"

No, not Castrocaro! That was truly the last beach. We were one of
the best bands in Italy. How could we show our faces in Castrocaro
with a bunch of young bush leaguers? Not only that, but the Homo
Sapiens were going to play one of my songs at the Un Disco per
l'Estate Festival, a kind of summertime Sanremo. How could I play
at Castrocaro? I saw it as a giant step backward. But Capecchi insisted.

"You've got to go. It's the only way for you to get a recording
contract!"

I borrowed a car from my uncle in Milano and drove to Saint
Vincent, where Un Disco per l'Estate was held. I didn't have a hotel
or a pass. I sat down outside the arena like a fan, and searched around
for a way to get in. I could have called the Homo Sapiens to get on the
guest list. But I'm funny that way. I just pick up and go. I don't like to
ask anybody for anything. I ran into Paolo Cattaneo, who back then
produced Matia Bazar. I had given him some songs, and although he
hadn't done anything with them, he said he liked them.

"Which hotel are you staying at?"

Hotel?

"Well then, come to my place. If you don't mind the couch, you
can sleep in my room."

Otherwise I would have been in the street. What luck!

Then I met up with Gianni Ravera, the leading impresario of his
time. He organized Castrocaro, the Un Disco per l'Estate Festival,

and Sanremo. A powerful man who everyone referred to with respect as *Il Commendatore*: The Commander.

"Ah, so you're Zucchero!"

Had Capecchi told him about me?

"They tell me you write nice songs. Why don't you come to Castrocaro?"

How could I tell him no? I didn't want to.

"Really, *Commendatore*, I think I'm a little too old for that."

"Don't you worry about age! You just come play!"

He got me in and although I wasn't thoroughly convinced, I signed up.

In the meantime, Capecchi sent me two artists he'd picked up at contests somewhere in Italy. One was Stefano Sani, a good-looking young fellow from Ponticino who sang like Massimo Ranieri, in a high register. I tried to explain to him that in Italy it would be tough, since the place was already full of people who did that. We had to come up with something different. I wrote a song just for him, with Joe Jozzo from Torino—something with lower tones, whispers, something out of the ordinary—called 'Lisa.' The other artist was Fiordaliso, for whom I wrote 'Scappa Via.'

The three of us—me, Stefano, and Fiordaliso—all wound up going to Castrocaro. Somehow, we made it through the opening rounds. At night, the record company people watched the performances and chose the singers they were interested in. Going into the finals, Fiordaliso and I were tied for first. Stefano Sani was second. Just before going on, while I was wandering around the hotel lobby, out of the corner of my eye I spied Ravera getting on the elevator. I darted into the elevator, too.

"Hello, Zucchero. How are we doing?"

Now it was time for me to soften the old fellow up a bit.

"*Commendatore*, good evening. You'll recall that I have a family to support."

I knew having a family didn't make any impression on him.

"I'm not joking around here."

In the end, Fiordaliso and I shared first prize. Ravera got us contracts with three different record companies and promised to bring me to Sanremo.

Castrocaro turned out to be a determining factor in my career. It got me my first recording contract, and I also became Stefano Sani's producer. I was given a very low percentage of royalties for the record, but I got to go to Sanremo for the first time, where I sang 'Una Notte Che Vola Via.' That year there was no distinction between the Big Artists and the Young Artists sections. I came in seventh and was satisfied. It felt like something was starting to move. The TV station Telereggio even sent a crew to interview my mother and father in Roncocesi. My mother was in the kitchen.

"Adelmo has always been a good boy," she said.

My father was in the vegetable garden.

"Are you happy about your son's success?"

"Let's hope it lasts," he said.

"Do you like your son's music?"

"No. I like waltzes and the mazurka."

It finally looked like things were turning around, but then there was my relationship with Angela. You can imagine how things were going. And at that time, right when I most needed her to believe in me, not a day went by that I didn't feel her withering glare on me and my world and everything I did. There was no need to talk. I saw and felt that in her eyes there was no hope that I would make it. Maybe she thought I was a loser. Or maybe she just hoped one day I'd give up. She was spiteful and jealous at the same time. I tried to make her happy, make her feel important. Get her involved. I asked her to come to Sanremo with me; I told her flat out that I needed her.

"With all those assholes? Are you out of your mind?"

That was enough to sway me. I was suffering like a dog.

"Come on. I'll buy you a fur coat. For Sanremo. An ermine fur."

I didn't have a dime to my name. But what did it matter? I was willing to try anything. What with the payment on the house, fur salesmen and ermines, a cool million went like *that*. But at least now she was smiling. I'd made her happy. And off we went to Sanremo, with Angela wrapped in ermine.

Another panic attack. I'd never heard of such a thing, and the more I wondered about it, the more restless I got. I attended rehearsals in a cold sweat. I sang 'Una Notte Che Vola Via' and it wasn't bad. Coming in seventh wasn't exactly rubbish. The record company, PolyGram, was pleased. The artistic director really liked it—and he was none other than Bruno Tibaldi, the record boss at EMI who'd turned his back on me that time I left him my demo when I was a kid. But despite my respectable performance at Sanremo, still nothing happened.

And that wasn't the end of it. One night at dinner with the brass from PolyGram, both British and Italian, I found myself in one of those situations where you need to strike a balance between hypocrisy and diplomacy, and do the best to sell yourself. I was chatting up the artistic director from the headquarters in the UK when suddenly my wife says—and not even in a hushed tone of voice—"That's enough! I don't want anything more to do with these assholes." Gee, thanks a lot. I told you I needed your support, that this is a delicate and important situation. I run up debt to buy you a house, ermine furs, and you can't even sit through a fucking dinner? "No. I don't feel well. Bring me back to the hotel." I couldn't believe it. Overflowing with shame, I got up and took her away, avoiding the baffled looks from the record company head honchos.

The first album I recorded for PolyGram was not my kind of thing, musically. They said to make it big, I'd have to give up the blues and sing more melodically, like Riccardo Cocciante. They had me parade through the offices, in front of the secretaries, to pick out a look for me. Hair combed back and looking good, dress shirt and sweater.

They wanted to make me a pop singer. I had other ideas in mind, but they were in charge. They titled the record—a true stroke of genius— *Un po' di Zucchero* (A Little Bit O' Sugar). Awesome! Suck me! On the front, my pretty little face with short hair. The finishing touch was the sugar cube on the back cover next to the list of song titles. What it came down to was there's this guy called Zucchero, with these honey-dripping, melodic songs, with a sugar cube on the back cover of his debut album. Where exactly is this thing going? Unfortunately, the critics wondered the same thing.

That year I went to Sanremo for the second time. I'd written a song for Richard Sanderson, which worked, because he was coming off the hit 'Reality' from the *La Boum* soundtrack. It was an anthem for kids in those days. I'd also written songs for Stefano Sani, who was back, and Fiordaliso, who was a hit with 'Non Voglio Mica la Luna,' which I co-wrote with Malepasso and Albertelli, as well as for Donatella Milani, who came in second with 'Volevo Dirti.' I, how-ever, did worse than the year before. I sang 'Nuvola.' It was a flop and PolyGram began fretting.

The Bluff

WHILE ANGELA CLEARED THE TABLE IN THE BACKYARD, I'D PLAY WITH Alice, hiding underneath, pretending to be Giovanni the Lion— *roar!*—or Theresa the Seal. I really enjoyed spending time with her. But I was tormented by our dire need for money, and kept investing my time in writing music, which up till then had led me nowhere. I was always down at my little ramshackle studio, playing away at the piano. We had bills to pay—electric, gas—the meters spun out of con-trol. I taped them shut so we wouldn't be charged. I didn't pay the TV tax. We had to eat and pay the installment on the house—five mil-lion—every six months.

I could see that things at PolyGram were cooling down. They called me less and less. I made an appointment with Tibaldi to get a bead on the situation. After my second appearance at Sanremo, 'Nuvola' was not a hit. *Un Po' di Zucchero* was pretty much a flop, too.

I went up to Milano, where they had me wait in the foyer. While I was waiting, Marcus Antonius, as we called the managing director, walked by, all clean in his little pink shirt and glasses. We hadn't quite figured him out yet, and took him for the Latin lover type. Tibaldi walked in before me and forgot to close the door all the way, which allowed me to eavesdrop.

I heard everything they said. Marcus Antonius hadn't even bothered to say hello.

"We'll leave this guy at home."

Crushing blow.

"Where's he going to go, with that voice? We're spending money for nothing here. No sense investing more."

What a Marcus Antonius. A real traitor.

"Let's get rid of him. If you really think you to, at most keep him on contract as a songwriter. But as far as becoming a recording star goes, forget about it—he's not worth a shit. No way."

Damn. I walked in. They offered to renew my contract as a songwriter for five million. Cold shower. Truly a cold shower. When you least expect it, you don't know how to react, and you wind up not reacting. I couldn't even open my mouth. I got up and left. By the time I got home, I was a wreck. Just the thought of Angela's scornful eyes was the *coup de grâce*. I didn't say anything about what had happened.

"I'm frazzled. You sleep with the baby in our bed, I'll go in her room."

I cried all night long. I didn't know what to do next. I was broke, and now I didn't even have a recording contract. I really had no idea where to turn.

The next morning, I took action. I found the strength to call

Tibaldi. Bluffing, I told him I had an offer from another record company, so I didn't want to sign their songwriter's contract. I would sell my songs elsewhere. Dealing with record company people is a lot like being in love: they're interested in you only if someone else wants you.

"You can't do that; you're still under contract with us," he retorted.

I poured it on: "You guys don't want me anymore anyway."

"Come to Milano, we'll talk about it."

I returned to Milano wearing a dark, gloomy face and sunglasses. This time I was going to sell my skin for a price. I told them I wanted to get to the point, and asked to sign a release so I could leave. Sergio Poggi, Tibaldi's assistant artistic director, spoke up, saying he could get 40 million out of the managing director. "That's the best I can come up with. And for that money, you've got to give us a record. It's your last chance."

It wasn't much (less than $20,000)—not much at all if I wanted to make a record. A ludicrous budget. But, desperate and broke, I said OK. I had no alternative.

I had already written the songs that I gave Guido Elmi to hear. He was the producer for Vasco, who'd just released 'Vita Spericolata.' They were demos of 'Donne' and 'Un Piccolo Aiuto.' I made them at Elmi's house. He led a bizarre existence. He would shut the place up, lower all the blinds in the middle of the day, so inside it was completely dark. He finally opened an hour after I got there, in his underwear. Maybe he had a disheveled woman or two in the back. The place was a mess. Who knew what they'd been doing all night? With an enormous pile of dishes to wash, the kitchen was in a frightful state. He played a Roland 808 drum machine and I played piano. We made some basic demos, but we really didn't conclude a fucking thing. Rhythm & blues and soul were my passion. I wanted to make a record reflecting my own tastes. But in Italy that was going to be tough. The record people said almost no one was into that stuff. I kept saying that, in England, Paul Young was a big hit singing soul, with his cover of 'Love of the Common People,' from the 1960s. He was white and sang soul, and doing very well with it. So maybe there was room for an Italian like me, too.

A Guy in San Francisco

THERE WAS A GUY IN AVENZA WHO HAD A SHOP WHERE HE REPAIRED heaters, across the way from us. After work, he'd come over to chat. He was a great lover of music and pretty much fed up with his job. He was fascinated by the world of entertainment. He gave me a lot of encouragement at a time when I was alone. Angela remained true to form and staunchly opposed my work. My parents had moved back to Reggio Emilia. I had no one to talk to except for the guy who came over every night after fixing heaters all day. He told me if I ever needed a ride somewhere, he could take me.

The Italian singers' soccer team contacted me after hearing I'd played goalkeeper as a kid. I'd be filling in for their longtime keeper, Paolo Mengoli, they said. I'd be doing them a favor, since audiences had already seen me twice at Sanremo, even if I didn't make that big a splash. But I didn't have money for gas to get there. So Agostino, the guy who repaired heaters, took me. Morandi, Tozzi, Mogol, Fogli, and Mingardi were all there. They scored three goals against me, one after the other. Pecchini, the team's secretary, had introduced me as a great goalie. Then they scored another. A producer who was playing fullback got totally pissed off: "Man, you know how to play or not?" That really hurt. What arrogance. I thought the match was supposed to be just for fun. But they wanted me to go to their training sessions and all that. I never played with them again.

Agostino's wife had a shop where she sold jeans. She won a trip for two to a retailers' convention in San Francisco. But they couldn't go.

First, he tried to sell me the tickets for a million. Where was I going to get that kind of money? In the end, he gave them to me anyway—he'd gotten them for free. "Pay me later."

I knew there was a great guitarist from Naples, Corrado Rustici, living in San Francisco. Before that, he'd played in England. He'd worked with Aretha Franklin and Narada Michael Walden, the drummer who played with John McLaughlin, the Mahavishnu Orchestra, and Jeff Beck. He'd even worked with artists like Whitney Houston and Herbie Hancock. Maybe I could contact him. Angela didn't want to come, so I took Giacomo de Simone, who filmed weddings for a living. At the Linate airport we met the whole group attending the convention. We'd give this organized trip the slip right away, and bring along a guy from Calabria we made friends with during the flight.

We got to San Francisco at four in the morning. Our hotel was beautiful. Along the promenade, with a view of Alcatraz and the Golden Gate Bridge. More bridges, the harbor, Haight-Ashbury—where all the hippies hung out—and crabs steaming in big pots. Late one night at Pier 39, I ate the best pizza of my life at a place run by Neapolitans. My friend filmed it all. I pretended to sing as if we were making a video. I found Rustici. We met at the hotel one afternoon. I played my songs for him, and told him I wanted to record them in San Francisco but I only had 40 million. If we could lay down the basic tracks for all nine songs in five days, we'd be in there. We gave it a shot. The next day I hooked up with Randy Jackson, who had played bass with Santana and Jerry Garcia and other high-caliber musicians, like George Perry on drums and Walter Afanatieff on keyboards. One after the other, we recorded the music for all nine songs.

Afterwards, I joined the retail jeans conventioneers and flew back to Italy with my tape. I sent PolyGram the recordings of the music, along with my dummy English vocals, since I still didn't have the lyrics in Italian. Only I sent it under an assumed name—a friend's, along with his telephone. I was testing PolyGram. They called my friend immediately and asked him who the singer was. They liked him and thought the stuff was really good. He told them he was the singer, and they invited him to sign with them. When I showed up instead, their jaws dropped. It was so different; they hadn't recognized my voice on the recording. At last I'd begun doing what I'd always wanted. There would still be compromises, but my own style was beginning to take shape. It wasn't yet the blues I'd been searching for, but it was a break from my pop debut. And it was up to international standards. It sounded great because I'd played on it with some real kick-ass musicians.

Target Practice

I HADN'T WRITTEN THE LYRICS YET, AND TIBALDI SUGGESTED ASKING Mogol (Giulio Rapetti) if he'd write with me. He was no longer working with Lucio Battisti, and maybe he'd be interested. Roll out the red carpet, crack open the Champagne. Mogol came and was treated like a prince.

"What am I supposed to do?" he began in his squeaky little voice.

"The lyrics, a direction, an interpretation."

"Yes, but…"

They sent me out.

"Come to my house at eight a.m. I get up early. At ten I go to Conti's."

What the fuck is Conti's? A gym, I later found out.

"If you're not there by ten after eight, I'm leaving, eh."

I set out from Carrara at five in the morning to make it to Milano on time. He lived in Piazzale Loreto. I couldn't find a place to park. It was five minutes to eight. Fuck, this guy's not going to wait. I finally parked the car. Elevator. Doorbell. Signora Carla, the governess, opened the door. He was in his robe in the bathroom, lathering up to shave.

"The old lion—I'm an old lion, Signora Carla. Bring me my *caffè d'orzo*."

A half hour goes by.

"Come on, let me hear something with the guitar."

I played and sang in my fake English. On the recording, just to give it a little flavor, I added in Italian, "*Ma l'aria è frescaaa*" ("But the air is fresh").

"For the love of God, don't sing in Italian," he said. "You're not right for the words. Now go home and do what Lucio did. Sit down with your tape recorder and do singing lessons eight hours a day."

"Singing lessons?"

"Yes. You've got to find your own way of singing and separating the notes. I hope you don't want to sound like Ray Charles and Joe Cocker. They're as old as pointy-toe shoes. They're ancient. We need stuff that's fresh."

I thought he didn't know what the fuck he was talking about—I wished I could sing like Ray Charles more than anything. And Joe Cocker had been an idol of mine ever since Woodstock.

I went home, practiced, and went back. Same old scene. Shaving. The old lion still roars. *Caffè d'orzo*. A half hour went by. Then he said, "Miraculously, I have saved you."

"Signor Rapetti, have you written the song?"

"Yes, but I'm not going to give it to you. You can't handle it. Vasco Rossi could, if he had it to sing, but not you."

"At least let me try."

"No way, this song's too precious."

The Italian song is like a target with concentric circles, he said. That was the metaphor he used. In the outermost circle, the black one, are the melodic singers, like the ones who go to Sanremo. The Roman singer-songwriters are in the circle after that. And in the next circle are the singers I've miraculously saved. In the bulls-eye there is only one. Guess which circle you're in. Two hours later, he told me: I wasn't in any circle.

"*Stasera se un uomo mi toccasse, forse non saprei dire di no. È tanta ormai la mia delusione che non saprei dire no.*" ("If a man touched me tonight, I might be not able to say no. I'm so downhearted, might be not able to say no.")

It came time to record. "Ma l'aria è frescaaa," I sang.

That was the first song he wrote for me, 'Stasera Se un Uomo.' At another session, he introduced me to his friend Alberto Salerno, who had written 'Io Vagabondo' and was married to (record producer and TV personality) Mara Maionchi. He agreed to write some lyrics for me as well, and penned 'Donne' and 'Un Piccolo Aiuto.' The rest of the lyrics were by Mogol.

Down to the Last Second

I PLAYED A CELEBRATION IN THE PIAZZA IN MASSA, AND WAS APPROACHED by a producer—a Neapolitan who'd played with Corrado Rustici's brother in Osanna, an excellent 1970s progressive rock band from Naples. They'd gone to England and then on to America. "I'm your producer," he told me. He spoke Neapolitan dialect with an American accent. He'd produced a few records and opened a pizzeria in Massa.

With his Italian-American style of management, he had the four "monsters" brought over to Italy—the four crack musicians I'd played with in San Francisco. He laid down the law with the record company—even with Mogol, who he asked to come up with more lyrics. I thought I'd finally found someone who was right for me. But the musicians went back to the States and he foundered, exposing all his insecurities. Lost in a world of incense, pizza, and Hare Krishna mantras, he couldn't get anything done. A bolt of lightning put the Dolby recording system on the blink for a month, and that brought a hasty conclusion to my relationship with Danilo Rustici. I replaced him with Fio Zanotti, and we quickly wrapped things up. The record company had decided to take me to Sanremo, this time to compete in the Big Artists section. I would perform 'Donne.' Mogol remarked that it was the most banal song on the album—the lyrics were written by his friend, Salerno.

I managed to get Corrado Rustici and Randy Jackson to come play with me at Sanremo. Randy Jackson is a superstar and was a judge on *American Idol*. On the album cover he's holding my second daughter, Irene, who was just a few months old. For live performance, he dressed in shocking pink and wore a yellow headband, and that gorgeous bass of his was out of sight. I also brought along my old standby, Gary, on drums. However, they just pretended to play—the music part was recorded, only my vocals were live. We also had a black keyboard player who lived in Bologna, and a sax player from Livorno, with a very dark complexion and dreadlocks—he was a "child of the war" who spoke only in a terrible Livornese drawl, but I pawned him off as a great American sax player. "Don't say a word"—was our agreement. Of course, that all fell apart at the press conference, when he told journalist Mario Luzzatto to take a hike.

The band had a cool black identity and came off as pretty badass. My look had completely changed. I got a pageboy haircut, and instead of a clean dress shirt and sweater, I wore jeans and a black leather jacket over a construction worker's tank top. I'd even found a sponsor from Reggio Emilia. The owner, who was also a country boy, agreed to pay me five million (about $2000) and said I could keep the clothes if I wore a skullcap with his company's name on it the night of the finals. I went to rehearsal the first day wearing the skullcap, and nobody said anything. Good, they'd get used to it, I hoped. Before the finals, I got a call from Ravera. "Hey, what do you think I am, stupid? Get rid of that cap!"

That worried me. The finals were broadcast live. I didn't want to have Ravera pissed off at me. Should I wear it? Should I not wear it? I had another skullcap, which was identical, only without the company's name on it. Down to the last second, I was backstage, holding both hats in my hand. When Pippo Baudo introduced me, I was in despair. Out of hunger, I put on the hat with the logo. It was a super stressed-out performance, because I was afraid I was going to get hell for that. But nobody said anything and I got my five million. I came in next to last.

The singer Christian cried bitter tears that made his mascara run. Why was he crying? Did he come in last? Where was I? Luckily there were also people like Ivan Graziani, Finardi, the guys from Banco del Mutuo Soccorso, and the New Trolls, who cared as much about winning as I did—which is to say, very little. The music of 'Donne' was new for Italy—it was soul, with lots of sax and choruses. The lyrics were captivating, full of energy. "*Donne in cerca di guai, negli occhi hanno dei consigli e tanta voglia di avventure, per volare ad alta quota, donne controcorrente.*" ("Women looking for trouble, there's advice in their eyes and longing for adventure, to fly high, rebel women.") It was an upbeat manifesto. A simple song, it was musically immediate. I played it live right after the festival, then never again, for years. I figured it belonged to a distant past. But 25 years later I started playing it again, by popular demand. I'm not ashamed of it. It's simple but elegant. And it was the first stone laid, the turning point of my career and my life. Luckily, it began to get airplay, and became a hit.

My mother said, "You were great, your father was very moved, his eyes were glossy. They all stop me at the cooperative to tell me how great Delmo is."

My mother began cutting out and saving the newspaper and magazine articles that talked about me. Photos, song lyrics. My first fan. She built a little altar in the house for all those things. My mom also loved her daughter-in-law and the girls to no end. Angela had only ever slept in Roncocesi once. She didn't come to Sanremo that year. I know she watched me on TV with Alice and Irene, who was just born, at her parents' house, and rooted for me like a hardcore fan. Of course, she would never tell me about that. On the contrary, she would belittle me: "But where do you want to go? What do you want to do?" In all the years we were together, she never told me she loved me, or said how much she cared. Never. Nor did she ever say that she liked any of my songs. Much later she did, though, whenever she comes to one of my concerts. "You've got an extraordinary voice that keeps getting better with age. It gives me the goosebumps. I'm moved." She told me in Verona, after a show on the Chocabeck tour of 2010. After we broke up, friends would try to console me and tell me that in reality, I was her life. But she wouldn't tell me that, and never did.

After Sanremo, Polydor thought there might be a glimmer of hope for me and released the album *Zucchero & The Randy Jackson Band*, which contains 'Donne.' Something of a disaster, only 11 thousand copies were sold. Angela wasn't happy. Angela was melancholy. Angela was devoid of feelings for me. When she laughed though, which was rare—and I always looked forward to those moments— she laughed with passion. She was beautiful. She lit up. I always tried to make her happy, even if we both should have sought our happiness elsewhere. And always, she was contradictory. And able to floor me. If I was at home writing songs, after a while she'd get fed up with it; if I was on the road playing and never there, I was only thinking of myself. It was a suffocating chain of double knots. Whatever move I made was the wrong one. The atmosphere in our house was a sweltering, muggy bog, in climate and mood. I loved her. I would have made love to her all the time. I was the one who always made the first move, and Angela would often refuse me. But we'd both wanted to have children, and she was a loving, attentive, affectionate mother.

Fifty Million

AFTER SANREMO, ANGELA TOLD ME SHE DIDN'T WANT TO LIVE IN Avenza anymore. I was away from home more than ever, and she didn't want to be left alone with Alice and Irene. "I want to go back to Forte dei Marmi," she said, "near my mother." She wanted a new house. I was flat broke. My bank account was 40 million in the red. Neither Sanremo nor 11 thousand records sold did anything to help my finances. And then, Angela became affectionate. She stood by me. She took the initiative, strolled around the house in her robe to provoke me, played footsie. We made love: I was crazy about her. In love and bewitched. But fully aware of the situation.

"Angela, we don't have any money."

She insisted. She wanted a house in Forte dei Marmi. She made the rounds of the real estate agents. She took me to see a house. Brand new, huge, beautiful, with three bathrooms and a backyard. A real deal. Five hundred million. A wicked dream for us—we lived in a hole in Avenza.

"Angela, it's unthinkable. I'll never pull it off."

"This is our house. I won't have any more problems here. I'll be happy at last."

She worked her charms on me.

I told the builder I didn't have any money. He said it was a great deal. He'd gotten back the deposit on the previous sale, a few million, and was willing to sell me the house for 450 million. That was a huge amount of money for me. Again, I told him I didn't have the money. He said I could pay in installments of 50 million every six months. Angela insisted. We bought the house.

An impresario guaranteed he could use my performance at Sanremo to get me gigs all summer long in the piazzas of southern Italy. He was a local powerhouse. I told him I needed an advance of

50 million by May. He said not to worry and promised I'd have tons of gigs. I believed him. I signed the deed to our house. Come on, we can do it.

I bought a lawnmower and cut the grass, like in American movies, proud of our new home. I thought I'd made Angela and our daughters happy—we had a house in Forte dei Marmi. A place, as I said, I always hated. I never felt at home there.

One night, I was headlining at a club nearby, in Lunigiana. I told Angela I'd be back after the gig.

"No way am I spending the night here alone. I'm going to sleep at my mother's. Either that, or I'll have her come and sleep here."

Once again, I felt humiliated and offended. Invaded, too.

"You still need your mamma? I come back from a show and your mother's here?"

I really had it in for her this time. "I've shown you I want to be there for you, that I have courage—the courage to make mistakes. I've run up debts for you. I'm a responsible husband and father. My family means a lot to me. I chose you because I loved you. And what do you do? Call your mother and violate our intimacy. Don't I mean a fucking thing to you? You call yourself a free woman? I've been waiting for a sign from you, but it never comes."

I didn't go back home that night. I slept at our old house in Avenza. More days of silence and rancor were to come.

I went to see the impresario in Rome to pick up the advance he'd promised. Instead he gave me all kinds of excuses: the accountant, the checks, the bank. He asked me for an invoice. I didn't even have a VAT number. How was I going to issue an invoice? OK, we'll straighten everything out tomorrow morning.

I got a room at the Hotel Clodio, near the RAI on Via Teulada, filled with the stench of fried food from the cafeteria below. The next morning at 11 I showed up at his office, as we'd agreed. But his wife was surprised to see me and said she knew nothing about the appointment. And that her husband had left for Mexico City with Luis Miguel.

By the time I got home, I was seething with despair, but I didn't tell Angela anything—just that I'd be going to write songs at our house in Avenza, my retreat. I had a red telephone there, which I used to call all the impresarios I'd worked with in Italy for my dance hall gigs. I was hawking a three-year exclusive contract for 50 million. Concerts, management, record royalties—I was selling it all. I was in fucking need. I had offers for 20, 25—reasonable sums for what I was worth at the time. 'Donne' was doing well. No one was outbidding the first offers, but I refused to give up. The payment on the house was due in two days.

I called Paolo Cattaneo, who was Matia Bazar's producer, and told him about my problems. He didn't have any money, but he pointed me in the right direction. "There's a young guy from Bologna, played drums for Gino Paoli. He set up Paoli's tour with Vanoni. I told him about you and he's interested. His name is Michele Torpedine."

Never heard of him.

"He's just starting out. But he did make some money with Paoli and Vanoni."

Torpedine. What kind of name was that? I was leery. I wanted someone people knew. I could sense blank checks floating in the air. The last thing I needed was more trouble. But Cattaneo insisted the guy was alright. I didn't want to risk wasting time by going to Milano and spending money I didn't have on something completely useless. I told Angela I wasn't coming home, that I had to work. She got mad. I called, I pondered, I didn't come up with anything. At midnight, I got a call from Cattaneo. He was a friend and concerned about me— he really cared. "You've got me totally upset. I can't sleep. If you're in the shit, don't bust my balls. Just get on the train tomorrow and go see this guy."

We met the next day at one p.m. at Bistecchino, a hole-in-the-wall grill near Polydor that served nothing but horsemeat. Torpedine was affable and sharply dressed, very elegant. He said he liked the blues. He'd seen me at Sanremo and could invest in me. And he knew how much I was asking.

"Are you ready?"

"Sure."

"To start right away?"

"Fine."

I told him we'd sign the contract at my lawyer's—to make it sound more credible.

Of course, I had no lawyer. On the road, I called Gary, my drummer friend, who I knew had a lawyer friend in Forte dei Marmi, by the name of Zavattaro. A divorce lawyer. I told him I needed a management contract that day. He asked me what it was about.

"Simple: There's this guy who's going to give me 50 million and I'm going to give him exclusive rights to my concerts and records. But it must be done right away, because I need the money." I also warned him, "The lawyer has to pretend that he's my regular lawyer and knows me well, that he oversees the legal aspects of my work."

Zavattaro got a contract from a fellow lawyer who worked in the entertainment field, and we signed. Torpedine came up with the money. I figured I'd pay him back with money from that summer's shows.

"Actually, I don't think you should do any shows this summer."

What do you mean? I thought. *When I finally have a record out that's doing something?* It was like having a Ferrari and keeping it locked up in the garage all summer.

"So where do you figure in all this?" I asked. I was starting to get worried.

"I'm not concerned about that now. Let me think. For now, just go back home and start writing material for another album. Use your head. Focus. Write the most beautiful music you've ever written."

Torpedine was always on tour with Gino Paoli and Ornella Vanoni at that time, in the theaters. He told me to contact Barbara, his secretary, if I needed anything. He took off. I got the money, thank God, and paid the installment on the house. I heaved a sigh of relief, but at the same time I was chomping at the bit. This guy splits, just when I figured I'd go out and play to promote my record. And he tells me to stay at home. What is this? Did he think he'd bought a horse just to leave it in the barn? I called Barbara. I told her I wanted to work. At last I heard from Torpedine.

"Why are you so on edge? You're not even working."

"Exactly! How am I supposed to survive? I paid off my installment on the house with the money you gave me, but how am I supposed to buy food? And pay the electricity and gas bills?"

"I'll give you 500 thousand lire a month. Will that cover your expenses?"

"I don't know."

I had no choice but to hunker down and start writing the songs for my next album, *Rispetto*. A month later, his tour over, Torpedine called and came to see me in Forte dei Marmi. While we talked on the beach, he suggested I play a benefit concert, Italy for Italy, to raise funds for victims of a dam that had burst in Trento. It was broadcast on RAI-3, and hosted by someone he knew: Gianni Minà.

"I may be able to get you to sing at least 'Donne.' The thing is, I want you there with an awesome band."

"OK, but I don't have an awesome band."

"Your drummer isn't bad. He'll do just fine. And I know these musicians from Naples who are gonna blow your mind."

It turned out to be true. He brought me Joe Amoruso, a piano player who'd played with Pino Daniele, and Julius Farmer, an awesome bass player from New Orleans who was working as a session man in Milano. There was also a hot guitar player from the band Napoli Centrale.

We put three songs together. Great sound. We went on last, after midnight, an endless wait. It was live, and time was running out. They would only let me do one song. I was livid. I walked onstage, introduced by Minà: "We're going to wrap up this live broadcast with a promising young star: Zucchero."

I sang 'Donne.' As it ended, Minà took the microphone and said, "Thank you, Zu."

I tore the mike away and said, "No, I have two more songs to sing."

"But, Zucchero, we're running late."

I protested that I'd waited all this time. So, I sang two more songs.

It was all broadcast live, except for the last half of the third song, which was faded out. They'd ganged up on me, but I held my ground. Sorry, Gianni, I know it wasn't elegant and that such things shouldn't be done. I put you in a tough spot.

But fuck, man, I'd been waiting the whole afternoon. I'd been waiting for you the whole summer. I felt like you thought I was some kind of bullshit upstart, so I said to myself, *fuck this shit, I'm singing!* That was my hot temper flaring up. I sang 'Donne,' 'Ti Farò Morire,' and part of another song, probably 'Un Piccolo Aiuto.'

I went home and launched into writing like a demon. I could sense that it was going somewhere, that people were interested in this new, unexpected version of Zucchero. The blues, at last. We played a couple songs at the Pistoia Blues Festival. The band included Julius Farmer on bass. I'd convinced my wife to let him sleep on our couch. But why give me a hard time? I couldn't afford to put him up in a hotel. OK, but just one night.

Julius Farmer was a helluva guy. He busted his ass. He drank at least 10 beers that night, then crashed out on our couch. Smoked like a fiend. But instead of putting his cigarettes out in the ashtray, he stubbed them out on the tile floor. The next morning, Angela had a fit. "Who does he think he is? I don't give a shit if he plays bass or not." And she kicked him out of the house.

The Miracle

SUMMER HAD COME. I SPENT IT WRITING SONGS. LATE ONE NIGHT in July, around four a.m., the doorbell rang. Ding-dong. I woke up. Fuck.

"Anyone home? Nobody's ever home. Everyone's abandoned me."

I opened the door.

"Giulio!"

It was Mogol.

"What are you doing here?"

"I took a boat from Punta Ala to Viareggio, but Morandi went home, and Gianni Bella went to see his wife. They abandoned me. Both of them. I said to myself, Let's see if my pal Zucchero wants to go for pizza with me. I'm starving."

"But, Giulio, it's four o'clock in the morning."

My wife: "Who is it?"

"It's Mogol."

"I don't give a shit about Mogol. What does he want at this hour?"

"Chill out, Angela, please. I can't mistreat the guy. I'll take him to Romeo's pizzeria in Forte dei Marmi, they're open till six a.m. Then I'll come back. Please, chill."

"You're crazy, man. At this hour," I said to Giulio.

"None of you people are free anymore. You used to be wild horses. Now everyone's got to go back home to their wives, kids, grandmas. I'm the only free man left. Come on, let's go for a pizza."

He was a sly devil and already had the whole thing planned. I took him to eat pizza, kept him company. He flattered me. He challenged me.

"Listen, we're both free. I've got an idea. Let's take a ride down the valleys, over the mountains. We'll cross the Apennine all the way to the other side of Italy, the eastern shore. You know how to drive an automatic?"

"No," I said. "I've still got a manual."

"Big mistake there, man. You've got to update. Automatic is awesome."

He wouldn't stop harping on it.

"You're behind the times, man. Like pointy-toe shoes. Get yourself an automatic."

"Hey, I get your drift."

"Come on. While you drive, put on the song you're writing now. And perhaps once again, I'll miraculously save you."

That was the way he talked. That was the way he was. Nice fellow, Giulio.

If I didn't come home, Angela was going to have a fit. But this guy was enticing me with promises of lyrics for my new song. So…

I called Angela. "Please be patient," I said, "but I have to go with Mogol."

Screams, teeth grinding, fuck you's flying.

I drove. It was five in the morning. Città di Castello, Perugia. We crossed mountainous central Italy all the way to Pesaro. From the Tyrrhenian Sea to the Adriatic. From sea to sea. That was the idea that had so thrilled Mogol.

Maybe he just needed a ride and had nobody else to take him. He was scheduled to play a match with the Italian singers' soccer team. He fell asleep along the way, so it was practically like driving by myself the whole time. He woke up when we hit the plateau before dropping down toward the coast and Pesaro.

"Ah, how pretty. Look, the sea!"

"'Ah,' yourself. You slept the whole way."

"I'm awake now. Come on, man, let's go for a sandwich."

We went to a deli. He wanted a sandwich with Negronetto salami.

"Do you have Negronetto?"

"We've got local salamis. They're very good."

"Negronetto's the best. Excellent. Thank you all the same."

And he left.

"Alright then, let's go get an ice cream."

"I'd like a Cornetto, please."

"Sorry, sir. We only have gelato here."

"Ah, what a shame. Cornetto. So good."

And he walked out of the ice cream store, too.

We resumed our journey.

"Come on, man, I'm in the mood. Put on your tape."

I drove on, said, "Finally," and put on the cassette. He started scribbling away, covering up the page like a nerd at school who wants to make sure you can't copy his math test. He never wanted to let anyone see what he was writing.

"Miraculously, I have saved you once again. The old lion can still scratch!"

I had a good laugh.

We reached Pesaro. All the soccer team singers were there.

"Guys! I've just saved him, miraculously."

"Hurray for Giulio!" they all shouted. "Bravo! Giulio, you're the best!"

"Thank you, thank you."

After the soccer match and dinner, he gave me the lyrics he'd written, and I checked them out. Just three lines about a molecule. "*Tu, molecola smarrita.*" ("You, lost molecule.") I put on the cassette and tried singing the words to the music. It didn't swing the way I wanted it to. But who's going to tell Mogol that?

As soon as I awoke the next morning, I got up and knocked on Giulio's door. I had everything I was going to say ready. Far be it from me to teach anyone how to do something, much less a master like him. The lyrics are beautiful. The idea of the molecule is great. But it just doesn't swing. There's something wrong somehow.

"Of course, there's something wrong! You don't know how to make it work."

He washed his face and went down to the lobby to join the rest of the singers from the soccer team.

"Ah, I don't work this way."

He called Tibaldi to tell him he wanted carte blanche. I could understand that—the guy had already written so many songs. While he was on the phone discussing the situation with Tibaldi, I snuck off. I left the hotel and took the first train out of Pesaro. I got back to Forte dei Marmi many hours later, after a long trip. I had the house payments hanging over my head. Everything was a mess. I was angry with myself. But now I was going to put myself to the test: "Damn it, man. Can't you write your own lyrics, instead of relying on someone else to do it for you?" I took up pen and paper, and wrote 'Rispetto' then and there. I was thinking of Mogol, but also of my wife. "*Quanti soldi vuoi per lasciarmi stare? Non c'è più rispetto neanche tra di noi. Per lasciarmi andare. Quanti soldi vuoi? Quanti soldi vuoi?*" ("How much money do you want, just to leave me alone? Ain't no more respect between us. How much money do you want? How much money do you want?") Then I say: "*Tira tira tira che si spezza, dài. Tira tira tira che si spezza dài. Stavo bene con gli amici al bar. Ci credi, ero lì. chiaro come il mar.*" ("Keep pulling and pulling, and it's gonna break. Believe me, I was there. It's as clear as the sea.")

It sounded good. It sounded perfect. A nice slogan, to boot: Respect! I'd become a writer. Of music. Of words. See that, you dope? You really can write your own lyrics. You don't need anyone to do it for you. It was a breath of fresh air, pure oxygen. I believed in myself. I reacted, and the reaction was triggered by none other than Mogol himself. A positive reaction. I had him to thank for it. I don't know whether he was mad at me, whether he liked me, or whether, or not, he was like that with everybody. He was like a hard-ass coach, the ruthless kind, the one who teaches you to never give up. He motivated me by being callous and harsh.

Summer went by and September came. I'd already written most of the songs for *Rispetto*, so now it was time to make a new album. The idea was that I'd return to Sanremo the following year. I had to have the songs I would sing there ready by November. Things began clicking with Torpedine. He introduced me to Gino Paoli, who wrote the marvelous lyrics to 'Come il Sole all'Improvviso': "*Nel mondo io camminerò, tanto che poi i piedi mi faranno male, io camminerò un'altra volta e a tutti io domanderò finché risposte non ce ne saranno più, io domanderò un'altra volta.*" ("I'll walk through the world till my feet hurt. I'll walk once more, and I'll question everyone till there are no more answers left, and I'll ask once more.") Salerno wrote the lyrics to 'Nella Casa C'era,' another beautiful song. The rest I wrote myself.

Then I called Corrado Rustici, who suggested I come to San Francisco to record, since it would cost less than bringing four musicians to Italy. So I took off for San Francisco. Corrado booked a week for us at Narada Michael Walden's Studio G. I worked with Narada, Randy Jackson, Corrado and Walter Afanatieff, who'd also played on the previous record, *Zucchero & The Randy Jackson Band*, and we laid down the instrumental tracks for *Rispetto* in a week. I returned to Italy, ready to hit the studio. I called a sound man in England to record the vocals and do the mix. Things went very smoothly and didn't take long at all. I even recorded the local marching band. I found two cute American girls, sisters who lived in Bologna, to sing backing vocals. We recorded a few solos by the saxophonist who's with me now, James Thompson, who was originally from Boston but lived in Bologna. It was all pretty much homemade. In Modena and Bologna. My means were quite modest back then. But the album turned out well. I'd finally focused in on my style, which took its cue from black music.

I performed 'Canzone Triste' at Sanremo, which people liked, although it didn't do anything that 'Donne' hadn't done already. I should have performed 'Rispetto.' But it was too transgressive, too new for the very traditional scene at Sanremo. 'Canzone Triste' was more melodic—and you know how record companies and the people who run

Sanremo are. Same old stories there. More than 100,000 copies of *Rispetto* were printed up for the release. I sang 'Come il Sole all'Improvviso' with Gino Paoli at Club Tenco, and more shows followed, with us doing duets of the song. 'Come il Sole all'Improvviso' became an enduring hit, a much-loved tune covered by many artists, including the beautiful version by Laura Pausini and Johnny Halliday.

Living Large

MY BROTHER-IN-LAW MARCO STARTED TO SEE BLACK SPOTS BEFORE HIS eyes. He was sick and getting worse. He'd always been something of a hypochondriac and was terrified at the thought of being sick. Maybe the poor guy had always known that he lived under an unlucky star. Those were the first symptoms. He was diagnosed with multiple sclerosis. He still played. But soon after the black spots he started having problems with his hearing. He heard noises in his ears: tinnitus. A scourge for a musician, a nightmare of constant buzzing. Angela freaked. She suffered, and so did I.

To try and help Marco, I contacted Dr. Rita Levi-Montalcini, who won the Nobel Prize for medicine in 1986. Gino Paoli and I donated all our royalties for 'Come il Sole all'Improvviso' to the Italian Multiple Sclerosis Association.

'Rispetto' came out that summer. Around that time, I began hanging out with fellow Italian singer Vasco Rossi. As soon as he heard 'Rispetto' he called me and said, "Fuckin' hell, Zucchero, that's a song I should have done. I fuckin' should have written it myself. Awesome song, man."

I'd never met him.

"When I wrote it, I was so mad, Vasco, that the words just came spewing out. 'Ain't no more respect between us…'"

My brother has a video of Vasco singing 'Rispetto' in a trattoria.

A mutual friend arranged for me to travel to Zocca, where he lived. I met him in a trattoria where he was a regular. In the hills, there was a stable next door. Truly God's country. He expressed so much respect for me. I thanked him from the bottom of my heart. I told him I thought he was great, too. It was all very simple, down to earth. We both hailed from the same region in Italy, Emilia. One from the mountains, the other from the countryside. We were provincial, shy. We began seeing more of each other. I used to spend a lot of time in Zocca, where Vasco introduced me to the barmaid at his regular haunt. She'd lived in France, but was originally from Zocca, and had returned to her hometown. She had the most sensual French accent. What a jewel—I was crazy about her! You're perfect, just the way you are. Keep talking to me. Give me your accent, your breath. We went out together nights, but there was no funny business going on. We'd mostly just go eat in the trattorias, do a little drinking, then everyone would head back to his or her own home. Vasco came to my house in Forte dei Marmi a couple of times. He'd bring one of his many women for a jaunt to the shore. For a while we saw a lot of each other.

One reason was because we both liked Franco Fanigliulo, a very original singer-songwriter who lived nearby, in Vezzano Ligure. Since by now the two of us had already had a bit of success, we figured we'd try to help him out, produce him and have him make an album for Vasco's record company, Bollicine. I would go see Vasco fairly often, and bring along Franco, so he could hear the songs and get an idea of what they were about.

Caterina Caselli brought him to Sanremo, where Franco sang: "*A me mi piace vivere alla grande già, girare tra le favole in mutande ma.*" ("I like to live large, though I'm not so keen on appearing in fairy tales in my underpants.")

He lived with his sheep, called each one by name. Forgot to pay the electricity bill. Never had a dime to his name. Never had a car. He just struggled by, any way he could. He was a poet, one of the most original Italian singer-songwriters of the 1970s, known for his theatrical interpretations. I was introduced to him through mutual friends, and we hit it off right away. He had a girlfriend from Florence, Sandra, but she was almost never around, since she worked as a seller in the markets up and down the Tuscan-Emilian Apennines. Franco would often show up at our house around dinnertime, especially in winter. He'd be hungry, but he was stubbornly proud, and always lied about having already eaten. Then, just for a taste, he'd eat a bowl of pasta. We were all fond of him. Even Angela, who rarely had a tender feeling for anyone.

"I just wrote an awesome song," he said one night.

"Let me have it, Franco. I'm going to Rome. I'll bring it to Ravera."

I knew Ravera would like it. I staked out his building and sat on a bench right beneath his office at around 7:30 p.m., waiting for him to come out and run into me "by chance." I convinced the *Commendatore* to listen to Franco's song in the hopes of getting him to perform it at Sanremo. And I was right: Ravera liked it. Then came a bunch of red tape: getting Franco officially signed, and the SIAE, the Italian Society of Authors and Publishers, to deal with, the copyright, besides getting the music together. I gave Franco the good news, but of course he didn't do a fucking thing with it. Ravera's secretary called me and said there was no sign of Franco's registration form. One afternoon, while I was in Carrara writing songs, Lucio, a friend of mine, came by with Franco. They were friends. We got the usual civilities out of the way, and Franco pretended like nothing had happened. I could tell there was something wrong. Lucio took me aside and said Franco didn't have the courage to ask me, but if he didn't pay five million by that evening, his house and what little furniture he had would be confiscated.

"He would never tell you this—you know how he is. If you could give him a hand."

Fuck! I was still paying off the house and other debts. I wrote him a check. Proud as always, he took it without much ado. Then, as he made his way down our front walk, he turned back and said, "Bye, brother. Don't worry, eh," and made a theatrical bow, like the great ham he was. In other words, "Yes, I'll make it a point to pay you back." And he left. Later that night, at around three o'clock, I got a call from friends. Franco Fanigliulo was dead. He'd suffered from arthritis, had a deformed hip, walked with a limp, and took gold salts for the excruciating pain. That evening he'd gone home and started feeling ill. He took two aspirins and suffered a cerebral hemorrhage. We went to see him at the hospital morgue in La Spezia. Then there was the funeral. Franco was a very strange person, but he had a big heart. He was unpredictable, but he had a lot of talent. Vasco Rossi recognized it, too. Franco was a hermit and could be tough to deal with. Caterina Caselli had a hard time dealing with him. When he had an appointment in Milano, he didn't show up two hours late, but the next day. He never got any gigs together, even just to earn himself a little cash. He could have worked—after all, he'd played twice at Sanremo.

He used to go to a trattoria, a stone building in the hills overlooking Sarzana, where they'd adopted him—they fed and took care of him. He'd met the owner's wife back in 1968, when she'd thrown herself headlong into the hippie culture and free love. She wound up getting married to a guy from Modena, and they rented this restaurant. They had a very cute daughter, Elena. Every evening, when Franco went to eat at that restaurant, I'd join him. We'd have dinner together. In those days, I wasn't sleeping at home—things were going down the drain. Anyway, they fed us in the kitchen. Franco was a good-looking man. All the ladies liked him. He was very vain.

One night we were at dinner in Lerici with friends of mine and their wives. "Hey guys, let's go skinny-dipping in Marinella!" He got there first. In the moonlight shadows, with his dick hanging out, he looked like one of the Riace bronzes. The girls had a blast and were all excited. We took our swim.

Around that same time, I was at Franco's friends' restaurant. I went to the bathroom and pissed black. I was afraid: blood in my urine. I went home to Forte dei Marmi and was struck with a stabbing pain in my back. Kidney stones. The pain was so bad it knocked me to the floor. I screamed like a baby. I kept pissing the color of Coca-Cola. I told Angela to call an ambulance. They took me to the San Rossore clinic in Pisa. Angela came with me in the ambulance, where they injected me with a tranquilizer. It had a bizarre, euphoric effect. The pain began to subside. I started laughing and couldn't control myself, like at school when you're not supposed to laugh but you do anyway. The injection produced a Viagra effect, and I was lying there with this raging hard-on. Weird reaction to pain. I asked my wife to intervene right there in the ambulance. Poor woman, she was never much inclined to such practices. There was always this strong sexual tension between the two of us. The pain, the sense of guilt, the fear—they all combined to make it so much more intriguing. A lusty ambulance ride. More of a mental trip than physical. When I got to San Rossore, the nurses put me on a stretcher and stuck an IV in my arm. A few days later, my father showed up at the door. He was carrying a large cardboard box, a care package tied with string.

"Papà, what are you doing here?"

"Your mother's worried. 'Go see what's wrong with Delmo,'" she said, "'because Angela told me he's in the hospital.' So, it's no big problem?"

"No. Just kidney stones. Nothing serious."

It was lunchtime. Sad hospital food.

"Papà, this is what I eat here."

"No, thanks. If you're OK, you might as well go back home."

He came to see me and left. He'd made the trip. His words dripped with unspoken love and affection.

Blue's

RISPETTO SOLD WELL, NEARLY 450 THOUSAND COPIES IN 1986. BEST OF all, the royalties began coming in every six months. They weren't astounding, but at least I could pay off the second installment on the house.

But just as I was catching my breath, a black crisis began, and things with my wife got worse. All I could do was keep my focus on the music. I put together a band with the guys from Forte dei Marmi, Pietrasanta, and Upper Versilia. We rehearsed at the Capannina— not the one Franceschi owned, but the one in Cinquale, where they gave us a room. They became my band and we started playing around. No more town square celebrations, like we did when I first appeared at Sanremo, in places like Lecce and Calabria, with all those religious processions and lights. Now we played at places like the Feste dell'Unita, and the Friendship Festivals. That's the way it's always been for me. Nothing great, yet I still got something out of it.

I set to work writing the songs for my next album, *Blue's*. I made the trip from Forte dei Marmi to Avenza every day. I was a musical working stiff. I'd wake up at 10 a.m., and by 11 I was in Avenza, where I stayed all day. For lunch, I'd grab a sandwich at the glorious old pensione across the street, which had a trattoria called Sergio's, where the quarrymen ate. I'd go back home in the evening.

Angela and I were on two different tracks, headed in opposite directions. I was focused on my work and bursting with energy. I felt that I was right in the middle of an extraordinarily creative phase. I knew exactly what I wanted—starting with the title of the new album, *Blue's*. As in the blues, black music, but with hints of Mediterranean melody. I was in the right mood, coming off *Rispetto*, which had provided a breath of fresh air. Now I wanted to write a great album, and make it more rhythm & blues. I fired off 'Con le Mani' and 'Senza una Donna.'

Things with Angela were rapidly going downhill.

I wrote the music for 'Senza una Donna' in one afternoon. It came to me right away. That night I stayed in Avenza because I was so pissed off with her, and wrote the lyrics. They just came spewing out. It's a love song about me and Angela. I figured it was all over between us and the end was near. But we were still together, and I wasn't thinking of putting it on the album because I didn't want to admit to what was already nostalgia. We hadn't broken up yet, and I was already trying to win her back. "*Io sto qui e guardo il mare, sto qui e guardo il mare, sto con me, mi faccio anche da mangiare, sì è così, ridi pure, ma non ho più paure di restare senza una donna, come siamo lontani, sto bene anche domani senza una donna che m'ha fatto morir, senza una donna, vieni qui, come on here!*" ("I'm here looking at the sea, that's how it is. Laugh if you want. But I'm no longer afraid of being left without a woman. How far apart we've grown. I'm fine, even without a woman—a woman who killed me. Without a woman. Come here, come on here.")

Corrado Rustici's manager, Pier Forlani who lived in London, set me straight. "You're crazy if you don't put that song on the album. The melody is so international that it could be a worldwide hit if it can break out of Italy." I wasn't totally convinced, but we wound up including it on the album. Fortunately.

I also cranked out the music for 'Hey Man' and asked Gino Paoli to write the lyrics. He helped me out and came up with the line "*Con le mani sbucci le cipolle*" ("You peel onions with your hands"). My relationship with Paoli was very productive. He spoke of me as if I were an unmade bed. I was disheveled, didn't comb my hair. I drank a lot, too, in those days, sucking down Averna on the rocks, whiskey, bourbon. I did it to relax, to keep me from thinking too much, and because I was fighting to get this record made and fighting with Angela when I returned home.

Anyway, Gino was into my music. The blues is always alluring, it's like a magnet for musicians. We wrote the lyrics to 'Con le Mani' and

'Hey Man' together, and he wrote the words to 'Bambino Io, Bambino Tu.' Sometimes we met at his house in Genova. Once he came to Carrara. We saw each other, though not often. I'd send him music through Torpedine and he would do his thing. Then we'd meet, and I'd say, "This works, this doesn't. Can we change it a little here and there?" We worked out the songs the way I wanted them. Paoli was easy to work with, very collaborative, and he never took himself too seriously. We were just writing songs. He was introverted, like me. He even called me Delmo. He and his wife, Paola Penzo, who's also Emilian, from Modena—very charming lady, superpositive attitude—watched me grow up. There's always been great energy between us.

Coming back from the shore one day, a line came to me after yet another fight with my wife. We fought every day. *I can't stand any more of you.* I was coming back in the car. *That's it! I really can't stand you anymore. Fuck!* I went to the studio. *I really can't stand you anymore!* A liberating cry. The music flowed from there. It came easy; I have no recollections of struggling with it. It was all very spontaneous. Then I found the connection to *"Solo una sana e consapevole libidine"*—my teacher's old slogan, which had remained in my memory. I wrote the music, the lyrics. After that came 'Hai Scelto Me,' which closes out the album—a short piece, less than two minutes. Piano and vocals. I think it's a gem.

The album came out and contained a barrage of hits. It sold 1.4 million copies. Bull's-eye. Enthralling rhythms and melodies, some delicate phrasing, spot-on lyrics. The tour we did for *Blue's* was magnificent. The band was hot, and we played in small stadiums.

"It Sucks!"

I MADE A DEMO WITH A ROLAND 808 DRUM MACHINE AND A KEYBOARD, with vocals, and recorded it live. I went home. This time, I thought,

I'd written a masterpiece. I admit, I was proud. I still think it's one of the best songs I've ever written, because it's the first true example of what I wanted to do with my music. The groove, the harmonic sequence, the chords, the hypnotic cadence, typical of rhythm & blues, the blues, gospel. Very American chords, very rhythm & blues. There was a bluesy beat to it, it was well articulated, with a purely melodic, pretty refrain. Very Italian, too. I was thrilled at having written something like that. This was mine—something the Americans and the British could only dream of, where the rhythm dissolved into a wave of melody. Eureka! This was my music.

"Angela, this time I've written a masterpiece. I've found my way with this one."

"It sucks!"

We still had a future together.

Along with her verdict, however, she brought up her brother, Marco, and said I should enlist him. "He's down in the dumps. I think he could write some good stuff with you." He was an excellent musician, and a very sensitive person. I gave him a cassette of the demos. He was glad. "Oh, I'll give it a try." Very humble. A week later he gave me his lyrics—full of beautiful imagery. "*Solcherò dune mosse.*" ("I'll furrow through blustery dunes.") There were words and expressions I had never used, like "*Colammo giù*" ("We melt down") and "*Si rimbalzò*" ("Bounced back up"). Nice. But overall, a bit obscure. So I took the things that to me were different, strange, that were awesome, like, "*Dai d'illusi smammai,*" which on the demo I sang as "I'm losing my mind."

He came up with that one—a stroke of genius: It sounds perfect, but it's not proper Italian. It does, however, convey the idea of wanting to break free from your illusions. Marco and I did the lyrics to 'Dune Mosse' together, and it went on to become my biggest hit, appreciated by fans and critics alike. Miles Davis was the first to remark: "Hey man, you have to sing in Italian." That was because I did the songs in English, too. Only they didn't have the same effect, the same allure, apart from the fact that the lyrics to lots of the songs are impossible to translate. How can you translate "*Solo una sana e consapevole libidine*" and get the same humor across? For the Spanish version, I called it 'Spanish Inquisition' to give people an idea of what I was talking about, since for Spanish-speaking audiences, 'Catholic Action' meant nothing; it wasn't funny.

Otis Redding kept his own personal glossary of slang terms. And I used lots of slang on *Blue's*—all sorts of expressions, dialect, even words I made up myself to sound like English. I cut words short. People could understand the basic meaning, but it was chopped-up Italian. That's another peculiar facet of my repertoire, and it started with 'Dune Mosse.' That was another key aspect of this song.

Pants for Clapton

I'D JUST FINISHED *BLUE'S* WHEN IT SO HAPPENED THAT ERIC CLAPTON came to Florence for a concert at the Palasport. I went because I wanted to meet him. At this point I was still just a fan, and I never figured that soon after I'd be playing with him. I was wearing black leather pants. "I love your trousers," he said. Then and there I took them off and gave them to him. He burst out laughing. It was a spontaneous gesture. He thought it was pretty funny, but he didn't want the pants.

Pippo, Che Cazzo Fai?

WHEN IT CAME OUT, EVEN ANGELA LOVED 'DUNE MOSSE.' PERHAPS because her brother had been involved on it, but I hope that wasn't the only reason she dug it. Then came another song, 'Pippo, Che Cazzo Fai?,' which signaled the beginning of the end.

Pippo and I had been friends since middle school, when we used to steal cigarettes and money from pinball machines. We hung out a lot. He fancied himself a drummer. Good-looking guy. Dark hair. There was something mysterious about him; he was something of an outcast. As time went on, the rest of us got sick of him playing the part of the misunderstood artist. He was also a painter, but he never sold a painting in his life. He spent his days just loafing around. Which is to say, he didn't work. Sometimes he'd go to the studio, but he had other things on his mind.

He got a kick out of trying to make it with his friends' wives. It was like, OK, here comes the charlatan, the misconstrued poet, the outcast artist. And since he was cute, the ladies showered him with attention. He was always on the sad and melancholy side. Wore mascara. Painted his nails. Like the emo kids would later—he was way ahead of his time. Sometimes he'd show up wrapped in a black cape.

One time I was playing with the band and our drummer said to me, "Fuck, Zucchero! My wife told me Pippo came to our house the other night at two o'clock and started throwing pebbles at the bedroom window. When she opened it and looked out, he said to her, 'Come down! I'm in love with you. I can't sleep. I need to talk to you. You're the most beautiful woman in the world!'"

He was an interloper and probably also suffered from depression. He had a wife and kid of his own, but was always after other guys' women. The thing was, the other guys' wives were happily married. They were newlyweds, they were happy, their marriages worked. Not mine, though. Things were completely falling apart. Angela was so fragile and always needed to be at the center of attention. I wasn't around much. I was focused on my music; it's true. But that was the only way I could support my family and pay off the house.

While I was away, Pippo would come over to visit Angela, usually around three in the afternoon. They'd drink coffee, smoke cigarettes, and talk about poetry. She was obsessed with all these writers, like

Nietzsche and Marie Cardinal. Especially the latter's *The Words to Say It*. Pippo was definitely a guy who had the words to say it. Strong feelings grew between the two of them. She thought she'd found someone much more sensitive than me, who was not at all a wannabe—because he never got his fucking act together, never busted his ass the way I did. They disparaged me: "You're just a hard-headed country boy from Reggio Emilia. All you think about is work. You're insensitive." The two of them had classified me as an ambitious striver. A life of music and work, and nothing else. What the fuck?! I had a family to support. Angela was convinced Pippo was this sensitive dude who understood her and made her feel like a woman. All the usual bullshit about two people understanding each other. Deeply.

I went to play a show in Gorizia, on the Italian border with today's Slovenia. I could see the train station on the other side, with the red star of the Yugoslav flag flying high. It came as a surprise to me. I was still in Italy, but it felt like I was in another country. This was Eastern Europe—like the legendary tales of my Uncle Guerra, set in Moscow, a wondrous, fantastical world inhabited by Lenin and the Communists. And now I was there, seeing the red star!

Before the show, I called home—I called every day. I tried to convey my enthusiasm for that star to Angela.

"Ciao. So…how's it going?"

"How do you *think* it's going?"

One of her typical mean-spirited replies. Followed by, "It sucks! The girls? Well, I'm the one who has to take care of them, not you."

Then I heard a man's voice in the background and asked her who it was.

"It's Pippo. He came over for coffee."

Ah, great. What the fuck?! Turns out he was coming over for coffee every day. I wasn't jealous. I trusted Pippo—we'd been friends since middle school. Still.

"What do you mean?"

"I mean what I said, he just came over for a cup of coffee. Anyway, why should you give a fuck?"

That was the kind of answer she always gave me. It was like getting stabbed. And this was just before going onstage.

After the show, I called her again. "You bastard!" she hissed. "You son of a bitch! You shouldn't have done it. You should've told me. You piece of shit! *Vaffanculo!*"

"Hey, what're you talking about?"

"No. You should've told me you were fooling around with a chick from Verona, that you're planning to set up house together, and that as soon as you get some money, you're going to leave me for her! That's what people are saying. That's what I heard—that this has been going on for the past year!"

I was clueless. I wasn't fooling around with anyone. Much less a chick from Verona.

But she believed the *fotonovelas*. She believed anyone but me.

Our drummer's wife was jealous, let's put it that way. We'd grown up together, gone to school together. She was up to no good, and made up that story. It was a lie, from start to finish. She was wicked. Provincial.

Angela cried and screamed, said I was a bastard.

Depression sunk in, I felt like shit. And I had more shows to do.

When I finally got home, I called the drummer's wife and asked her to come over and repeat her accusations in front of Angela and myself.

"No, I was just...I mean...I wasn't sure It was just stuff I heard."

I kicked her out of the house and haven't seen her since.

Of course, this nasty episode had repercussions on my relationship with my drummer. I had no idea what was going on. A shitty deal all the way around. This misunderstood, melancholy poet hanging out with my wife, plus the drummer's wife making up stories about me—probably because she wanted to fuck me herself.

One day, Angela accused me of shooting up—I hung out with a bunch of junkies, she said. More gossip, people talking shit about me because they were envious of my success.

Angela and I had started out as a couple of street kids. But now my career was about to take off. I was talked about, even considered a sex symbol. That's the way it goes whenever a new singer comes out. Fans, groupies, gossip. I was young and not even that bad looking. The young chicks liked me. More gossip; more shit.

"And now you're a fucking drug addict! You disgust me!"

Idle gossip, calumny.

A lot of people probably thought I really was a junkie, or that I spent my time boozing it up, from morning till night.

I couldn't take any more of this bullshit.

I became obsessed with Angela, who would not for the life of her approve of what I was doing, despite my newfound success, which had been so sought after and which had finally come.

I'd call her.

"What the fuck do you want? What the fuck do you care?"

And Pippo kept coming to my house to drink his fucking coffee.

Blue's provided the only gratification. For the first time in my life I'd made the kind of album I wanted to make, with music I felt was really my own. It stayed at the top of the charts for months and months. I came home for Christmas and decorated the tree with the girls. I noticed one of the gifts had already arrived. A painting. Of Angela's face.

"Who painted your portrait?"

"That's a gift for me."

"OK, but who painted it?"

"Pippo. It's a present."

"What do you mean? Your portrait? Pippo…"

I was starting to get confused.

"You said you were friends. That I can understand. But is there any more to it?"

"Why the fuck should you care?"

That floored me. Instead of reassuring me, she told me to fuck off.

It was time to get to the bottom of this.

I called him up.

"Ciao, Pippo! Thanks for the wonderful present you gave my wife. Why don't you come over for a cup of coffee? Bring your wife along, too."

I wanted to rid myself of this terrible foreboding, and sort it out among the four of us.

Pippo showed up, but without his wife.

He and Angela were embarrassed—I could feel it in the air.

"So, Pippo, tell me where things stand."

"What things? What are you talking about?"

He was clearly embarrassed.

"Angela told me you guys have been hanging out together. That you're good friends. Is there anything else I should know? I have the feeling my wife isn't telling me everything."

He jumped up.

"For starters, her name is Angela, not 'my wife.'"

Pathetic. It was like saying: "She's a person, above and beyond anything else." Please, this is no time for hypocrisy and political correctness. Besides, she was my wife, wasn't she? I'd already sussed things out. But I wanted to wrest the gory details from my boyhood friend. It was Angela who spoke up.

"If you want to know whether we've fucked or not..."

I was dying inside.

"...my answer is neither yes nor no."

I had no idea what the fuck was going on.

"Then *you* tell me!" I howled at Pippo.

"No. If that's all she has to tell you, then I'll do the same."

There was no doubt about it, then. I was in despair.

"Get out of my house. Either tell me what's going on, or get out!"

"How dare you?" screamed Angela. "Who do you think you are?"

He left.

The storm in our house raged on. Angela and I argued all night long over the fact that she refused to tell me anything. That episode caused our relationship to deteriorate even further. The situation dragged on like that until June, when I was scheduled to go on tour. One morning, at nine o'clock, the doorbell rang. I saw who it was on the closed-circuit display in our bedroom: Pippo.

"What does he want?" I asked Angela. "What am I supposed to do, open the door?"

"Do whatever you want."

Nice reply. Encouraging.

I answered.

"Can you come out?" he said. "I have to talk to you."

When I got outside he told me: "You know, I think I'm in love with Angela."

Yes, asshole, I already figured that out.

"What about her?"

"I think she's in love with me, too."

I had to set off, on tour. But I was suffering like a dog.

"Listen, I need to work this out with my wife. We'll talk about it when I get back from the tour."

Can you believe it; he got pissed off!

"Who do you think you are? God? That we have to wait for you to finish your tour?"

Fuck it. I went back inside and confronted Angela: "He says he's in love with you. What about you?"

I had a desperate desire to cry.

"I...no...I don't know. What the fuck do you care? Go enjoy yourself on your tour!"

I was blind with rage. I grabbed my gym bag, threw in some socks and underwear, and without a word got in the car and drove to Avenza.

Our house there hadn't been lived in for years. It was falling apart, filthy, full of mold and mildew. The only thing left inside was an old cot.

"Now Pippo will come back, once he sees you're not there. He'll be back, you'll see." Talking to myself. The typical thoughts of a desperate man.

Days passed.

The phone rang.

"The headlight on my car just blew and I need to use it. I'll bring it to your mechanic in Avenza and tell him it's yours—that way they'll fix it right away. Because you're Zucchero, right?"

She was taking the piss out of me.

"Just do whatever you want."

"Alright, but if they don't fix it by this evening, I can't walk back home. What am I supposed to do?"

"Why don't you just call and ask them? See what they say."

They couldn't do it in a day.

"Come on, let's go out for pizza tonight. I'll sleep here and pick up the car tomorrow morning. How's that sound?"

I was shocked. Did it make any sense? I was about to cave in.

I took her to the best restaurant around. She was oddly sweet. On the way home in the car, she leaned her head on my shoulder. In a whisper, she showered me with compliments, something she'd never done before. A part of me was mad, because I felt like she was teasing me. But I could see she wanted to make love, and my adrenaline was pumping. I was touched. We went to bed and were making love when the phone rang.

"Hello, this is Pippo. Is Angela there?"

Damnation.

"Angela, it's Pippo."

Like a chump, I handed her the phone instead of telling his ass to fuck off.

She came back to bed.

The next day she left.

I set about recording *Blue's*. I had Corrado Rustici and Randy Jackson brought over from America, as well as David Sancious, for the first time, and Giorgio Francis, also from America. We recorded at Fonoprint Studio in Bologna, which back then was located on Via dei Coltelli, beneath the porticoes.

I moved to Bologna with Torpedine and the musicians. I wanted a horn section that knew how to play rhythm & blues—the sound I had heard as a kid in Roncocesi, when the guy from Memphis played it for me on his tape player. He turned me on to Otis Redding. I wanted a horn section. Graziano Uliani, a man on the scene in Bologna who was crazy for the blues, came by the studio and told me I should hook up with the Memphis Horns.

"Who are they?"

"Wayne Jackson on trumpet and Andrew Love on sax. The best rhythm & blues horns in the world. They played with Elvis Presley and on Peter Gabriel's latest record. They played for Stax Records. They appeared on some of the most famous rhythm & blues hits of all time, from 'Soul Man' to 'Hold On, I'm Coming.' You think they would do?"

They came. One was short and white, with glasses thick as Coke bottle bottoms. The other guy was black. We brought them in, had them sit down. It wasn't like we had to tell them what notes to play. We just let them hear the songs, and they were ready. They had their own special sound, straight out of Memphis. They'd whip off riffs crafted for each song. They gave each song what it needed. No more, no less. A lot of it was simple stuff, but they had their own special touch and a wealth of experience.

After Uliani had picked them up at the airport in Milano, they pulled into a rest stop on their way to the studio in Bologna. He later said, "Guys, no one's going to believe this, but I took a piss with the Memphis Horns!"

We had a blast in the studio. Wayne Jackson, the trumpet player and the smaller of the two, drank two pints of Jack Daniel's a day. Always very chipper, clearheaded. Things went smooth as silk. We presented the album in Bologna. Torpedine had found a trattoria with a little pond out front, in the hills overlooking the city. A feast for all of us, featuring typical Emilian fare like fried gnocco, cured meats, and *tagliatelle*.

Angela asked me to come back home. She said she wasn't seeing Pippo anymore.

"Please come home."

I later learned she was double-crossing both me and Pippo, and left us both in the lurch. She had a talent for tearing men apart, making them crumble. She drove Pippo crazy when she said he was a failure, a good-for-nothing who would never go anywhere. "Unlike Zucchero, who's famous now." She told him I was a great person, and that killed him. Then she played the opposite game with me when she told me I didn't understand, that I was insensitive—whereas Pippo was this very sensitive guy who understood her. The dirty double-crosser. She stoked our jealousy, denigrated us. Insanely jealous, a wreck, torn apart with frustration, Pippo lost it.

Meanwhile Angela asked me to come back home. And like a chump, I went. It wasn't easy, though. I tried, I really tried, but it was just no use. A week into it, we were back arguing and bickering and messing everything up. Same old shit. One afternoon she said, "Pippo needs to talk to me. He said he's going crazy."

It must have been about three o'clock. I was pissed off.

"Are you a fool? Tell him to fuck off, no? Or maybe you're still interested in him. Maybe you've still got something going on with him. Why did you beg me to come back home if you've still got something going on with him?"

"No, no, no. Look, he just needs to talk. I have to go."

She was frantic, possessed.

She had a Citroën 2CV, which I had given her. I had a black Mercedes, which I could finally afford. She took off. Pissed off as I was, I followed her. I wanted to look Pippo in the face. Angela was totally out of her mind. She began swerving on the interchange for the Autostrada. She dodged oncoming cars like bowling pins. Then she suddenly slammed on the brakes. I rammed into her from behind. She turned around and threw it in reverse, and started barreling down the wrong side of the road. It was suicidal. I followed close behind. When she got home, she grabbed a knife and hurled it at me in a violent rage. I grabbed a family-size bottle of Coca-Cola and sent it flying in her direction. She dodged and it smashed to pieces against the wall. We calmed down. Relatively speaking. We'd gone too far this time. Total madness. And I hadn't drunk anything, wasn't on any drugs. Neither was she. Somehow that just made it worse. It was awful. I suffered like a dog. It still hurts to remember.

A Piece of Paper

WE WERE SO CHILDISH. UNPREPARED. WE DIDN'T KNOW HOW TO handle my popularity. Success, the big time, so sought after and at last achieved, was eating us up from inside. We were both going off the rails, unable to deal with all the upheaval undermining our identities. I'd reawakened Angela's insecurity. She felt like she didn't matter as much to me anymore. And that translated into more rancor and violence.

155

We had a cute young babysitter, and she complicated things by going around saying she worked for me, strutting her stuff in town. It seemed like she would have let me have my way with her, too—maybe she was in love with me. She was there when it came to me keeping in touch with my daughters. One day, she told me word was going around town—and it was a small town—that Pippo was getting it on with my wife. Nasty gossip spread like wildfire. Perfect for the dreary winter. Pippo, the painter who had a studio somewhere, called our babysitter and asked her to pose for him.

"I went," she confessed, "and posed for him. Then he asked me if I would fuck him, and I did. He's cute. But I couldn't give a shit about him."

Wretched girl—I think she did it just to piss off Angela.

We were all pretty much out of our minds. I called Angela and told her that her lover, that supersensitive guy, the one who really cared about her—while I supposedly didn't love her, etc.—had fucked the babysitter. Low-down revenge. As usual, Angela hit the roof. Scenes beyond belief. She went to Pippo's and dragged the girl along with her. Angela was in rough shape. She tore apart our marriage. Maybe she believed him. But the first thing he did was cheat on her. She unleashed her wrath on him as well, then showed up at my house in Avenza at eight o'clock the next morning. She banged her fists against the shutters and shouted, "Wake up, you son of a bitch! Wake up!"

She fired a barrage of insults at me: "What a fucking asshole you are. What a piece of shit. Pippo never fucked her. She made it all up. I brought her to his house, and she admitted it was bullshit."

She had it in for everyone—Pippo, me, and anyone else who crossed her path. We were all sons of bitches. That was the result of those days. Sad days. Over-agitated days.

She didn't come back home. She was supposed to pick up the girls at school at one o'clock. I started to worry. Her mother called me. The girls? They were still at school. Angela? No news of her. She'd gone off to some mountain. Mt. Marcello? I didn't know. She'd lost it and had no idea what to do or who to believe. Suddenly, she was alone. It all came crumbling down on her. She could never have me back, and Pippo had betrayed her.

She came home that night, though. I'd been worried about the girls, and her, as well—I didn't want anything bad to happen to her.

We decided on a formal separation.

Deep down inside, despite everything, I wanted to make up and get back together. All I needed to know was whether she and Pippo were through. I was willing to give it another try.

I asked Gino Paoli if he knew a good lawyer, someone on the ball who wouldn't fuck her over. He hooked me up with a friend of his, an attorney from Florence. Great guy. Angela didn't want to hire a lawyer of her own. "It's just a piece of paper," she said.

At which point, we got back together. I burst into tears. I didn't want to split up.

"Come on, it's just a piece of paper."

She also shocked my lawyer when she said to him, "Whatever he decides is fine with me."

That's how a chick like that floors you, every time.

We walked out of court. Both of us sad—me more than her. Then she floored me again.

"Let's go on vacation. We deserve it."

"Vacation?"

I asked her to repeat herself. I didn't think I'd understood.

"Yeah, let's go away for a few days. After all this stress, no?"

"For years, when we were married, I asked you time and time again to go somewhere with me. But no—you were always afraid of this and that, and stirred up all kinds of problems."

"I've changed my mind."

I insisted: "Do you want to bring along the girls? As a way to prepare them for our separation and make it less traumatic for them?"

"No. Just the two of us. Me and you. Take me to the Maldives."

Wow! I thought there was still a chance we'd get back together. I was happy and still very much in love with her.

In three hours I had the tickets and couldn't wait to take off.

We landed in Malé. Fishermen brought us to an amazing atoll in their boat. We checked into a bungalow. Angela was gorgeous. Happy, at last. She laughed. She frolicked in the water. Played with the fish in the coral reef. Dinner at night. She was sweet. Romantic. Like never before. I tried to be the best ex-husband I could be. I anointed her with suntan lotion, brought her breakfast. We took fabulous swims— like we hadn't done in ages. We slept in the same bed, naked. My hormones were doing flips.

"You're not thinking of trying anything on with me, I hope!"

I'll never understand women and their dynamics. The second I get close, longing for her and totally turned on, she refuses me. Torture.

It was hot, very hot. I came close, to give her a caress.

"Don't you dare touch me. Leave me alone. Otherwise, I'm going straight home. We're separated, you know."

My desire raged. I kept trying. She put me off. I didn't get it. She floored me again.

I woke up early the next morning, and went to the village to buy some little bananas and a pineapple cake. She had her breakfast. She went for a swim in the sea. She was happy.

Sunset. Walking on the beach. The moon comes up. What a sight. I looked at her and said, "I love you." I tried to give her a kiss.

"Leave me alone."

On the plane on the way back home, she put her head on my shoulder and said, "You're a wonderful person. I really enjoyed this. Come back home. Back to us. We'll start over, starting tomorrow."

And we'd just separated.

Miles Davis: *Ta-Pum*

I HAD JUST FALLEN ASLEEP WHEN THE PHONE RANG. IT MUST HAVE BEEN three or four in the morning. Mimmo d'Alessandro, a promoter from Viareggio, was on the other end. I've always figured managers never sleep.

"He heard 'Dune Mosse' and asked who it was. Then he said to call you. He wants to play it with you." I couldn't figure out if I'd just missed what he was talking about because I was too groggy, or whether I was already supposed to know. It wasn't till later I realized that Mimmo was putting together Miles Davis's upcoming tour in Italy.

"It's three in the morning, and you're making crank calls?" I can't stand that sort of thing.

"No, Zucchero. You've got to be in New York on April 1st to record with Miles."

Yeah, right. Some April Fool's joke. I hung up. A half hour later, the phone rang again.

"Zucchero, listen. Miles Davis wants to do this song with you. We have to be in New York on April 1st."

For Christ's sake, it was three a.m., March 25th!

"We have to be there."

I couldn't believe my ears.

Strange days. First Angela asks if we can get back together, now Miles Davis wants to play with me.

I'd been waiting for Angela to come to my place in Avenza with the girls, as we had agreed. It really looked like she wanted to come back to me, and we were all ready to sign the girls up for school. Then one morning she says: "I thought it over and I'm staying in Forte. The girls can go to school here."

I count to five, but she doesn't tell me to come join her there. It's over. And this time for good. Music and my wife, two titans battling it out inside me. Always the same. Music wants me to go to New York. So, I go see Miles Davis.

Back then, there was no digital. The 48 tracks of 'Dune Mosse' were recorded on analog tape, old-school style. I set out for New York with a suitcase full of reel-to-reels and the pieces of my broken heart.

We landed in New York and took a yellow cab to Hotel St. Moritz, on Central Park South, right next to where Sting and Pavarotti lived. I went straight to my room and crashed.

The phone rang. "Hey, Zucchero. You've got the tape, right?" Torpedine asks. Why does this stuff always happen when I'm asleep? Anyway, turns out I didn't.

"Fuck, I left it in the cab."

He tries to stay calm and says he'll find it.

He and Mimmo went to the police, who of course laughed in their faces: "We only work on homicides." They went to a private investigator. Mimmo remembered the name of the cab driver from his ID: Nikolas Stratos, a Greek guy. The PI shook his head. "There's two thousand cab companies in New York, and each one has a fleet with a hundred cabs. All yellow. I'll give it a shot, but I wouldn't count on it." He set to work.

By the time we got to the studio, we were at the end of our rope. Then the phone rang: "I don't know if I found what you're looking for, but the wife of a taxi driver with the name you gave me says her husband left a rectangular box at their house, and she doesn't know what it is. There's a logo on it, with notes written on the box, and the words Dune Mosse." It was the label copy.

There was just enough time for the sound engineer to set up. Luckily, Miles walked in an hour late. Black leather, black gloves, black shades, black hat. Not a word to anyone—I'd been told he was a grouch. He opened his black case and pulled out a black trumpet, I swear.

"Play the song," he says without even saying hello. "Play the song."

I start playing and barely get out three notes before he stops me: "You're playing in the wrong key."

"Hi, Miles," I say.

He doesn't reply. He just repeats that I'm playing in the wrong key. I don't get it. I start playing again.

"What the fuck are you doing?"

I freeze. What does he mean, what the fuck am I doing? I was the one who wrote the song. How could I be playing it wrong?

"No," he says, "not B minor. It's B-flat minor."

"Sorry, Miles," I say, "but I'm the one who wrote it and it's in B minor."

"No!"

He was pissed.

I broke into a cold sweat. A doubt crept over me.

"Listen, Miles, you think maybe the batteries in your tape player were low when you listened? Maybe the song was slowed down, so you heard it in a lower key."

Miles reflected. "Could be."

I heaved a sigh of relief.

It was only later it dawned on me that Miles was one sly son of a gun.

Since his trumpet, like most of them, was tuned to B-flat, it was easier for him to play the song in B-flat minor.

He picked up his sheet music and quickly rewrote the whole thing in B minor.

"OK, I'm ready," he said.

He sat down with his trumpet in front of the mike. I got up to go sit in the sound booth and listen. Just sit and enjoy. But he stopped me.

"Where do you think you're going? You stay here. Sit down."

He had some attitude. I sat down next to him. He placed two fingers on my throat.

"I need your energy," he said. "I love your voice."

Every 20 seconds, Miles would stop playing and curse. "Fuck! Shit!" Then start back up again. He would drain the saliva out of his trumpet, spit, curse. At one point, he walked across the room and changed instruments. The new one was cherry red.

Finally, we recorded. I still have that recording, which I put on the version on *Zu & Co.*, where you can hear his voice say, "Yeah, I'm ready. Yeah, yeah."

I blushed when he told me, "I love your voice. I love your song."

He kept getting up, changing his jacket, picking out a different color trumpet. In the end, though, we found the right mood.

An hour went by. Then he asks, "Are you happy?"

He shuffled his feet and said, "This song makes me cry. Your voice makes me cry."

"Damn, thanks!"

Happy? You bet! He recorded seven different versions, one after another. Different solos, improvisation, counterpoint. He really got into it. When it was over he said, "You want more?"

"No, but which one do you think I should use? Which is the best?"

"Whichever you like. Maybe the next to last is more in the air. Just don't take the wrong notes. Although my friend Gil Evans used to say that there are no wrong notes in jazz and blues."

Miles says I should add a snare drum to the beat. "Listen." *Ta-pum-pum ta-pum-pum ta-pum-pum.*

"I got you," I say.

Miles looks at me. "No, you don't." *Ta-pum-pum ta-pum-pum ta-pum-pum.* "You have to put in a snare. Understand?"

"Yes!"

"No. You don't." Then he said it again. I've got it all on this crazy recording. I'm listening to it right now.

"I understand."

"No. You don't."

I thought, *How the fuck does he know whether, or not, I understand?*
"Listen, Miles. I really do understand."

I start mouthing back to him, *Ta-pum*—when a big glob of spit shoots out of my mouth and hits him in the face. He tells me to go to hell. I want to laugh. Whenever I'm embarrassed, I get the urge to laugh, and so I burst out laughing. And he's cursing away. I was really embarrassed.

Then Miles disappeared—nowhere to be found. His driver came up to me, a big guy, and said, "Miles wants to go have dinner with you in an Italian restaurant."

He ushered me out of the studio. It was night. The neighborhood was deserted. No streetlights even. The big driver opened the door of the black limousine for me. Black leather upholstery inside. I went to sit down in the back and I heard Miles shout, "What the fuck are you doing?" I had sat down on top of him, all huddled up in the corner. I couldn't see a thing, what with everything being all black.

When we got to the restaurant, Miles relaxed. He took off his shades and his mask. His eyes were dark green and beautiful. Turned out he was slightly cross-eyed. He ate like a bird. It wouldn't be long before he was dead.

I kept that fantastic recording in a drawer, and released it many years later.

Not long afterward, Torpedine and Mimmo were both like, "Awesome! Three concerts. Miles Davis and Joe Cocker have both signed on."

Mimmo also managed Joe Cocker.

"And you're the headliner."

At the time, I was more famous in Italy than they were. Sure, they were legends, but in those days, I was the one bringing in the crowds. I saw the posters: Miles Davis, Joe Cocker, Zucchero—all in the same size letters. We played Rimini Stadium, Viareggio Stadium, and San Paolo Stadium in Naples.

Hey, Friend. You're Back!

JUMP BACK A FEW YEARS.

Everybody knew Joe Cocker had had big problems with drugs and alcohol. He'd been away from the music scene for years because he was so fucked up. But he came back with an album called *Sheffield Steel* in 1982—he was born in Sheffield. It had a song by Steve Winwood and Will Jennings, 'Talking Back to the Night,' and one by Leo Nocentelli, the guitarist from New Orleans and founding member of the legendary Meters, titled 'Look What You've Done.' Leo Nocentelli may not be a household name, but I guarantee you he's a living legend.

Joe was haggard, aged, but for me it was like seeing the rebirth of an old friend. I dedicated these words to him in my song 'Nuovo, Meraviglioso Amico': "*Ehi, meraviglioso amico, sei tornato, ti credevo assopito invece sei ancora qua.*" ("Hey, wonderful friend, you're back! I thought you were washed up, but instead, you're here!") I was at home with Angela in Forte dei Marmi one rainy Sunday afternoon watching *Domenica In* when the opening credits announced that Joe Cocker was going to be a guest. Holy hell! He'd disappeared ages ago. But he was back, and in Rome. I jumped in my broken-down white Mercedes at two o'clock and, driving through torrential rains, got to Rome at six. I called the promoter I knew at EMI to ask where I could find Joe, and he gave me the name of his hotel. I waited for him in the lobby. I saw him walk in with his record company people and Michael Lang—he had co-created the original Woodstock and was now Joe's manager.

"Joe!" I cried, going up to him like a fan.

His manager gesticulated, trying to get rid of me.

"Joe! I'm Zucchero, an Italian singer. You're great!"

He turned away and walked up the stairs to his room.

His manager, somewhat irritated, said to me, "Maybe when he comes down, you can have your picture taken with him."

I waited. An hour. Two. He finally came down.

"Joe wants to take a picture with you," his manager said.

"So, you're a singer?"

"Yes."

"Italian."

"Yes."

"Then why don't you come have dinner with us?"

I was surprised. Shocked is more like it. They took me to an awesome restaurant. I ordered spaghetti with clams. I couldn't believe this was happening. "*Hello, little friend. Ti credevo una storia finita. E invece hey. Proprio quando non t'aspettavo. Tu, e una canzone nuova nasce già. Sei qui per me o ti sentivi solo? Per me, eh?*" ("Hello, little friend. I thought you were through. But instead hey! When I least expected you. With you a new song is born. Are you here for me, or were you feeling lonely? For me, eh?")

Back at the hotel I blew my guts out from the excitement, the thrill, the tension of meeting Joe Cocker. Barfed up all that spaghetti with clams, like some kind of crazed fan.

Strange Night Tonight

WE DID THE FIRST IN A SERIES OF SHOWS FEATURING THE THREE OF US: Joe Cocker, Miles Davis, and me. The stadium in Rimini was packed. After the show, we went to a pizzeria. Angela came along.

"I'm fucking tired of this shit," she screeched. "I want to go to bed."

"Oh, we're going to have dinner," I said. "Didn't you want to see Joe?"

"I've got a stomachache. No way. Take me back to the hotel."

We'd just kicked off the tour and this was the moment when we were coming together as a team—and she forced me to leave. I took her back to the hotel. Another of our epic battles. She offended me.

She excited me. I wanted to make love. To hurt me, she replied: "Call Vasco. Call him. I'll fuck him, but not you. You can't touch me."

The worst vibes. We didn't sleep all night. The next day we had a show in Viareggio. In the morning, I was a wreck. Joe was up too, wearing sunglasses. The night before he'd drunk all the alcohol in his minibar fridge. He had a bag with three beers inside. He whipped out a bottle opener and opened one. It was morning. He lit up a cigarette. Took another sip, had another cigarette. Smoked and drank. It was a wonder he was still alive. He'd abused all kinds of nasty shit. It would have killed a bull. But he was still rocking.

On the plane to Pisa for the Viareggio concert, he let me hear his new album. I loved it and told him how great I thought it was. Then, during a bout of turbulence, I made an off-the-wall remark: "If this plane crashes, I'll be proud to be on it with you." That same night on-stage, he repeated my comment to the crowd.

"You know what Zucchero told me on the plane today?"

We arrived in Viareggio that afternoon. I went to Forte dei Marmi with Angela. She didn't want to stay for the show. I hadn't slept the night before. An hour after we got home, Angela said, "Alright, I'll come to the show tonight. I'll bring Marco."

Her brother was a big Joe Cocker fan. She accompanied him in his wheelchair. She was cool, very mellow.

We were failures compared to the dreams we'd had. I was completely undone by Angela's mood swings: a roller-coaster ride of feelings, a maze that put me at a loss because of my own psychology, more simple and direct than hers.

We got ready in the dressing room. I drank some beer, not much. Joe drank at least 10. It was time for the show. We hit the stage. At one point, during 'Hey Man,' I put my arms around him. Last song of the night. Fantastic show. The stadium in Viareggio is surrounded by residential districts, and we were only supposed to play until one a.m. We stayed on till 1:30, at which point police in riot gear, carrying shields, stormed the stage and kicked us off. I was right in the middle of a song. The crowd booed and began hurling whatever they could at the stage.

The next day we went to Naples for a show at San Paolo stadium. Angela stayed home. I flew down with Joe. He'd lost his voice. He could barely utter a word. It was August. It was hot. I had the taxi driver crank up the air-conditioning. Joe sat there with his face up against the vent, sweating.

I was like, "What the fuck, Joe? Your voice sounds like death."

"I don't care, I don't care."

He didn't give a fuck.

When we got there, I said to him, "Joe, it's two o'clock. I'm going to take a nap. I'll see you at six for the sound check. With that voice of yours, you should take a rest too."

"You're right. Rest. I need a rest."

We checked into the Santa Lucia hotel in Naples. I went to my room, Joe stopped off at the bar. I saw the bartender, a young Neapolitan fellow, serve him a large mug of beer. Joe spoke English to the guy, and they seemed to understand each other. He drank, coughed, oozed phlegm. When I came down from my nap he was still there. He hadn't taken a rest, but kept on drinking and talking to the Neapolitan bartender who didn't speak any English.

"No," he said, "I'm not doing any sound check."

He had a bucket of beers on ice brought backstage.

"Maybe I should eat a little something, too."

We ordered pizza for everyone. It came. Good Naples pizza. Thin crust. He ate one slice; that was it. But he kept drinking beer after beer.

I started my set. At a certain point, we were supposed to break into "With a Little Help from My Friends" and introduce Joe, who'd made history with his howling at Woodstock. It was all planned. The stadium was packed. When it came time for 'With a Little Help from My

Friends' I turned around to see if Joe was ready to make his appearance. Instead, there was Michael Lang saying, "Keep playing!"

What the fuck—I'd just finished our set. We played for another 15 minutes. The crowd was getting impatient. I turned around and saw Joe staggering behind an amplifier, wearing a skullcap and sunglasses. He could hardly stand up. Michael shouted to him, "Go!"

"Ladies and gentlemen, Joe Cocker!"

He hit the stage with his belly sticking out.

"Ahhh…Eeekkk…" he tried to howl, but all that came out was thin air, no voice.

He fell, crashing into one of the monitors.

"Help me," he cried. "Help me up!"

I helped him to his feet.

The crowd booed.

"Strange night tonight," he said and made his exit.

I'd never seen such an angry crowd. They threw everything they could at us.

In the dressing room, a massively irate Michael Lang chewed out Joe.

"What the fuck are you doing?" he said. "You drank all the beers!"

All Joe said, holding ice cubes to his temples—his head must have been in a wretched state—was, "Fuck you, fuck you!"

Sex vs. Music

GIVEN THE CHOICE BETWEEN SEX AND MUSIC, I'VE ALWAYS OPTED FOR the latter. After a while, sex bores me. Sex is always asking you questions, whereas music can give you answers. But sex always demands something in exchange.

Music is eroticism and sensuality. If there were no erotic tension, it wouldn't be music. Elvis Presley used precisely those two elements to create his music and his fame. Eros is like harmony. It's sound and rhythmic movement of the pelvis. With seven notes, you can express every sense and sentiment imaginable. Music is melancholy, it's rage, it's energy, it's drama, it's cheer, it's dancing, it's flavor, it's color. Music is life. *Andante, adagio, con brio*, and all the rest are common terms in Italian to describe music. Music is all those things and more. It transcends those things. Just as life does. Those descriptions— *andante, adagio, con brio*—can apply to sex in the same way they apply to an orchestra. And when a song comes out just the way you imagined it, the feeling is orgasmic.

Music is a ritual, a celebration. It comes to life, germinates, and blooms in an orgasmic exchange between you and the audience. It's a high-tension zone, where huge amounts of energy are consumed and dispersed in the Dionysian spasm of the crowd. The audience and I study each other, there's an exchange of vitality. They give me strength, and I give it back to them, amplified and in a nutshell, contorted and refracted. You can feel all that energy coming back at you, and what you give, the crowd amplifies a thousand times over. That's what's so miraculous about concerts.

Gold, Champagne, and Ducks

WINTER 1988. I'VE ALWAYS PREFERRED TO WRITE SONGS IN AUTUMN. I don't like to compose in summer. There are too many distractions, and I detest the heat. I need the intimacy of autumn to concentrate. When the days grow short and the first chill rustles the fallen leaves— that's the best time for me in my studio. The year was coming to an end, and I was writing material for my next album, *Oro, Incenso e Birra*.

Angela was living in Forte dei Marmi; I was in Avenza. I called an architect and had him restructure the house. He had free rein—I was busy working away in my studio in the backyard—a prefab concrete shed, basically, with an old rug on the floor and matchboarding on the walls. I had my piano, an electronic keyboard with a drum machine, the red telephone, and a dresser with a TV on top. I spent the winter in there, and since there was no heat, I hooked up butane gas tanks to one of those heaters with the red spirals that light up. They're dangerous. I got myself a double bed and a down comforter. That was it.

That's how I lived while the house was being renovated. Every morning I would go wash and have breakfast at the pensione across the street. On my first record sleeves I thanked the lady who made me those breakfasts—"Aunt Rita," I called her. They took me in like I was their son. On Saturday, I would take my weekly shower there—they let me use one of the rooms. If I needed to use the bathroom, even at night, I'd go there. If I just had to piss, I'd go outside.

Once in a while, a friend of mine, Lucio Menconi, another crazy artist type, would stop by. We're still good friends.

"Oh-oh, Fornaciari," I remember him saying. "Oh-oh, you've made one phenomenal record."

He always exaggerated everything. Sometimes he'd be depressed, then the next minute euphoric. But he's always given me lots of support. *Blue's* had just come out. One day I was coming back to the house in Avenza and I saw a broken-down white Mercedes parked out front. Lucio got out of the car. Dressed exactly like me. He called me "Maestro" and kneeled before me. Crazy guy.

"Your music touches the soul. My partner and I would be honored if you were to grace us with your presence at dinner. Bring along anyone you wish—friends, family. We'll dine on lobster and Champagne."

He imagined I had become some kind of gourmand, and ate only the finest foods and drank the most expensive wines.

"I know a phenomenal restaurant in Lido di Camaiore," he boasted.

He was deranged. I got a kick out of him, although sometimes he got on my nerves. He came back the next evening. And the one after that. He kept insisting on taking me and my friends out to dinner. I finally broke down and said, "OK, we'll go one of these nights."

I rounded up 30 friends or so. It was kind of a dirty trick on my part, but he and his partner strutted around like peacocks, showing off how rich they were. Lucio pulled up in a Ferrari Testarossa someone had loaned him, with a gaudy gold Rolex around the cuff of his shirtsleeve like *l'Avvocato*, "The Lawyer," as everyone called the boss of Fiat, Gianni Agnelli. He was a caricature of the little world of Versilia, where appearance is everything and substance is totally lacking. A world of well-heeled pleasure seekers who flock to the shore to live it up at the Capannina—I can't stand them. One of the friends I'd invited happened to be a millionaire for real, so I asked him to play along. "You're an expert on lobster and Champagne," I said. "So, every time we open a bottle, you taste it and say it's no good." Moët & Chandon, Cristal, Dom Pérignon. He sent them all back, one after the other. What did it matter? Lucio was paying!

I lost track of Lucio for a while, but he became my best friend after I moved out and separated from my wife. He was the only one who would come by evenings to visit. He gave me a lot of encouragement.

One night I was in the shed writing and the phone rang. It was that bastard, Pippo. He hadn't given up. He started insulting me over the phone.

"Who do you think you are? I'm in love with your wife, and nothing can stand in the way of love. I'm at your house right now."

I asked him to put Angela on.

"What the heck is he doing there at this hour?" I said. "The girls are in bed—they'll hear all this. How dare he set foot in our house?"

"You don't understand," said Angela. "Insensitive, as usual."

For them my presence was unwelcome; I was an obstacle to their relationship. They imagined that now I was successful, I had all this money and power, and would sic a gang of lawyers on them and wreak havoc. Provincial lunacy.

New Year's Eve came, the first since Angela and I had separated, and I wanted to spend it with the girls. I took them to a beautiful abbey in the Siena countryside, along with some friends. I was just coming off a time when Angela had broken my balls with all her Nietzsche shit, analyzing and picking apart his works at that infamous dinner when they all started talking about *Thus Spoke Zarathustra*. "What the fuck does this Nietzsche say anyway?" I couldn't stand the guy. It was Angela's fault. I even tried to read some of his books, but I couldn't hack it. 'Nice (Nietzsche) Che Dice?' I dunno. That was the first song I wrote after we broke up. I was sad, alone. "*Ho bisogno d'amore, perdio.*" ("I need love, by God.")—a line from 'Overdose d'Amore,' the song that came next. I wrote them both in just a few minutes.

I was reading a book of poetry by poet and singer-songwriter Piero Ciampi, *Ho Solo la Faccia di un Uomo*. I really loved it, especially these two lines: "*Il mare impetuoso al tramonto / salì sulla luna e dietro una tendina di stelle.*" ("At sunset the stormy sea /climbed upon the moon, and behind a curtain of stars.") I contacted his widow and got the rights. I came up with another famous line, one of my fans' favorites, when after the chorus I added to Ciampi's lines in a whisper "*Se la chiavò*" ("It fucked her").

I wrote 'Madre Dolcissima' and 'Diavolo in Me' one night when I couldn't sleep. Just picked up the guitar and they came to me in the blink of an eye. From 'Diavolo in Me': "*Le strade delle signore sono infinite lo sai. Gloria nell'alto dei cieli, ma non c'è pace quaggiù, è una questione di peli, sei proprio un angelo tu.*" ("The ways of the Lord are infinite, you know. Glory to the heavens on high, but there's no peace down here. It's a matter of body hair. You are truly an angel.") From 'Madre Dolcissima': "*Niente di nuovo, tranne l'affitto per me.*" ("Nothing new for me except the rent to pay.")

The song 'Iruben Me' was another story. That one took a lot of work. What I had in mind was a kind of weather report of the emotions. Pouring rain, flashfloods. That was Angela all over. It was me saying: I hurt. The song came pouring out like tears; don't you understand? In the finale, I cry out how much I miss her.

I'd written the music for the opening of 'Diamante' 10 years earlier, as part of the stuff I'd composed on the piano and then set aside. At the time, I was hanging out with Mino Vergnaghi, a talented singer who'd won at Sanremo. Wonderful person. He was fed up with living in Italy and moved to London with a friend of his, Matteo Saggese, who wrote music. They sent me a song that didn't quite convince me, but there was a group of notes that weren't bad—a verse. One morning, I sat down at the piano as soon as I got up and stuck that verse to the opening I'd written ages before but never did anything with. This became the music for 'Diamante.'

Corrado Rustici and I decided to record at the best studio in Europe: Peter Gabriel's Real World Studios, outside of Bath, an hour's drive from London. At the last minute, I put another song together, 'Wonderful World.' The best songs are like that. You stumble onto them one or two days before a recording session. I'd worked out the guitar riff, but still didn't have the words. I'd gotten in the habit of writing the music first, then recording the basic tracks in the studio, singing in *maccheronico* English just to sketch out the vocal parts. After that, I'd write the lyrics—or get someone to write them for me. That became my method. Other people write the music and lyrics together, and then, when everything's ready, they go to the studio to record. But I like to compose the music first, then find the lyrics. A useful technique because it allows you to add lines that you come up with in the studio, or things like counterpoint choruses; I could even change the melodies a little, based on the arrangements we did, so songs would transform and become even better. Sometimes I'd throw in words in English. There were sessions when one of the musicians might say, "Ah, a word that sounds such-and-such would work here."

This helps me go home with a clear picture in my mind of how the album will be. That's the method I've always used. It's the music that inspires the words. I'm of the conviction that music already has the words. It determines the words and evokes them. All you have to do is find them. They're intrinsic. It takes skill to develop a concept and find the right lyrics among all the possible combinations. Poetry works the same way.

Real World is situated in the beautiful English countryside. It's a residential recording facility along the Bybrook River that features an avant-garde studio with glass walls and reinforced concrete buttresses. Peter Gabriel has always been an innovator. He had it built by the best engineers and it was the premiere studio in Europe. We all had our own rooms; there was a living room with a big table and a fireplace. Definitely good vibes. It was winter and cold outside, but cozy and warm inside Real World. I got there at night. The next morning, I went to the kitchen for coffee and saw him, with his back turned to me, feeding the ducks in the pond. He turned around. It was Peter Gabriel. What a warm welcome he gave me. A real gentleman, as polite and kind as you'll ever meet.

As we worked, we realized that, holy fuck, we were making amazing music, even better than the stuff on *Blue's*. This was more innovative. In a studio like that, once again with Gordon Lyon as our sound engineer, it sounded great. Some musicians, like Brian May and Eric Clapton, consider this one of my best records. They're still big fans.

We recorded the music. February 23rd was Angela's birthday. I thought it might be a good chance to see whether we might... since her romance with Pippo seemed to have fizzled out. I invited a bunch of friends to Bath. They got her to come, too. I booked dinner for us all in an old English restaurant near the studio, with a majestic entrance lined with centuries-old oaks, and wood tables inside. They also had awesome rooms for all 20 of my guests. She couldn't believe it. At last, all this money. Blue's had sold well. I could afford to give her a birthday party in high style. Roses, dinner. Happiness. We went to bed. I was devoured by desire. Strong attraction. Outright refusal. That was our infinite conflict in a nutshell. True, we were separated at this point. But what's wrong with a little transgression? We slept. I didn't touch her. I was totally bummed. All this tension, this alchemy, this understanding, this identification. Always backward, always broken. An impossible relationship.

She went back to Italy. I returned to the studio to work on the record. We recorded the music, and then I went back home to write the lyrics. In Carrara, alone. Every day I'd get in my car and compose lyrics while I drove. It was like being inside a mechanical uterus. I come up with my best lyrics while driving. I'd put on the cassette with just the music, and I worked them all out, apart from 'Diamante,' then wrote them down in Marinella, a little town along the coast. I'd always wanted to dedicate a song to my grandmother. Set back in the postwar years, when I was growing up. But I was afraid of ruining beautiful music. I didn't think I was up to the task of writing a song about my grandmother. I didn't think I could ever come up with the poetry she deserved.

I wanted a gospel choir. I also wanted the Memphis Horns back, plus Clarence Clemons. This music cried out for it. We went to Memphis and visited the legendary Sun Records studio where Elvis Presley had first recorded, which had been turned into a museum. There was the old recording equipment, but no one recorded in the studio anymore, apart from some old bluesmen. Eight-track. We recorded on 48-track sound boards. But the memory of all the great soul, rhythm & blues, and country artists that began their careers there lingered.

Disappointed, we took snapshots like all the other blues tourists. Then we found Ardent Studios. Modern and up to date. We were staying at the Peabody Hotel, the wildest and most outrageous hotel in Memphis, where every morning a valet in full uniform would roll out a red carpet in front of the elevator, and four ducks would walk down it to the fountain in the middle of the lobby and splash around. Incredible. I asked my mentor, the father of Memphis blues, Rufus Thomas, what it was all about. He told me the ducks lived in the Royal Duck Palace, on the roof. Twice a day they flew down to the fountain, where Japanese tourists snapped their picture. There were signs that read: DO NOT STEP ON THE DUCKS' FEET. Rufus told me that the owner of the Peabody chain left his fortune to these four ducks. His heirs wouldn't be entitled to their shares until the ducks had died a natural death. Which is a fantastic story, even though it's not true. Double-decker tourist buses plowed through downtown Memphis all the way to Graceland, the fabled home of Elvis Presley. We paid a visit. The legendary Beale Street was behind the hotel. Lined with bars and clubs with outrageous three-piece blues bands. I ate some awesome steaks there, too.

Eric Who?

BEFORE LEAVING FOR MEMPHIS I WENT TO THE POLYGRAM OFFICES IN Milano to tell them we'd finished recording the basic music tracks and I was heading for the States. In the hallway, I ran into the actress Lory Del Santo, a big fan of mine, who was crazy about *Blue's*. I had no idea what she was doing there.

"Zucchero!" she cried. "Guess what: Eric's coming tonight!"

"Eric who?"

"Eric Clapton."

Lory was Eric's girlfriend. She invited me to have dinner with them, and we talked about music. We talked about ourselves. To round out the evening we went to a piano bar in Milano's Brera district. As soon as the pianist realized we were in the audience, he started playing our songs—'Cocaine,' 'Dune Mosse.' People couldn't believe their eyes when they saw Eric Clapton, me, and Lory Del Santo. Later, in our taxi, I got a brilliant idea. I had a cassette with the new demos with me. Before the two of them got out at their hotel, I played 'Wonderful World' for Eric on the taxi's scratchy sound system. Eric was so kind. He said he really liked my music. I gave him the demo and told him I was going to Memphis the following week to record it.

"If you like," I added, "maybe you could play a few licks on it."

Oh, well. I tried.

A week later I was in Memphis with Clarence Clemons, Corrado Rustici, Uliani, and Torpedine as well. A call came from the reception.

"Mr. Zucchero, Mr. Clapton is on the line."

Holy cow!

"Ciao, Zucchero!" said Eric. "The song is great! I love it! So, how can we do it? I wanna do it."

"I don't know. When you come back to Italy…"

"On your way back to Italy, why don't you stop in New York, and we can record my guitar parts at the Hit Factory?"

I didn't need to be asked twice.

"Yes! How much do I owe you for this?"

Our budget was running low. I was a little worried and didn't want to seem like an asshole.

"What? Not a fucking thing, man. I'll do it for free. It's a pleasure."

This was all so wild. Not even the record company knew what we were up to. We just did it.

Rufus Thomas—Memphis, Tennessee

MEANWHILE, WE WERE STILL IN MEMPHIS. ONE SUNDAY MORNING, Rufus Thomas took me to a church service because we were looking for a gospel choir—the kind where the singers are all dressed in purple. He came to pick me up in his car, which had fake leopard-skin upholstery and Tennessee plates that read RUFUS THOMAS. We attended the service. They had an organ, drums, a guitar, and a wonderful gospel choir all decked out in purple. I was the only white person there. Lots of big, beautiful women. Some wore leopard-print miniskirts, high heels, with lots of makeup. At one point during the sermon, the preacher began rhythmically inciting the crowd.

"Hallelujah! Without the Lord, we're lost in the fog!"

He sounded like James Brown. As he raised his voice, the rhythm got more syncopated. Then he started singing. The girls in miniskirts wiggled about, danced, writhed, legs open, faces covered in sweat. It was like a collective orgasm. Tina Turner had nothing on these chicks.

"Good God almighty! In the name of God!"

I had seen stuff like this in the movies and always dreamed of seeing it in real life.

We called in the Ardent Gospel Choir, directed by Lester Snell, featuring singers from the Seventh-Day Adventist church. Working with Rufus Thomas, they belted out 'Overdose d'Amore,' 'Il Mare Impetuoso,' 'Madre Dolcissima,' and 'Il Diavolo in Me' to perfection. It gave me goosebumps.

Rufus also got the mayor to give me the key to the city. He showed up with his entourage and said, "Welcome to Memphis. You are an honorary citizen." He presented me with the key. Photographers took pictures. I was nobody. This was my first time in Memphis. To get that kind of recognition was an enormous pleasure, and a great honor.

Recording continued. Clarence Clemons was there. So was Jimmy Smith, one of the greatest organists alive. But when the time came that he was supposed to show up, I saw no sign of him, only his Hammond organ, which I figured he'd had brought in by someone else. Then I saw a tiny man soldering wires underneath it. It was him. A legend like Jimmy Smith, fixing his organ himself! In Italy, someone that famous would have had bodyguards and a staff of technicians at his command. But he didn't put on any airs. He came to play for a pittance, yet this was Jimmy Smith. He whipped off a slick version of 'Overdose d'Amore.' Next was 'Diavolo in Me.'

"What key is it in?" he asked.

"E major," I replied.

"No way, man. I don't play in E major."

"Why not?"

"Cause that's a guitar player's key."

Oh, well. At least I had Jimmy Smith playing on 'Overdose d'Amore'—what more could I ask?

That same day I was told that Stevie Ray Vaughan, one of the greatest blues guitarists around, was in the studio next to ours. He was a Texan. Much admired by Eric Clapton. I couldn't pass up this opportunity. That's typical of how my musical collaborations work. And without much ado, he gladly brought his mini-amp over to the studio we were in. I played 'Madre Dolcissima' for him.

"What a great song!" he said.

He played an awesome solo for it.

Rufus Thomas was my tour guide in Memphis. He introduced me to the black community. He took me out to eat black beans, chicken, and all kinds of hot and spicy soul food specialties. We explored the Memphis underworld, juke joints, clubs. I felt like I was inside the film *The Color Purple*. This was my world. I felt good there.

Then I got one last, crazy idea: Ennio Morricone. Why not go for it?

"Maestro, I'm in America. I'd be proud and honored to record one of your songs."

"Style?"

"Old America, blues, a little soul—stuff like that."

"I'm super busy right now and don't have time. Call me back in a week. I might have something for you."

"Just something short. A minute. A minute and a half, Maestro. I'll write the words to your melody."

A week went by and I called back.

"I've already recorded it," he said.

He'd written the music and recorded it with an orchestra in Rome. And since he had no faith in rock musicians, he arranged and conducted it himself. That was it. He sent me the multitrack recording. I wrote the lyrics to what would be 'Libera l'Amore': "*Libera l'amore o liberatene per sempre.*" ("Free your love, or free yourself from it forever." It closes out *Oro, Incenso e Birra.*

A Real *Diamante*

I ALWAYS RECORD MY VOCALS IN ITALY, WHERE I CAN BREATHE. IT HAS to be in places like Emilia, Reggio, Modena, or Veneto, or at least in Tuscany. I need to sing in nice places, with lots of land around: vineyards, fields, light, colors, and smells that inspire me. My childhood. The scent of my grandmother. A village setting.

So, we went to Montale in the Modena countryside, to have Umbi record the vocal tracks. He's like a brother to me. He'd watched me grow. Umbi recorded the vocals for *Blue's*, too. He had a room for me, where I slept. His mother made us amazing food: *le tigelle, lo gnocco, la pastasciutta*. We had a great time.

One day, Francesco de Gregori showed up (Bob Dylan once called him a "an Italian folk hero"). Torpedine had contacted him about writing a song with me.

"You got any ideas?" he asked. "What do you want it to be about?"

I told him the story of my grandmother Diamante. A farm woman dressed in black, with blue eyes. Sensitive and sweet. I spent a lot of time with her when I was a kid. She would take me by the hand and we'd walk among the haystacks. I remember the smell of the barns, barnyard celebrations, my mother and father dancing. I remember tanks rolling by when there was trouble, but this was 1955 and the war was over. Though I did see tanks. That was the world I wanted the song to describe. A beautiful, simple, archaic world. A connection between life and death—she was no longer with us. But she was looking down upon us from on high.

"Oh, I'll give it a try!" said Francesco. Real mellow.

He grabbed a can of beer and shut himself in a room upstairs. An hour and a half later he came down to show me what he'd written. I was fucking blown away when I read: *"Respirerò l'odore dei granai…"* ("I shall breathe in the smell of the barns…") Then all the imagery of the brides dancing silhouetted in light, soldiers and brides hand in hand, and my grandmother along with them. Stupendous! Just what I wanted. Only Francesco hadn't mentioned the actual name Diamante, which I had decided would be the title. We had to find a way to fit it in. A line came to me: *"Dall'alto di un cielo, diamante, i nostri occhi vedranno."* ("From way up high, in the sky, Diamante, your eyes and mine shall see.") Fuck, that fit perfectly. When shit like this happens, it's like a miracle. 'Diamante' is a special song for me, as special as the grandmother it's dedicated to. I didn't want to mess it up, and didn't trust myself with the lyrics. So, I asked a poet like Francesco. Who, by the way, later declared, "Zucchero came to me because he's insecure and doesn't realize how good he is. He doesn't believe in himself."

He said the same thing to me.

"Why did you ask me to write lyrics for you when you yourself were capable of writing the words to a song like 'Così Celeste'? What do you want from me?"

Insecurity. It's humility. De Gregori wrote incredible lyrics for that song. Truly a Gregorian chant.

We made a beautiful video of 'Diamante' directed by Stefano Salvati, on an old farm in Carpi, outside Modena. Hayloft, farmers, women dressed as brides. A short film. I was in it too—I saw myself growing older. I come riding in on a horse, scraggly beard, cigar in my mouth. My grandpa Cannella all over. The priest and the wedding scene. It was my co-star Maria Grazia Cucinotta's debut. I chose her out of a group of 30 girls in casting. I've got an eye. She'll go far, I thought (as did the Bond movie producers, who put her in *The World Is Not Enough*). In one scene, we get married and we're supposed to kiss. I couldn't wait because it was supposed to be a kiss on the mouth. But she didn't want to. OK, cut. We tried to convince her, but she wanted no part of it. I managed a fake film kiss for the camera.

The Bishop of Soul

IT'S NOT OVER. I STILL HAVE TO TELL YOU ABOUT THE GREAT SOLOMON Burke, known as the Bishop of Soul—who of course never took any vow of celibacy. I was introduced to him by Rufus Thomas, the father of Memphis Blues and a man who ushered in many of the future heroes of soul music. It was thanks to him that I got a chance to work with Solomon. We were recording *Oro, Incenso e Birra* in Memphis, and staying at the Peabody Hotel—the one with the ducks. It was there Rufus first spoke to me of this outrageous character who called himself a bishop and had fathered 15 children—others claimed 20—around the world. After each tour, another one would be born. "God bless them," he said, and recognized them all. A legend. Rufus claimed he said, "When I started reading the Bible, I opened it up and read a verse at random. It said, 'Be ye fruitful and multiply.' That's what I did." To me, though, it sounds like a tall tale.

Rufus arranged a meeting. Solomon, who was a very large man, came up to me, gave me his hand, and said, "I'm the king of soul." The scene in *The Blues Brothers* with John Belushi and Dan Aykroyd singing 'Everybody Needs Somebody to Love' popped into my head—Solomon Burke wrote that song (along with Jerry Wexler and Bert Berns). The positive energy flowed—we clicked, right off the bat. The second time I met him was at a special edition of the Pistoia Blues Festival, featuring Steve Winwood, Solomon Burke, and the Blues Brothers Band with Eddie Floyd. I wanted to do a version of 'Diavolo in Me' with the Blues Brothers Band and Solomon on vocals. Before that we did an awesome version of 'Everybody Needs Somebody to Love.' Solomon swaggered onstage in a purple cape and a crown. At the end of the show, he put the crown on my head and declared me "prince of soul—not the king. There's only one king, and that's me!" We went our separate ways, with the promise that we'd be seeing each other soon.

Time went by. Once in a while I got news of Solomon through Graziano Uliani. He toured with the Rolling Stones in the United States. When Eric Clapton gave me his new album, *Don't Give Up on Me*, which I loved, I made up my mind to call him.

"Solomon," I said after we'd exchanged pleasantries, "can I ask you something?"

"Whatever you want."

I was overjoyed. Then shattered.

Solomon said he couldn't sing a song called 'Diavolo in Me.'

"I'm a bishop, man. I don't have the devil in me."

That threw me for a loop.

But he tried to come to the rescue.

"Can I change the words a little?" he asked.

"Sure, as long you preserve the spirit of the song—it's supposed to be funny."

He added his own words. Then he added more. And more after that. There was no room for them all.

"I need them, Zucchero, because I'm telling the devil to get out. He lures me with his deceptive, seductive ways, tries to knock me to the ground, but I won't fall. He's the one who's got to go. I'm gonna beat him at his own game, but first I've got to convince him with my words."

We worked out a new version in Los Angeles. Later we played it together when Solomon made a surprise appearance at the Nice Jazz Festival. We also performed together at the Royal Albert Hall in London. By then he'd put on even more weight, could no longer walk and was confined to a wheelchair. But onstage he was still an extraordinary animal. He really did seem to have the devil in him, but always managed to cast him out with his sweat-soaked performance.

"Why Don't You Leave the Chorus in Italian?"

I WAS AT OLYMPIC STUDIOS IN LONDON MIXING THE ALBUM. ONE morning I walked into the kitchen for breakfast and ran into Paul Young.

"You're Zucchero!" he said to me.

"What an honor!" I replied. "I'm a big fan of yours."

"No, man. You got it backwards: I'm *your* fan. When I was on vacation in Italy and heard 'Senza Una Donna,' I thought it would be a great song for my next record. Of course, with the lyrics in English."

"Why don't you leave the chorus in Italian?" I suggested off the top of my head. "I think British audiences would find it alluring and exotic."

"You might have an idea there."

I upped the stakes. "We could even try doing a duet together. What do you say?"

"I say that would be great! Let's see how we can work this out."

We practically made a game of it, letting the music tracks roll while we sang on top of them. I knew a songwriter, Frank Musker, who lived in London and spoke Italian. He gave us a literal translation of the lyrics. The next day we tinkered around with them and recorded our duet, mostly just to see how it sounded. It came out rather well.

"Now what?"

"I dunno. Send it to your record company and see what they say. I'll do the same with mine."

A week later, the record was released. I never had to work so little for so much success.

We didn't make a video until the song had already become a worldwide hit. We hadn't even done a photo shoot. We released the record with a picture of Paul and me singing in the studio. Three weeks went by and my telephone in Avenza was ringing off the hook. It was my record company giving me constant updates: "It's Number Two in Germany, Number One in France, the United States, Canada, and South Africa." No marketing, no promotion. All we did was send it out to the radio stations. I was asked to do a European tour and ride the wave. But I was depressed, dealing with all the usual shit—a broken marriage I couldn't fix. I said no and passed up a golden opportunity. That's the movie of my life. It was like I could never seem to enjoy the best moments. Moments I'd worked so hard for.

Once, in Spain, on the terrace of my room at the Hotel Plaza in Madrid, I felt so lousy I even contemplated throwing myself over the railing. A flash: Nothing made sense anymore. In Paris, I had a panic attack. In London, too. Violent attacks. One day I was supposed to drive to Umbi's. It was early summer. I got in my Fiat 500 SL and set out from Avenza on my way to Modena. I'd just about reached Sarzana when I started passing a truck. But halfway through, wham! Another panic attack. "Oh, my God. I can't do it. I can't do it. I can't…" I had to pull over and stop in the emergency lane. The next exit, Aulla, was too far. I rolled down the windows for air. I was stuck between home and Modena. I had to call my friend Lucio, the lobster and Champagne guy, to come and pick me up. Another time I was on my Harley Davidson, going to the shore in Forte dei Marmi. I stopped at a red light. Panic attack. I had to get off my bike and try to keep my cool—there were people around, looking at me. For them I was a star. I, though, thought I was going to die.

Sister Hunt

FLASHBACK: LISA HUNT.

After we finished working on *Blue's*, Torpedine and I, multitrack recording in hand, missed our flight to Bologna. It was hours until the next one. We were near Covent Garden when our taxi driver suggested we should get out and take a look around. We stopped at a place to eat and in the distance spotted this big black chick singing into a microphone hooked up to an amp, accompanied by a blond kid on the guitar. She looked like an African matriarch. I approached. She was busking in Covent Garden and singing her heart out. Gospel numbers, a little Aretha Franklin.

"Hi. I'm Zucchero, an Italian singer."

"Hi. I'm Lisa. What kind of music do you do?"

"Blues."

"An Italian who sings the blues? Ha! Ha! Ha!"

That gave her a good laugh.

"I'm looking for a background vocalist. You're great. I'd love to have you come on tour with me."

"No, I live here in London...I don't know...maybe."

At that time, I could only afford to pay her 150,000 lire per show. But for her, that was a lot.

"OK. I'll come tomorrow."

I'd missed my flight and by chance found her busking in Covent Square. And one of the most beautiful friendships I've ever had with a woman was born. Ever since that day, she's been like a sister to me. Lisa's so likable, and everyone adored her. When she opened her mouth, she was extraordinary. She had droves of fans. And she liked Italy so much, she wound up moving to Massa, where she and her big ass would hop on the Ciao moped she'd bought and cruise to the beach by herself. She worked with me up until 2001 and the *Shake* tour. After that, she married a good-looking, skinny Australian guy with blond hair and dark eyes, and they moved to Sydney. It was great having her along for the ride because she was always so upbeat and positive. Of course, being a Scorpion, sometimes she would get on my nerves. She could be touchy. And I would come back with stuff like, "Come on, gimme a break, you big ol' butterball." At which she'd burst out laughing and that was the end of our bickering. There was a lot of cohesion in the band, and we all had lots of great times together. Especially when my record sold two million copies and we started playing sold-out stadiums.

The band was big, tight, and hot as hell. Our music was innovative. The scenography was done by Paolo Gualdi, from Modena, and projected huge images surrounding the stage during concerts. I performed against a backdrop of sunflowers, intense skies, enthralling sunsets, and blue seas. I closed out saying, "Mass is over, go in peace. May God bless you. May God forgive us."

I never talked to audiences much during my performances; I mostly just sang. Never gave any big speeches. I just took off like a train for a roaring two-and-a-half-hour ride with the band. An explosion of body and soul. Sounds in contrast and harmony. The sacred. The profane. I never cared about explaining concepts to audiences, or peddling any kind of message, or giving sermons. I let my music do the talking.

From 'Back 2 U': "*Calma è la sera, salvezza del mio blues.*" ("The evening is calm, salvation of my blues.")

From 'Papà Perché': "*Ho sempre un po' di blues in fondo agli occhi, c' è sempre un po' di blu in questo cielo.*" ("I've got the blues in the back of my eyes, there's always a little blue in these skies.")

Voice of Leather

WE PLAYED IN PALERMO, AT THE STADIUM. THIS WAS THE *ORO, INCENSO e Birra* tour. Next was the stadium in Rosarno, Calabria. But by the time the show in Naples was over, I'd lost my voice. I'd overstrained it playing concert after concert in the heat. Every time I swallowed it felt like a nail driving through my throat. I called Torpedine and Sconocchia, and said, "Guys, I can't sing in Rosarno tomorrow. I need to see a doctor. I've lost my voice. Notify everyone right now. Don't let the trucks leave. I can't sing. And I'm not taking any calls."

I tried to get some rest and was almost asleep when the phone rang. I heard a voice with a strong Calabrese accent say, "Is this Zucchero? This is Pesce, from Rosarno."

"Didn't they tell you I can't come?" I said. "And how'd you get this number, anyway?"

"Don't worry about that. Pesce is one of the biggest families. You've got to come to Rosarno, it's a matter of family honor."

"I'm sorry. We'll make it up. But right now, I can't sing, I've lost my voice, as you can plainly tell."

"You're coming to Rosarno." He repeated it: "You're coming to Rosarno."

I immediately called Torpedine. I was scared shitless.

"Send the trucks down. Tomorrow I'm singing."

I got to Rosarno early the next afternoon. This Pesce had some face. He showed up with his goons.

"Come with me, I'll take you to the stadium myself. I'll show it to you. It's important for you to see it."

"Look, I'm not getting ready until eight o'clock. I go on at nine."

"It would be better if you came to the stadium."

They showed me my dressing room, and then locked me inside with a mountain of watermelons and cantaloupes. Kidnapped. Pesce wanted to make sure I didn't get away.

Finally, at around seven o'clock, they let me out of the dressing room and took me to a camper behind the stage so I could have a shower. I was super pissed off. While I was having something to eat, I was told there were some cousins of mine outside who wanted to say hi to me.

"Cousins? In Rosarno? I don't have any cousins here."

"They're pretty insistent. They claim to be your cousins from Reggio Calabria."

Ten or so people walked in, whom I had never seen before. They were all dressed in black, with white shirts and hats. The biggest one, the boss, said, "Hi. I'm Cesare, your cousin. How's Peppino doing?" That was my father. "How is Aunt Rina?"

Holy fuck, they knew everybody.

Then Cesare began introducing me to the others.

"This is Adelmo."

"What do you mean, Adelmo? I'm Adelmo."

He looked just like me: the shape of his face, his eyes, his hair. Practically identical.

"This is Rina." My mother's name. "Then we have Pino." My father's nickname. "And here's Lauro." My brother's name. "Alice." My daughter's name. They all had the same names as my family did. "And last, but not least, there's Grandpa Cesare who wants to meet you." Who's Grandpa Cesare? "Yes, come with us. Unfortunately, he can't walk anymore. He's in the car waiting for you, along with Grandma."

Outside was a black car with tinted windows. Like out of some mafia movie. I went over to the car. A shock. Grandpa Cesare looked just like my grandfather Roberto, nicknamed Cannella. He had a strange manner of speaking: a Calabrese accent with words from the Emilian dialect mixed in. He said to me, "I heard you had a few problems with Pesce. Why didn't you call me? That guy's just a little fish."

I couldn't believe it. The head of the family told me the whole story. I'd never known anything about it. At home, no one had ever told me.

During the war, my grandfather's brother—I didn't even know he had a brother until then—instead of being repatriated to Reggio Emilia, had been sent to Reggio Calabria by mistake. At least they got the Reggio part right. While he was waiting to be sent to the proper destination, he happened to meet a girl. They went out one evening, and next thing you know, the girl's parents forced him to marry her. So he had to stay and live there, in the wrong Reggio. Welcome to the south! He married her and they had all these children I'd never seen before. Of course, they were all Fornaciaris. And they'd become an important family; they ran all the gas stations from Vibo Valentia to Reggio Calabria. The next day they brought me to one and gave me bergamots, oranges, lemons, chili pepper, sausage with chili pepper, 'nduia (a Calabrese specialty, featuring cured pork and chili pepper)—they were incredibly hospitable. Kisses, hugs, people crying.

As for the concert, my voice was shot for the whole show. I couldn't even finish. But I managed to pull it off.

My next stop with that awesome band was the stadium in Agrigento, Sicily. While I was getting dressed, someone made the announcement that Clapton was there.

"Go on! Eric Clapton? In Agrigento?"

"Yeah. He's with a chick."

It really was him, with Lory del Santo. They were on vacation in Sicily. He saw the show and afterward told me he'd heard great music played by a great band. He asked me to go on tour with him, as his opening act. Our managers hammered out a deal. Clapton was managed by Roger Forrester, who was very well known and respected; my manager, Torpedine, still couldn't believe it was happening.

We played arenas all over Europe. We kicked off the tour at the Royal Albert Hall in London: 12 nights in a row. Then Finland,

Denmark, Sweden, Germany. I was so excited I would have done it for free. This was my chance to get out of Italy and have my records distributed in Europe.

So, we made our debut in London at the temple of British music. Torpedine was a little on edge the first night. In Italy I played stadiums, my popularity was a big draw, a guarantee. But here? The only song in English I had was 'Senza Una Donna / Without a Woman,' the only song of mine known on the British market. They applauded that one. But as for the rest, the audience was pretty cold. I suffered. Torpedine suffered.

"You see?"

Capturing the esteem of British audiences is tough. I was starting all over again. In the UK, I was nobody. The next day Eric comforted me. He was totally psyched. It was our sixth or so show when a review came out by one of the top critics. It went more, or less, like this: "You all know Clapton, but I suggest you go check out this Italian mad hatter, with a voice of leather." Roger called me and said, "I hope Clapton doesn't see this. Otherwise he'll get jealous." He was just kidding. The audiences grew, even during my opening act for Eric. The record company began putting up my posters around town, and released what I call my *White Album*, featuring English versions of all the songs from *Oro, Incenso e Birra*, plus 'Senza Una Donna,' my hit and the only song of mine anyone in the UK knew. The cover was all white, with me in the corner, wearing a hat. That became my image. I saw posters of that cover all over London. No small victory there. I was proud to see my face plastered all over town. People stopped me on the street. They considered me part of the Italian trinity: Schillaci–Pavarotti–Zucchero. Eric and I really clicked, he was totally supportive, and the tour went great.

Every date was sold out. It was Clapton's return to the stage after a good many years.

At the Hallenstadion in Zurich, Roger Forrester took me aside and asked if I'd like him to manage me, promising we'd hit Europe big-time.

"Eric would be thrilled. He loves your music."

"Yeah, but I've got Torpedine. I can't just get rid of him."

"Sure," he said, "I understand. But this is an opportunity I'd jump on if I were you."

"Yeah, but I'm loyal."

"That's stupid loyalty," Roger said, passing judgment.

The Genius of Ray

FOR THE GIG AT VERONA ON THE *ORO, INCENSO E BIRRA* TOUR IN September 1989, I'd convinced Ray Charles and his friend Dee Dee Bridgewater to join me onstage.

Our appointment was at four p.m. The hours dragged on and no sign of Ray. When he finally showed up, there was no time left to rehearse, so we ended up inside a dressing room with a cassette player and a piano. He listened to 'Come il Sole all'Improvviso.' It was the first time he'd ever heard it. He followed the chords with one hand on the piano and sang on top. He went through it three times. It was wonderful.

"See you onstage," he said on his way out of the dressing room.

Hmm, he'd only heard the song three times. Was he going to remember the chords? I couldn't conceal the fact that I was a bit perplexed.

We had two grand pianos onstage. As soon as I walked on, I began to worry he wouldn't show up. Should I introduce him? Not introduce him? His song was on the set list. I decided not to introduce him, just to avoid any blunders.

It came time to do the song. I went into the first verse, thinking it was a good thing I hadn't introduced Ray. It was impossible to remember a song after hearing it only three times. Five seconds later I see him walk on, totally cool. He sat down at the piano as calm as could be, and began his part perfectly on cue. I was ecstatic, singing almost in a state of shock. He was the greatest singer in the world. When Ray Charles opened his mouth, there was passion, energy, and joy.

Working Your Way Up & Rock 'n' Roll

IT HELPS TO HAVE TO WORK YOUR WAY UP. IT HELPS YOU TO BE READY, to react. And to respond. When Eric Clapton called me at the last minute to sing 'Tearing Us Apart' with him at the stadium in Bologna, I went. And I went fast. I'm often asked why I seem to prefer singing with foreign artists over working with Italians. Well, I sang with Luciano Pavarotti, and he sang with me because he had a very open mind, a yearning to put himself to the test and challenge the status quo, a longing to overcome insecurity and break down barriers. I've had lots of dealings with Italian artists who come up with excuses: "I don't know, I'll have to see what my manager says." "Let me check my agenda and I'll get back to you." "What? The concert's in two weeks? That's not enough time for me to get ready. I thought it was in two months." What do you mean? You call yourself a professional musician and you can't even learn one song in two weeks?

80% Sweat, 20% Inspiration

THERE'S ANOTHER ASPECT OF THIS JOB: HARD WORK. I'M NOT SOME KIND of genius who gets up in the morning and fires off a masterpiece at the drop of a hat. I need to work at something if I want results. I need a workshop atmosphere where I can ply my trade, because the more you ply your trade, the closer you get to art. Experience has taught me that the best songs always come at the end of a long, intense process, when it's time to hit the recording studio. They've been the songs that went on to become my biggest hits. Sometimes a flash will come, a phrase, a riff—like that time when I visited the mansion they used to film *Gone with the Wind*, or while sitting on a plane. But that kind of sudden inspiration is rare for me. Instead, I approach creativity like a job, and I'm always working at it. I got out of bed at four o'clock in the morning to write 'Diavolo in Me'—just grabbed my guitar, went into the kitchen, and cranked it out in five minutes, including the basic idea for the lyrics. But it wasn't just a stroke of luck. It came because I'd plied my trade and, like a sponge, soaked up so many different things, they sprouted like mushrooms at the last minute! It's always been like that. If I sat around waiting for inspiration, months would go by without any decent results. Sure, I might suddenly come up with an idea, and quickly record or write it down. But most often, ideas come when you spend time hammering out a song. You work through it, listen to the music, and work through it some more. Of course, you may not like what you've done. But you go back and listen to it the next day, and maybe there's something in it you like, something you can use, and you scrap the rest because it sucks. There have been songs where I had a good riff for the verses and recorded it a hundred times over, but there would be something about it that didn't quite convince me, so I wouldn't put it on the album I was working on, but set it aside for later use because it was a good riff. For 'Il Volo' it was just the opposite: I came up with the chorus, but it took me five years to find the right verse. I was in a parking lot in San Francisco, on my way to Corrado Rustici's to work on some demos. I had to pick up groceries at the supermarket. And there, the verse just came to me. I went to Corrado's and recorded it. I'll be damned! It was perfect. Vice versa, on the album *Chocabeck*, I used a verse I had discarded for the song 'Il Volo' in the song 'Alla Fine' and it worked like a charm. It's work that involves piecing things together and chiseling away at them. And, of course, it requires patience. You set aside the ideas you can't use at that moment, and when the time comes you may find a place for them.

Panic at the Kremlin

NO ROCK SINGER HAD EVER PERFORMED AT THE KREMLIN. EVEN Gorbachev didn't give his speeches there anymore. I was perplexed. No one in the Soviet Union knew who I was—my records weren't even distributed there. Yet a request came through ATER, the theatrical association based in Modena, which organized exchanges with the Soviet Union, normally involving opera singers and dancers from the Bolshoi Ballet. I was to play with the Vivaldi Orchestra, and the show would be broadcast live in Italy on *Domenica In*.

With all our vans and trucks loaded with instruments and equipment, it was like setting out for the invasion of Russia. We froze our asses off every night rehearsing with the orchestra. It was the tenth anniversary of John Lennon's death, and I brought along Randy Crawford to sing 'Imagine' with me. We also brought in Toni Childs, who I adore.

But then something inside me broke. I had an incredibly violent panic attack. I didn't want to do the show anymore. Someone suggested I try a massage. A thickset masseuse from the Bolshoi Ballet showed up. She took me into a big, antiseptic white room and had me lay on an aluminum table. It felt like being inside a morgue. She began manhandling me. Strong as an ox. Crack! Crunch! Ah! Ouch! She wracked every bone in my body. It didn't help. I asked for some chamomile tea.

Soon we were going live via satellite. Damn it!

I felt awful. My head was split in two. Half was saying, "Run away, get out of here. What the hell are you doing in Moscow? At the Kremlin? Who do you think you are, Lenin?!" The other half rationally urged me to go on and just sing whatever words I could remember. Watching *Live at the Kremlin*, you wouldn't think I was in the middle of a humongous panic attack. I was just standing there with my microphone in a cold sweat, my strength completely zapped. I thought I was going to topple over. I could hardly move, but I made it over to our bass player, Polo Jones, and leaned on him. I kept thinking, "What am I doing here? Run, man, run!" I was a wreck, but my adrenaline finally kicked in a half hour into the set. The two parts inside my head seemed to reunite and I could finally concentrate.

After that came a beautiful duet with Randy Crawford, and another with Toni Childs. The audience stayed sitting down; they didn't even applaud. It was so quiet at the end of each song you could have heard a pin drop. Why hadn't anyone thought to tell me it was the custom at classical music venues to applaud only at the end of a concert? The KGB was there too, with an agent in every 10 rows of plush red velvet seats, keeping an eye on things.

At the end of the show, the crowd broke into a 20-minute standing ovation. Kids came up to the stage to bring me flowers, a hat, a jacket. It was unreal. But over.

Before leaving the hall, I turned around to take one last look. I wondered if Gorbachev ever had a panic attack.

Zucchero Who?

I FIRST MET STING AT A PARTY AT HIS HOME IN MIGLIARINO PISANO. IT was 1990.

I was curious and happy on the way there, but also a bit worried. I wondered what kind of fellow Sting was.

He gave me a warm welcome: "Zucchero, I love you, I love your music." He was cordial, friendly, open.

We sat down at the table and next to me was this blond gentleman who didn't say much and wore a sullen look—he never smiled. After a while, he asked me a few questions in English.

"Who are you?"

"Zucchero."

"Zucchero who?"

"Zucchero, I'm an Italian singer."

"What kind of music?"

"Blues."

"Blues?" he said with a look of disgust. "An Italian who sings the blues in English?"

"No, in Italian."

I guess that really irked him, because he turned the other way and went on eating. It was Miles Copeland, and little did either of us know that he was soon to be my new manager.

After dinner, Sting asked to hear the songs from my new album, *Oro, Incenso e Birra*. He liked 'Madre Dolcissima.' Then he played his new songs for me, the ones for his upcoming record, *The Soul Cages*.

"Why don't you stay over tonight? Tomorrow's our daughter Coco's christening. I'd like you to be her godfather."

"What? Why?"

"Because you strike me as a very good, sincere, genuine person."

The next day we went to the little church in Migliarino Pisano for the ceremony.

Many people consider Sting a narcissist, a snob. But with me he's always been very simple and kind. He comes from a humble background, and I respect that. True, he's not Bono. Bono is outgoing, a real charmer who's very straightforward, whereas Sting is sophisticated, polite, elegant. Sting's a real family man. He gets along great with his wife, Trudie, and the two of them are always having loads of fun together.

We met up in Capri later, so I could teach him how to sing the lyrics to 'Muoio per Te,' the Italian version of 'Mad About You.' We worked on it till four in the morning, when Sting slumped over and groaned, "Zucchero, stop, please."

"OK, but your pronunciation still isn't perfect. You'd better work on it, otherwise you're going to sound like Mal from the Primitives."

Eldorado

BY THE END OF THE *ORO, INCENSO E BIRRA* TOUR, I WAS A MESS. I FELT like I had nowhere to go, nowhere to live. I couldn't stand Avenza anymore, and so went back to my parents in Roncocesi.

"Delmo, what are you doing in bed at this hour? Get up and let's go to work."

My father didn't realize what my job involved. The night before I'd gotten back from a concert at four a.m. He woke me up at seven, expecting me to give him a hand in the fields.

"Delmo got home late last night, let him sleep," my poor mother pleaded.

But my father was relentless. "There's work to be done," he insisted. And every morning he'd wake me up at six on the dot to go out and work with him. I lasted a week before I went back to Avenza. It was the house where our daughters were born, and being there made me sad. I was depressed, riddled with anxiety, in the middle of a wicked identity crisis. There was also another problem: my life. I was a star.

I was invited to a dinner at Forte dei Marmi, given by a trendy architect. There, I met an extraordinary woman: Rosa. She was a hairdresser who, in the summer, ran a beach club in Fiumetto, near Marina di Pietrasanta, called Eldorado. A beautiful place with a wooden cottage and porch, big glass windows looking out onto the sea, surrounded by palm trees. I was telling my friends how bad I felt and how I didn't know where to go next.

"Maestro," said Rosa—that's what she called me—"I'd be honored if you stayed at my house here at the shore. I'd be proud to have you write your music there."

I was supposed to be working on material for another album, but was reluctant to accept her proposal. I was uncomfortable about going to live in a strange place. Besides, the sea has always frightened me. It makes me restless and puts me on edge. I prefer a winter paradise to a scorching summer. But Rosa insisted. Summer was over and a mild October had set in.

"Nobody will bother you there, and you can stay until May, just like it was your own home."

She insisted and I caved in. Why not? It must have been the numbing effect of my depression. It zaps you of strength, leaves you frazzled. Even the simplest, most routine and banal everyday tasks are impossible. That's how I felt then, so I just let myself be carried along with the tide.

I took my bicycle, my piano, a guitar, a recorder, and moved in. I even got myself a dog—a little mutt called Olmo.

Fiumetto's near Forte dei Marmi, so at least I could see my daughters whenever I wanted. I spent my days listening to operas by Puccini, the grand master from Torre del Lago, alone, while reading Charles Bukowski, which was soothing since Bukowski was worse off than I was. I alternated Puccini with U2's latest album, *Achtung Baby*. I could only take so much opera.

I walked along the beach with Olmo for hours. We played. I would toss pieces of driftwood and he would fetch them.

I was alone. There were moments of great serenity—occasional, but truly stupendous reprieves, when I'd sit down at the piano and lose myself in music.

Word had got around town that I was living at a beach club in Fiumetto. Soon there was a procession of girls and women jogging past my window in their sweat suits on the beach. They looked inside as they went. I'd see them go by, then retrace their steps and jog past again and again, looking in each time, hoping to catch a glimpse of me. One morning a pretty blond woman knocked on the door. She stepped inside with lots of cheeky candor, first apologizing for having bothered me, then asking if she could take a shower.

"Sure, help yourself," I said, feeling rather embarrassed. I found her impertinence unsettling. I suppose she figured it was a legitimate request. I kept playing, trying to develop an idea that wasn't working. I was concentrating on my music. Then, a soft pattering of feet, furtive slithering. And there she was standing beside me, wearing my robe. Her hair was wet and she was gorgeous. I later found out she had a son who went to school with my daughter in Pietrasanta. I didn't want to be bothered, but I didn't want to be impolite either. I kept playing, looking for the right idea, the right harmony, a phrase, a sound. She gave me a cross look and snapped, "I guess I'll be on my way." She got dressed. I saw her again one day at our kids' school when I went to pick up my daughter.

You know how gossip spreads. Soon my lonely retreat had become a port of call. Women friends, acquaintances, friends of Angela, girls I met maybe one time. They all showed up—even my current partner, Francesca. A radiant woman—independent and cosmopolitan, a true citizen of the world who spoke a slew of languages. At the time, we knew each other, but we weren't together yet. Sometimes she would come visit and find me with another woman—there was a cavalcade of women. I was depressed, yes, but I was also totally free and didn't have to answer to anybody.

One night I was watching a movie on TV with Olmo snuggled up beside me when I heard a loud racket coming from the beach. I went to see. A group of German kids had built a bonfire. They had gone swimming and were all naked and drunk on beer, dancing around the flames. None of them knew who I was. We all ended up eating spaghetti at my little wooden cottage at three in the morning. I played for them and we all sang. One tall, beautiful blond chick said to me, "Hey, you're good. You should be a singer."

Another night, a British friend of mine, Rick, a VJ on the Italian music channel Videomusic, called. His Italian was approximate and he spoke with a strong English accent.

"Hey, Zucchero, there's a new Mexican restaurant in Vittoria Apuana"—that's the next town down from Forte dei Marmi. "Come on, let's go!"

In the grips of my suffering, I didn't have the least desire.

"No, I don't quite feel up to it."

"What the fuck, man? Come on! I'm taking you out, you fuck."

He won out, and we went to the Mexican restaurant. It was swarming with chicks with their tits hanging out, wearing holsters with shot glasses instead of bullets, pouring tequila boom-booms, rapid-fire. I drank, six, seven, eight. That's when things got crazy. People were dancing on the tables. Rick, who wasn't as drunk as I was, managed to pick up a couple of chicks.

"Come on, we'll all go back to Zucchero's house!"

I was drunk and sad. We got in the car and I cranked up Puccini's *Turandot* on the stereo. There was no traffic along the coast road, and I hauled ass. We sped over the bridge in Forte dei Marmi. The speakers were pumping Puccini. I slammed on the brakes. They screeched, tires skidded. The girls shrieked, scared shitless. We came to a stop no more than a meter from the sea. Shattered and numb as I was, a sudden feeling of calm came over me. We went inside my cottage. I lay down on a mat in the living room, while Rick went into my room with one of the girls. I was with the other. She had a dark complexion and spoke Spanish. She was on top of me. I can't remember anything else. The next morning, the cleaning lady found me lying naked and crashed out on the floor.

It was a little like the rock 'n' roll life I'd lived back when I played the dance halls and clubs. There was a lot going on now, and I hadn't had so many kicks since I'd broken up with my wife. Whatever happened to that magical slogan "Sex, Drugs, and Rock 'n' Roll"? It's gone, everybody's become politically correct.

How many chicks passed through Eldorado while I was there? A helluva lot, because I was free. Sensuality—oh, how I adore it. Flirting and seduction are key to any sexual relationship; they add spice. And the perfect music to make love to is soul music. In that cottage on the beach, I feasted on sexual repasts with Barry White in the background. His smooth, cadenced rhythms and hypnotic voice accompanied yes's and no's, and lots of moaning.

I was alone. I felt like shit. But I had tons of women. It was a weird, painful, effervescent combination of suffering and freedom.

I rode bikes with my daughters, Alice and Irene, in the pine forest of Versilia. There were good times, but bad times too. Light. Darkness. Over, and over again. It was a drag.

But a toast to life! I still hoped to put the pieces of my life back together. I tasted the pain of solitude and the pleasure of freedom.

After listening to all that Puccini, one day I came up with 'Miserere.' Strange song, I'd never written anything like it. A mix of pop and opera, with a little gospel thrown in for good measure, in 6/8 time. The tenor part was very operatic. Lyrics in *maccheronico* English, as usual. The words "*Miserere, misero me, però brindo alla vita*" ("I may be in bad shape, but a toast to life!") came to me with the music, just like that. Then I set it aside. And the idea of having Pavarotti sing it came in a flash.

"This is Brian. Brian May."

ONE DAY WHEN I WAS DOWN AT THE SHORE, TUCKED AWAY IN MY LITTLE cottage, getting *Miserere* ready, the phone rang. Three in the afternoon. Strange, I thought. Only a few people had this number.

"Hello."

"Is this Zucchero?"

"Yes. Who's this?"

"This is Brian. Brian May."

Queen immediately came to mind, and stupidly the first thing I said was, "*The* Brian May?"

"Yes," he said, "at least I think so."

He had seen me at the Royal Albert Hall with Eric Clapton and had become a big fan, he said. That was a good time for me; 'Without a Woman' had just hit the charts in the UK. He invited me to play on the Freddie Mercury Tribute bill, with Guns N' Roses, David Bowie, Elton John, Roger Daltrey, Annie Lennox, and George Michael. I accepted at once. Two minutes later I began feeling queasy. Panic attack. Would I be up to it? My anxiety spiked when I heard the list of songs I had to choose from. All the best-known songs were already taken. I ended up going with 'Las Palabras de Amor.'

We rehearsed in London for a week, in a big warehouse. My anxiety wouldn't go away. As we say in Italy, pull out the tooth to relieve the pain. I wish. I was ice cold. Terrified. Lost.

The night of the show, I saw Bowie calmly talking to everyone. I looked out onto the stage, saw the crowd going wild for Roger Daltrey. I took a tranquilizer and convinced myself I'd remember all the lyrics and wouldn't pass out on satellite TV. Maybe. The speaker screamed out, "Zucchero, five minutes." I headed for the gallows. Why did I ever agree to this?

There was a huge crowd. I walked onstage and felt myself die a little. I looked around. I was waiting for my acoustic guitar and it wasn't forthcoming. Just as I felt like I was on the verge of vomiting, Brian May gave me the eye. Letting me know everything would be alright and he would do the intro. Alright, my ass! Even now as I write this, I break out in a cold sweat. Luckily, I relaxed after the first few bars. By the end, I didn't want to leave the stage. After sharpening my sword, I fought on equal footing. When we went into the soulful grand finale, the crowd burst into a standing ovation. In short, it was a nightmare, a terrifying experience that I wound up enjoying afterward, but not while it was unfolding.

Since then, Brian and I have become friends. I call him quite often—to invite him to my birthday parties, or when I'm playing. He's played with me in Bologna, Germany, and London. And every time he just walks onstage without even rehearsing, because I always ask at the last minute. He's great. Always says yes, walks on, plugs in his guitar, and plays. A true legend. Once, when he invited me to London to see the musical about Queen, *We Will Rock You,* he asked me to join the band. That's right, Queen. For a tour. I told him he was crazy. Replace Freddie Mercury? High treason. Being in Queen would have been nice, but I'd rather try for the crown of the King of Soul, at least in Italy.

I've performed with Queen lots of times since. I invited them to *Pavarotti & Friends 2003,* where I sang 'We Are the Champions' with them. Brian fell in love with 'Così Celeste,' and I fell in love with his simplicity.

That same year he asked me to play at the concert in South Africa, for Mandela. I know what you're thinking—that we spend our time inviting each other to play at our shows. Well, it's kind of like that because the stage is the best party possible. I don't know of anything that can beat it. So, we did this huge tribute, and afterward we all went out to dinner together.

The next day I was on my way home to finish writing the songs that would be on *Miserere.* There was 'It's All Right,' which, along with 'Dune Mosse,' I consider one of the best songs I've ever done. There was 'Ridammi il Sole,' which is pretty sad and melancholy; there was 'Un'Orgia di Anime Perse' and 'Pene.' Those songs were a mirror of the darkness and light I was going through at the time. There was also 'Il Pelo nell'Uovo,' the first song of mine that Pasquale Panella wrote the lyrics for. I asked him, and he was quick about it. He came up with a whole bunch of different versions, and this one was the most beautiful, so I recorded it. The first track on the album starts off with vocals by Leo Ferrè, sampled from a song called 'La Solitudine.'

The album opens with the words "*Io non sono più dei vostri, io vengo da un altro pianeta, da un'altra solitudine. Non sono più dei vostri, aspetto dei mutanti.*" ("I no longer belong to you, I come from another planet, from another solitude. I no longer belong to you, I'm waiting for the mutants.") Then the music comes in, accompanying these melancholy, reflective, psychotherapy-sounding lyrics.

Atomic Bomb

ONE DAY I GOT UP LIKE I DO EVERY MORNING, AT MY OLD FRIEND UMBI'S studio. They'd organized the whole thing the night before: hidden TV cameras in the hall, in the kitchen where I had my breakfast, and one outside. They'd come up with a perfect plan. Umbi's mother, the musicians, even Corrado Rustici were all in on it. Of course, the only fool who had no idea what was going on was me—as the victim of the prank, I played the lead role.

I got out of bed and walked into the hall. In the video, you can see I'm still pretty groggy, scratching my head. Yes, I was certainly out of it—actually, still suffering from a bit of depression. Symptom: When you get up in the morning and first thing you say is "What a pain in the ass!" You can see me going into the kitchen, having coffee. But I was just one big complaint. Then I start writing, putting the finishing touches on the lyrics of 'Miserere.' At one point, it must have been about eleven o'clock, *BOOM!* I hear this explosion. I thought it was a canister of butane. Then Umbi's mom comes running in, screaming like a madwoman, "We've got to get out of here, we've got to evacuate! A nuclear missile just exploded!"

"Huh? What do you mean?" Here as well, I just didn't react. "Oh, well. A nuclear missile. Who cares?" That's how gone I was.

I went over to the window and looked outside. Holy fuck, there really was a missile, stuck in the ground out in Umbi's field.

"Everybody out!" cried Umbi, scared out of his wits.

Torpedine: "Everybody out! They said to evacuate the house! Contamination, contamination!"

Huh? I just kind of followed along.

Meanwhile I caught sight of a white van driving down from the riverbank onto Umbi's field. Four men in protective suits got out. They were wearing gas masks and carrying radiation detectors that made funny noises.

"Let's move! Everybody in line. Contamination! Danger! Danger!"

Then Umbi's neighbor shows up. I knew him, I used to go over and eat his peaches. He walks up, carrying a hen whose feathers are all ruffled and…dark green! It looked rotten.

"Umbi, what's going on? Look at my hens! They're all dead! Look! They're green!"

They had put movie makeup on him. Feigning despair, he pulled chunks of fake hair out of his head, the rubber skin on his face began to peel off. I still couldn't believe it, but I was no longer laughing. It was the farmer who fooled me, holding that dead green chicken.

Then they lined us all up and tested us with their little machine that went *pee-pee, pee-pee, pee-pee.* First, they did Rustici, then the drummer, then Torpedine.

"No, no. You're OK, you're OK, you're OK."

Then they get to me and I hear them shout, "Get away, everybody. Move away now! This guy's 100 percent contaminated!"

They were very serious.

"You've got four days to live! If you're lucky! Everybody out of here!"

Two things went through my mind. First thought: the girls. In a fraction of a second I saw my life flash before my eyes. This can't be possible. Next thought: Why me and not them?

"Run, run!"

They evacuated the others. Then one of the men told me, "We're going to take you to the hospital. But there's only one surefire way to lower the level of radioactivity: fish broth. No, sorry. I mean fish gelatin."

Fish gelatin?

"On your knees!"

I knelt, fully dressed. They grabbed a bucket filled with fish gelatin and threw it on me. Yuck! And I'm still kneeling there like a dope, thinking, *Fish gelatin? Why fish gelatin?*

"Zucchero! You're on *Candid Camera*!"

Vaffanculo!

You, Maestro, Will Be Sitting on Your Couch.

I'D COMPOSED ALL THE SONGS. MY MANAGER, MICHELE TORPEDINE, along with one of the bosses at my record company, Universal, came from Bologna to hear the new material. I played it all for them, except this weird piece that alluded to the music of Puccini and gospel, titled 'Miserere.' When they'd finished listening, Torpedine said, Yes, there was some interesting music there—and asked if I had anything else. I was coming off of *Oro, Incenso e Birra*, an album that was a big hit in Italy and around the world. That album was rock- and blues-based, and the operatic mood and melodies of 'Miserere' had nothing whatsoever to do with that kind of thing. I had no desire to play such an off-the-wall song for them now. But Torpedine insisted. I played it. "Awesome song, man! You're crazy if you don't want to put it on the album." They were both convinced. I wasn't.

To raise the stakes on them, I made what I thought was an impossible request: "This song would only make sense if we had Pavarotti singing tenor on it."

207

"Fuck, man, don't you think you're asking a bit much? He's a classical singer, the Number One tenor in the world. He's never done a duet with a rock singer."

I insisted. This song would only make sense if we had him on it. I was adamant. Otherwise, forget it. My final offer. The boss from Universal proposed asking around at Decca, the company's classical label. At least Pavarotti and I had the same record company. They took the demo and managed to make an appointment with Pavarotti, who was in Philadelphia. They caught up with him there, and when they got back to Italy, they told me Pavarotti had liked the song and sent his compliments. He even said he was a fan of mine. But that didn't mean he wanted to sing with me.

"Oh, well. That's that. I'm not putting it on the album."

"Let's think it over. Maybe we'll find some other tenor."

"Either it's him or the thing just doesn't make sense."

Meanwhile I was putting together a new demo that would give a better idea of what I was trying to do, with a tenor on vocals. Then maybe I would go pay Pavarotti a visit. I asked Umbi if he knew some kid who could sing tenor. A few days later he said he'd found three or four who were studying opera singing in Modena, and one from out of town, who performed in piano bars but could sing classical tenor. Andrea Bocelli. By singing pop songs in piano bars, he'd developed a looseness that classical tenors usually didn't have. The other kids were too academic, but Andrea knew how to swing. We pieced together a demo as best we could, with me playing keyboards and a little bit of everything, and him singing.

I waited a few days, worked up my courage, got his phone number from the record company, and one morning I called Pavarotti at his home in Modena. Titti, one of his daughters, answered. I told her who I was, then heard her whisper in awe, "Mamma, it's Zucchero." Adua, Pavarotti's first wife, got on the phone and I asked her if I could talk to *il Maestro*.

At last I heard the famed, thundering voice, booming with his usual generosity: "You're brilliant, champ! My compliments!"

I didn't know how I should address him. Maestro? Signor Pavarotti? I opted to keep it simple and went with Luciano. Of course, I still used the polite form of address, which in Italian is *Lei*.

"I'd like to pay you a little visit."

"Of course. Come to Modena tomorrow morning at eleven. I'll meet you at my home."

Holy fuck, that was easier than I thought. I showed up at his house and we talked about all kinds of stuff—everything but the song. I told him I was originally from Roncocesi, near Reggio Emilia, and about my family. I told him I loved horses too. And naturally, we talked about food: *Al persott* (prosciutto), *i turtléin* (tortellini), Parmigiano Reggiano, balsamic vinegar, Lambrusco. We laughed and joked about the double entendre of the saying in Emiliano dialect: *Pan e persòtt, fic e lambròsc*—literally "Bread and ham, figs and wine," but in Italian slang, fic also means "cunt."

"Come on, stay and eat with us."

At lunch, there was also Panocia, Pavarotti's best friend, the one he played cards with—*briscola* was their game. I didn't dare explain the reason for my visit yet. After lunch and a nap, still sitting in his chair at the table, Pavarotti really softened up.

"Zucchero, how pleased I am that you've come for a visit."

"I'm here to ask a favor."

"Tell me, what is it?"

"I've written a song with you in mind."

"I know, I know. Your people from the record company came to see me in Philadelphia. But you know I can't do it. The music is really beautiful, but I beg you to understand: I just can't."

"I understand. But unless I record it with you, there's no reason for it to exist."

It was early February. The logs crackling in the fireplace made a beautiful fire that warmed the room, the table, and our hearts. I made a scene straight out of a Neapolitan melodrama.

"No, there's absolutely no reason for this song to exist."

I threw the cassette with the demo sung by Bocelli into the fire.

"You're crazy!" Pavarotti screamed. "Now what are you going to do? Such a beautiful song, and you've destroyed it forever. Why did you do it?"

Overwhelmed by the insistence of my request, the warmth of the fire, the abundant libations of Lambrusco, and my melodramatic gesture, he genuinely thought that tape was the only copy I had. But I had five more out in the car.

He continued, fraught with despair. "Even if I did want to do it, look. My schedule's full, I don't have time. You see? The only day off I have is August 19th."

"Fine. We'll do it August 19th. Maestro, I'll be expecting you."

My deadline for finishing the album was at the end of the month, which meant I was taking a big risk—but it was worth it.

Snorting and cursing, Pavarotti erased something on his calendar and wrote in pencil on the 19th: ZUCCHERO.

I did it!

"OK. But I don't know how this works. I've never done this before."

"I'll take care of everything. You, Maestro, will be sitting on your couch."

"But I'll be on vacation in Pesaro, at our summer house."

"Then we'll go there with Maurizietto Maggi's mobile studio— he's Umbi's younger brother. Corrado Rustici will engineer the recording. You'll be sitting comfortably on your couch. We'll boom a mike through the window, right to your face. We'll put headphones on you so you can hear the orchestra perfectly. The music will be prerecorded, so all you'll have to do is sing your part."

"OK. But what about the conductor?"

"I'll be the conductor, right by your side, Maestro. When I touch your arm with my hand, you start singing. When I step on your foot, you stop."

"You're a madman. But we'll give it a try. And stop calling me Maestro. It's getting on my nerves."

I returned home victorious.

August 19th

AFTER WE'D FINISHED RECORDING THE REST OF THE MUSIC, WE went TO London to lay down the orchestra tracks for 'Miserere.' The conductor was Michael Kamen, who, among his many accomplishments, did the orchestral arrangements for Pink Floyd's *The Wall*. He was a very modern, rock-oriented conductor with long hair, and gave us a fabulous arrangement for a 60-piece orchestra, which we recorded live.

We went back home to wait for the fateful day. By 10 in the morning on August 19th, the sound staff had everything set up and ready to go. We'd planned to record before lunch, so we wouldn't be bogged down by the meal.

Luciano had a different idea. "Let's take it slow, eh? And let's not start with that you-have-to-sing-now stuff. Otherwise we won't get very far."

Nicoletta was there. So was Signora Anna—fantastic. She'd been Pavarotti's nanny when he was little and his parents would bring him to Pesaro for summer vacations. By now she was an old woman, but she still cooked for Pavarotti.

"First, let's eat," said Pavarotti.

We sat down at the table. Rustici, Torpedine, and Tibaldi were there, too.

He yelled: "Signora Anna! *Tagliatella!*"

She came in carrying a huge platter of steaming *tagliatelle alla bolognese*—with the weather so hot and muggy we were melting. But there were also rivers of chilled Lambrusco. You were asking for trouble if you didn't eat and drink. As soon as Pavarotti's pasta got the least bit tepid, he didn't like it anymore. He wanted it steaming. When it began to cool, he'd toss it out the window, past the hedge, down a ditch facing his house, and call out, "Signora Anna, more *tagliatella!*" And she'd come in with another giant yellow trayful, yellow and steaming with the scent of *ragù* (meat and tomato sauce). He ate happily. Then came the second course, and to finish up, a couple *ciccioli* (fried pork rinds).

By now it was three o'clock. I was beginning to get jumpy, while Pavarotti took his nap, wrapped in his enormous colorful shawl. No one said anything. We just had to wait till he woke up. An hour later he woke with a start and remembered our recording session.

"Ah, yes, we have to do that thing. Come on, let's go in there."

We moved into the living room, the sound staff was ready. Pavarotti walked in wearing his headphones. We start, using the method we'd agreed on: arm and foot signals. I'd already recorded my vocals. Corrado Rustici made a rough mix and played it for us. Luciano raised a fuss.

"Nooo, that's not my voice. That's not what I sang. You guys had better watch out: No fooling around here."

I was embarrassed. And Pavarotti was known for having a hot temper.

"Maestro, it's the same level as Zucchero's voice."

"No, nooo. My voice doesn't sound like that. No more bullshit."

"But, sir, I'm the producer…"

"No more bullshit. Change it!"

An icy chill descended over stifling Pesaro! He didn't like the recording—he would never give his approval.

Corrado went out to the mobile studio and raised Pavarotti's voice a couple decibels higher than mine—it practically drowned out my voice. Then he came back in and played it for Pavarotti.

"Oooh, that's better!"

I kept the recording, which was technically unacceptable, with his voice much higher than mine in the mix. I sound like a nightingale compared to him. But we could work out a balance more or less, so that was the one we used.

"Fine, fine. That's enough, now."

The recording session was over, but he kept on singing. He was in a good mood, so I felt brave enough to make my final request.

"Listen, Luciano, now we've got to make a video of this song."

"What's a video?" he asked.

I had the whole thing already organized.

"There's a church called San Francesco del Mille, less than an hour's drive from here. All you have to do is come there for half an hour and do some playback."

"What's playback?"

"It's when you pretend to sing, but you just move your lips."

His curiosity grew—he knew absolutely nothing about the world of pop music.

"Luciano, you come there, pretend to sing, and they film you."

"Gee, I dunno. Alright, I guess."

It was time for dinner. He liked drinking his Varnelli dry anisette, a liqueur produced in Pesaro, in a glass full of ice. Then he lit up a Toscano cigar. Here he is a tenor, the greatest in the world—I didn't think he drank or smoked. He crashed on the hammock, fell right to sleep. We didn't even manage to say goodbye.

The next day Tino, our Peruvian driver and assistant, a real good guy, took Pavarotti to the church we'd chosen for the location. *Il Maestro* had a portable chair, a sort of trestle that he sat on—his weight caused his hips to ache—while we surveyed the location. He refused makeup, telling the makeup girl, "Bring me some corks." When they brought them back, he burned them and painted himself with the residue. He was happy, singing all the while. He put burnt cork on his beard and on his bald spot—like the old theater performers from once upon a time. I couldn't believe it: Pavarotti, the world-famous star, the global tenor, coloring himself with pitch-black burnt cork. He sang, was very patient, happy, and so glad that I even managed to have him put on a monk's habit, like me. A couple of fat friars: happy, crazy, shuffling the *briscola* cards of the world in a carnival from Modena to Reggio, the tenor and the rock singer, opera and the blues.

We were on our way home. It was eight o'clock.

Luciano: "Let's eat, eh?"

We stopped at a simple trattoria with yellow paper napkins, the kind I used to wrap cold cuts in when I was a boy.

"Luciano, it would be nice to present this song together, me and you, with the orchestra. And maybe we could even invite some of our artist friends—you could get someone from opera, I could ask Brian May from Queen, or Sting. A pop and opera crossover—that sums up 'Miserere' to a tee."

"Zucchero, you sly dog. That's a wonderful idea. Yes, let's do it!"

We took a red pen and began jotting down ideas for the show on a sheet of yellow paper.

"Let's have it at my farm," he said. "Pavarotti International."

It was in Modena, on via Stradella, with its own restaurant.

"We'll do it there," Pavarotti said. "I'll call the orchestra. Who are you going to call?"

We planned the whole thing just like that, in two shakes of a lamb's tail. Nicoletta and Torpedine, being quick, immediately realized how big this could be. As did Polygram. Soon everybody was rushing around to make it happen. Torpedine and Nicoletta were in charge of the organizing phase: stage and lights. Polygram invited all the European general managers; someone called the BBC and proposed a live broadcast. The whole thing came together in record time. I called Brian May, he accepted; Sting said yes, too. Luciano invited

Lucio Dalla. This was the kind of thing that happens, because it has to.

Everything was set. Then the night before, Luciano suddenly asks, "I don't have to sing, do I?"

It was my fault for showing him playback, wasn't it?

"I can't sing this live because in five days I'm having a concert at the Metropolitan. I can't risk straining my voice."

"But Luciano, we'll all be singing live. And you're the world's most famous tenor."

"No, no. I'm doing playback—it's just television."

He was adamant. There was no way to change his mind, so we had a round piece of Plexiglas set up in front of the microphone, a transparent disk that hid the movement of his lips so you could only see the rest of his face. He was no expert at playback. Apart from our video, he'd never done it before. With the TV cameras in front of him, behind him, and all around him, you could tell he was just pretending to sing. So not to risk straining his voice, he made a fool of himself.

It was a dreadful night, under a stormy sky. It had rained non-stop from that morning to nine p.m., just before showtime, and we were at his farm, which was definitely not the place to put on such a big show. Mud everywhere. Ladies in evening gowns and high heels, from England, Germany, wives and girlfriends of record company big shots, the press—everyone in the muck. No dressing rooms for the artists. After all that; the downpour, the mud splashing all over the place, and the playback, the first edition of *Pavarotti and Friends* did not make what you would call a stunning debut.

Grappa and Prozac

AFTER THE RELEASE OF *MISERERE*, I DID TWO DATES AT THE FORUM IN Milano and two at the Palaeur in Rome, all four shows sold out. A summer full of stadiums awaited. But something was happening to me, I didn't know what. I was in deep shit again.

Corrado Rustici, the band, and the Americans were coming to Italy. The stadiums were booked, the posters were hung. Sixteen concerts in Italian stadiums. A nightmare. The famished maws of the people opening wide, thousands of teeth gnawing at me, tearing me apart.

I awake soaked with sweat. Afraid. In the clutches of an outrageous panic attack. I get up. It doesn't stop. The literature on the topic says if a panic attack lasts more than 15 minutes, the risk of suicide increases. The stronger and longer they are, the more you succumb. Mine weren't that violent, but they were constant. They would last all day—I was afraid of going on tour, onstage, of dealing with people.

This thing has always haunted me. Today I can handle it and control those fears, because I know what I am. Back then I didn't.

I asked Torpedine to cancel the tour. He said I was crazy. The posters, the rents for the stadiums, the musicians under contract. There would be penalties to pay, tons of problems.

"We'll have all the promoters in Italy sending doctors to examine you. Sixteen, as a matter of fact. You can't cancel a tour over panic attacks—they don't even know what panic attacks are. Maybe a broken arm or leg, that might work. But you're rich and famous; they all want you. It's gonna be tough to prove you're depressed. So, dear Zucchero, canceling the tour would be a major financial loss, as well as a stain on your image."

I decided to check into the hospital in San Rossore. I went to see Dr. Cassano, a luminary in his field. An austere man, normal to excess, almost unpleasant. He receives me. I tell him my story.

"No. Mr. Fornaciari, you must do this tour. If you cave in now, you'll never have another chance."

I was bent on checking in.

In the meantime, Mino Vergnaghi, a friend of mine, flew in from

London. I'd asked him to be one of my backup singers on the tour and act as my right-hand man. We go to dinner. I'm pale and taciturn. Convinced the only solution is hospitalization. I'd already told Angela I couldn't take care of the girls.

We eat. Mino pours me some wine.

"I'll be with you. One way or another, things will work out."

No way, I still wasn't into it.

He kept pouring wine in my glass, then this sweet grappa from Bassano del Grappa, in one of those long, dark bottles—I still have some at home. We partied until the wee hours. I was stoned on grappa and Prozac.

Mino asks me, "Would you go onstage now?"

I was like, "Yeah, I'd give 'em hell!"

He'd found the key. I could do it. We rehearsed and set out. On one condition: We started the tour in Bassano, where we loaded five cases of magical grappa onto the truck—the trick that got me through the tour.

At five o'clock, Mino would come into my dressing room while I was having my massage. We'd eat, then he'd start pouring me grappa. This went on until nine o'clock: showtime. At which point I thought I was doing fine. But every night, as soon as I got to the third song in the set, "Il Pelo nell'Uovo," I had a panic attack. It lasted the whole song. Every night, all 16 dates.

I Believe So

OF COURSE, PAVAROTTI COULDN'T JOIN US ON TOUR, SO I NEEDED SOMEone to replace him for those 16 shows. I thought of the tenor Andrea Bocelli. Talented and fun. He clicked with the group right off the bat—a really great guy.

When his moment came, he would be rolled out on a platform,

sitting at a piano, and he would sing 'Miserere.' I fell in love with him as an artist at rehearsal. He's able to combine a marvelous temperament with a voice that gives you goosebumps. When he sings, he conveys overwhelming emotional power. I told Torpedine how much Andrea impressed me. It might not work in Italy, but the pop-opera crossover might appeal to American audiences.

"I believe so," Torpedine said.

Too bad no one else was interested in it—or rather, no one understood it. None of the major record companies, or my manager really understood. For the time being, anyway.

Caterina Caselli, of Sugar Music, saw my determination and enthusiasm, and while she didn't totally believe in the project, she agreed to a record with Andrea on the condition that I would write and produce it. I agreed, so long as she would make sure the single was presented at the Young Artists section of the Sanremo music festival in Italy. She said that would be impossible. I insisted. I called her from Salzburg—from Mozart's hometown, I was still pushing for Andrea.

"If you bring him to Sanremo, I'm ready."

"I'll try," said Caterina.

I wrote 'Il Mare Calmo Della Sera' ('The Calm Evening Sea') together with Giampietro Felisatti and Gloria Nuti. I brought it to Caselli and she got it on the program at Sanremo. Standing ovation for Andrea when he hit those high notes during the finale. He won the Young Artists section, which meant the following year he'd have a chance to compete in the Big Artists section.

The next year though, "I'm not going. I'm not going to Sanremo with this song—I don't like it," Andrea said as he walked into my house before that year's festival. "The arrangement is all electronic, there's a drum machine. I don't like it. Why should I go to Sanremo? I want to sing something different."

The song was 'Con Te Partirò' ('I'll Leave with You'). It was a pretty powerful song.

Bocelli hadn't understood the song's potential and didn't like it. I insisted and insisted some more.

"You've gotta go with this one, Andrea. It's an awesome song, believe me."

He wound up doing it. The first night he sang without much conviction. I called him at his hotel at two a.m. and said, "Look, Andrea. If you're going to sing it like that, you might as well go home, because you're not convincing anyone. You don't believe in it, and it shows. Do whatever you want, but as long as you're there, put some energy into it; pour some blood into it!"

The second night went a bit better. I called him again at two a.m.

"We're still not quite there."

The third night went great. Then came the finals. Andrea gave a wonderful performance. Standing ovation. I was blown away, tears in my eyes. He was a big hit.

Lunisiana Soul

BEFORE SETTING OUT ON THE *MISERERE* TOUR, I MET ENRICO FERRI, then mayor of Pontremoli. He wanted me to move there. Why?

"Because it's good living here. And having someone like you would be a boon for the community. I'll make you an honorary citizen."

He began hounding me and taking me around to see the local marvels: old mills, castles, ancient villages, and villas flaunting frescoes. Wonderful places, I have to admit. But at the time, I was dying of solitude in that little house of mine in Avenza, and couldn't see myself sitting in one of those huge halls all by myself. It wasn't for me. I'm not the type for luxury; it's not part of my culture.

That May, my surveyor friend Lucio and I rode our motorcycles toward Pontremoli. We climbed a hill, and from there I saw a valley with a river flowing through it: the Verde, a tributary of the

Magra River. There was also a run-down farmhouse, an old mill. It reminded me of Ireland. I wanted to see this place. I parked my bike and lay down on the grass. The sound of the water, the cool air of the valley, the birds in flight. My childhood. I felt as if I'd always been there. For the first time in a long time, I was at peace. I was getting a grip on myself. It took me six months to buy that neglected property and its tumbledown homestead. It was owned by 13 siblings who had emigrated to France, Belgium, and the UK, and the mill had been in disuse for who knows how long. Sometimes sheep grazed there.

For the moment, I left Lucio to begin the renovation and went on tour. He had a new roof put on where the old one had collapsed, and things began taking on a semblance of home. After the tour, I moved to Pontremoli and got directly involved. It was great playing architect and going around to the second-hand shops looking for furniture. This will be the nightstand; this, the armchair; this, the bed. Setting up house the way I wanted it provided soothing relief for my suffering. At last I had a new interest. Creating an atmosphere that reflected my past in the countryside of Emilia, with a blend of New Orleans style, was a dream come true.

Donkeys and Paparazzi

I HAD A DONKEY MARE. SHE WAS HUGE, A BLACK-AND-WHITE PINTO. Beautiful animal. An old-timer had given her to me; he couldn't keep her anymore. I kept her alone for a couple of weeks, then said to myself, she needs a male for company. I got her a male Sardinian donkey. But I hadn't considered that she was big and he was so little. He'd chase after her with a raging hard-on, braying away. He'd try to mount her, but *wham!* All he got was a kick in the face.

I called him Camillo and her Lucia, after two of some of my dearest friends. Very outgoing types. Poor Camillo. He was after Lucia all day long, suffering like a dog, with his massive dick sticking out.

"We've got to help him," I said to Mino Vergnaghi.

We pretty much made a game out of it and put her in a ditch—that way Camillo could reach her. Then we had to help Camillo. At university, they taught me: "Take hold of the donkey's penis and guide it into the female. That's the best way."

I tried, but it still wasn't working.

"Mino, we need to build a ramp for Camillo."

We built a wooden ramp. Then we tied Lucia to a tree. I knelt to grab Camillo's dick. It was hot as hell. I was in my bathing suit, wearing gloves. Mino was holding Lucia, but then he suddenly took off.

"You bastard! You son of a bitch!" he cried.

It was a paparazzo.

Mino leaped over the fence, grabbed him, and beat the shit out of him. He got the roll of film back, and good thing, too. The guy had taken pictures of me in my bathing suit, kneeling beside the donkey with a hard-on!

"We Have to Write a Hit!"

HENRY PADOVANI CALLED ME FROM PARIS. HE'D BEEN THE ORIGINAL guitar player for the Police and was still good friends with Sting. He used to drive the van for the band, back in the day—he was the only one sober enough to get them to the hotel at the end of the night, where they all crashed in one room. Now he was working with Miles Copeland, drummer Stewart Copeland's brother and Sting's manager. He'd left the Police before they made it big. Unlucky him. Every year Henry and Miles held week-long workshops at Miles's chateau in Bordeaux, amid the vineyards. It was a fairy-tale setting—songwriters and singers all brainstorming. Miles got publishing rights.

I arrived at the chateau at dinnertime. A huge table was laid out, with a throne at the head—that's where Miles sat. Cher was there, along with other American and British artists. I went to bed. The next morning at eight, Padovani woke us all up, knocking on everyone's door, yelling, "Wake up! Wake up! Wake up!" After a frugal breakfast, the songwriters were paired off at random—one for music, one for lyrics—and sent off to rooms with a drum machine and a keyboard to write a song. I couldn't work that way. I work the way I fucking want to. And what was this eight o'clock in the morning bullshit? No, all these rules weren't for me. But I gave it a shot.

They teamed me up with a red-haired guy called Robert. He'd written lyrics for Aretha Franklin. He was gay and somewhat overenthusiastic.

"Come on, Zucchero," he said, "give me some beats on the drum machine. Let's work out a melody. We have to write a hit!"

"This isn't the way I write hits," I said. "This stuff takes time."

But he was the typical American: "We can do it! We can do it!"

I played a B-minor chord, a little bluesy, and started to get into it. He leaped like a cricket and started singing.

"Holy fuck!" he cried. "We've got a hit!"

"Hey, man, I just started."

"If the Divinity herself hears this one"—he was talking about Aretha Franklin—"she's gonna have a hit on her hands!"

I felt like I was in a madhouse. I'd played one freakin' chord, for God's sake.

One night after dinner, Miles Copeland asked me, "What are you up to?"

"Making a new record."

"Have you got a manager?"

"Yeah, but his contract's up. I don't know what's next. I'm checking out various—"

Miles took me by the arm and announced with a theatrical gesture, "I'll be your manager!"

He was already Sting's manager. And the brother of Stewart Copeland, the drummer from the Police. Very intelligent man. Degree in economics. Even spoke Arabic. His father had been a CIA agent, his mother worked for the British secret service. He managed R.E.M., and Sting after the Police broke up.

Naturally Torpedine was pissed off. I was sorry, too. He had done so much for me in the beginning. But now I needed someone with a broader view, someone to help me gain access to the world. Copeland lived in Los Angeles and wanted complete control over operations in North and South America. Padovani would head the attack in Europe, and Torpedine would take care of things in Italy.

Dad's Still Cutting the Hedge

I WAS IN AVENZA WHEN ONE DAY MY DAD CAME BY. MY MOTHER WASN'T with him. He was alone and had taken the train. My brother had warned me: "Dad's walking with a slight limp. He says his pinky toe hurts." I'd seen him hobbling around, but I never figured it was anything to worry about. Another time I got a call from my mother. She was all worked up: "Papà was riding his bike back from Cavazzoli and fell in a ditch. He came home with one arm all bloody and torn up." My father didn't drink. I was beginning to grow concerned. It was summer. He loved to cut the hedges by hand, with shears. He came to cut mine in Pontremoli and ruined them all. Without saying a word to anybody, he'd be out there at six in the morning, chopping away. I wanted to let them grow, but no, they were "too wild!" he said. I let him have his fun. He too appreciated the countryside of the Pontremoli Valley. It reminded him of our roots in Emilia.

One morning he went for a bike ride on his Graziella. He came back with his knees all cut up, carrying the broken handlebars. Another fall. My brother Lauro made an appointment for him at the hospital in Reggio Emilia. X-rays, CAT scan. "It was like lying in a coffin," he said.

Diagnosis: Progressive supranuclear palsy.

"What's that?" I asked the doctor.

"It's a rare degenerative disease of the nervous system. The electric circuits in the brain shut down. He still wants to do things, but his brain can't make his body do what he wants it to do."

The doctor explained what the illness would entail.

"He'll reach a point where he tries to swallow, but the food may enter the lungs instead of the esophagus and his stomach, and that could cause aspiration pneumonia, if an infection were to develop."

I spoke to my dad on the phone. He was losing the power of speech. He screamed but had trouble pronouncing the words. I had no idea what he was trying to say.

We had to explain the situation to my mother. We were as delicate as we could be, but the news came as a terrible shock to her. My father could still manage to do some things, but began spending more and more time on the couch, just watching TV. When he did go into the garden, he had trouble getting around and had to lean on something. He got worse. We had a woman brought in to give him assistance. My mother grew depressed. Luckily, my brother Lauro was always there for them. He took care of our dad as if he were a baby. Lauro was married and had a couple of kids—they helped cheer up my mom a bit. I could only help financially, since I was always on the road. I'm profoundly grateful to my brother for what he did. Without him, things would have totally fallen apart. "OK, champ," he'd tell our dad, "let's go for a ride!" and take him out in the wheelchair. He spoon-fed him.

My father never complained. He had lots of visitors, too. "Hey, Pino. How's it going?" And even though he could barely talk anymore, he still laughed. He would muster up his strength and stammer to my mother, "Fix coffee for our guests." He was always very hospitable.

When things got very bad, we had him brought here, to Pontremoli. He'd have his caregiver wheel him out to work in the vineyard early in the morning, just as he had always done. He ruined half of it, but again, I let him have his fun. It helped him to be in a place like this. I could tell he enjoyed being here.

Woodstock

MILES COPELAND WAS INTENT ON BECOMING MY MANAGER. HE traveled from Los Angeles to my house in Avenza and asked what it would take for him to get the job.

"Woodstock," I said. "I want to play at Woodstock."

I figured it would be impossible, but I was testing him. Yet, despite it being late, with the lineup already decided, Miles Copeland brought me to Woodstock (it was the 25th anniversary of the original festival, in August 1994). First he arranged a promotional tour in South America, where I received international star treatment. Then it was off to Woodstock.

From the helicopter above the festival I could see an enormous mass of people, all camping out. A crowd of at least 400,000. I couldn't get over it. And I was the only Italian artist on the bill! All my idols were there: Santana, Joe Cocker, Crosby, Stills & Nash, Bob Dylan, Peter Gabriel. My dressing room was next to theirs. The Red Hot Chili Peppers were there too—that year they were really big. Along with Aerosmith and Radiohead.

I played for 45 minutes. My set included 'Diavolo in Me,' 'Madre Dolcissima,' 'Con le Mani,' and 'Diamante.' I sang a little in English, a little in Italian. Miles had brought the bosses from A&M to see the show. They wound up signing me—one of the most important American labels. They later distributed *Spirito DiVino* in the United States. Full steam ahead!

Woodstock was a truly important experience. In August 1969, I was just a kid flunking my way through middle school, but the music played at Woodstock echoed around the world and fired the imaginations of provincial kids like me. It was the epic musical event of my generation, the height of hippie culture, bringing together the youth of the world for three days of peace and music.

I got the original album and played it so much I wore it out, listening to songs like Richie Havens's improvised version of 'Freedom'; Jimi Hendrix's 'The Star-Spangled Banner,' performed with such power and all those eerie sounds, protesting the violence of American policies in the Vietnam War and on the social front at home; and the howls of Joe Cocker. Sounds and images that have been carved into our memory. Twenty-five years later, I was there too—along with Michael Lang, who'd organized the first edition, and lots of other heroes from the world of rock music.

It's hard to explain the sensation of taking part in an event of such magnitude, one that goes way beyond your wildest dreams. I was there, at Woodstock. Representing Roncocesi, Italy. Probably the only other time I experienced the same sensation was when another dream of mine came true: the construction of the big wheel for the water mill on the north side of my property, Lunisiana Soul in Pontremoli. I was obsessed with it, and hired architect Tiziano Lera and a team of engineers, who made infinite calculations. Nowadays anyone can build a skyscraper, but lost are the technical secrets of building a water wheel like the one that makes the water at my house sing like the Mississippi, inspiring me to write new blues tunes.

Spirito DiVino

IT WAS TIME TO WRITE THE MATERIAL FOR MY NEXT ALBUM, *SPIRITO DiVino*, and I spent the entire winter in Avenza doing just that. I had

Miles Copeland and Henry Padovani listen to the demos, and they were psyched. There was a balance between soul ballads and blues energy. We met in Los Angeles with Corrado Rustici, who lived in San Francisco. We worked inside the A&M Records studios, located in the old Charlie Chaplin headquarters. Miles was glad to have us in Los Angeles, where he lived and could have direct control. I wanted to do an album with the flavors of New Orleans. I wanted to go to Louisiana. They hesitated at first, but finally gave in. Then, as usual, we would go to Umbi's in Modena to record the Italian vocal tracks. The final mix would be done in London—just to keep things simple—at Beatles producer and arranger George Martin's Air Studios.

We began recording in Los Angeles. Stewart Copeland, the drummer from the Police, was also there. After I got to my hotel the first night, there was an earthquake. I saw the armoires rattling against the walls. A good start. Dan Aykroyd invited me to perform at the House of Blues and introduced me with these words: "You know how rarely I come down from the hills anymore, but tonight I'm here to present to you an Italian blues brother." He liked me because I was Italian, and because I'd played with Miles Davis, Eric Clapton, and Ray Charles. The concert was a tribute to John Belushi in a veritable temple of the blues, and taking part in it was a true blessing for a bluesman.

From there I flew to New Orleans. I had never been there before, though naturally I had heard a lot about it. I had the feeling I'd always lived there. We worked in a broken-down studio called the Boiler Room. It looked like someone's garage, but it was efficient. Bourbon Street. Bars and cafés on every corner, where people played live music. Incredible musicians. I didn't go back to New Orleans for many years after Hurricane Katrina, because I was afraid it wouldn't be the way I remembered it. It has a tormenting allure—the strip joints, clubs, restaurants.

I'd heard a song by Peter Gabriel a few months earlier, 'Digging in the Dirt,' and it had this funky guitar that drove me crazy—a beautiful sound and rhythm. I went to look up the credits and saw the name Leo Nocentelli. I thought, "How can it be that I don't know this guy if he's Italian and that good? Maybe he moved to England when he was little. Otherwise I'd know him."

So, I went to find out who Leo Nocentelli was. Which was when I discovered that he'd been the leader of the Meters, a pioneer funk group from the 1960s who inspired so many others that followed. Leo was from New Orleans. His father was Sicilian; his mother, Creole. He still lived there and was very well known among local musicians. I asked around. One night by chance I met up with Julius Farmer in a café, and he helped me find Leo.

"Hey, man, how are you? I'm Leo."

"I've heard some of your stuff. It's great. Congratulations. I'd like you to play on a couple tracks for my new album."

"Sure!"

In the meantime, Leo's wife showed up. A blonde.

"I'm Leo's manager," she said.

"So are you the one I need to talk to?" I ask.

"Yes."

We discussed his fee.

"Would five hundred dollars a day be too much to ask?"

She was embarrassed because they had never been paid that much before.

"Is it too much?"

"Not at all!"

He came to the studio and did some beautiful things. And with that voice of his, I even had him do the opening vocals on one song, 'Senza Rimorso.'

The record also contains 'Pane e Sale,' with beautiful lyrics by Francesco De Gregori. I'd gone to a concert of his at the Ponchielli Theater in Cremona to ask him to write them. There's 'X Colpa di Chi' and 'Il Volo,' which was a big hit in Europe, Number One in France. There's 'Papà Perché,' dedicated to my father, whose illness had already begun. And 'Così Celeste,' which is one of the best-known and best-loved songs among my fans, along with 'Diamante.'

Here's how 'X Colpa di Chi' was born: Sisto Fontanili, a friend of mine, came over to my house. He's got an ear for Emilian dialect and anthropological sensitivity. He told me there was this madman by the name of Calcaterra, who called himself the World President of Ecology. He went around proselytizing. Sisto said it was crazy stuff. He put on a tape: "Wake up, the world is sick. Wake up! And whose fault is it? Cock-a-doodle-doo! Whose fault is it?" He went on ranting and raving about ecology, the environment.

I said, "Fuck, man. That's perfect for the opening of a fast, powerful song." And I wanted his voice for it!

"I'll bring him over."

One day Calcaterra shows up, totally off his rocker. He was one of these guys who stands in front of the Parliament all day to protest. He was slovenly. I brought him up to Umbi's in Modena and had him record that rant of his. Then I gave him some money—it was only right—and he was all happy.

"Oh, make sure you give me a credit for this," he said. "I want my name on it."

That's what gave me the spark for 'X Colpa di Chi'—I had already written the music for it. "*Chi chi chi chicchirichì! Stanotte voglio stare acceso e dire sempre di sì... Oh, avanti o popolo con la Lambretta rossa, che intanto il tempo passa e lei non torna più.*" ("Cock-a-doodle-doo! Tonight, I'm gonna be fired up and keep sayin' yes...Rock on, people, in your red Lambretta, but she's not comin' back.") Humor, sarcasm, funk. "*Funky gallo, come sono bello stamattina. Non c'è più la mia morosa e sono più leggero di una piuma.*" ("Funky rooster, I'm lookin' good this morning. My love is gone but I'm feelin' light as a feather.") The borderline that unites—or perhaps divides—the sacred from the profane. In a kooky, upbeat way I explore a world where deep roots and healthy values coexist with revelry and transgression. "*Oh, avanti o popolo con la Lambretta rossa...*"

One day when we were in New Orleans, I asked to go visit the mansion where they filmed *Gone With the Wind*, which was still intact. Inside there was a piano, clothes, furniture; outside, cotton fields, big oak trees along the driveway, and the banks of the Mississippi. The river flowing by. That's where I got the idea for the musical phrase "*Per colpa di chi, chi, chi, chi, chicchi chiricchi.*" And holy fuck, it worked. I used that madman Calcaterra's words to begin the song.

Afterward we took a boat ride in the muddy waters of the alligator-filled swamps along the Mississippi. We ate crawfish and fried catfish, typical Louisiana dishes. Much the same as in Boretto, on the River Po in Italy, where my father used to take me. We went to a church service to hear a gospel choir, the same one that appeared on the record. I called Johnny Johnson, Chuck Berry's legendary pianist. Clarence Clemons was still around as well. I also called Jeff Beck, the guitarist who can pick up an out-of-tune guitar with a crooked neck and make it sound astonishingly good. He'd replaced Clapton when he left the Yardbirds. All these great musicians contributed to make a fine album, which, as always, we finished at Umbi's and had mixed in London.

And the funky rooster? Easy. I'd been given a Leghorn rooster, not too big, typical of the Italian variety. He was young and lively, bursting with energy. Every morning he'd start mounting the hens and be at it all day long. The others were much more laid back. He was the only one I saw fucking all the time. That's how that line popped into my mind: "*Funky gallo, come sono bello stamattina...*" It was born out of scenes, images. Funky rooster because the rooster was amusing. Plus, it sounded good in Italian: *Funky gallo*. It really caught on and became a catchphrase for a lot of people in Italy. Kids especially started calling me *Funky gallo*. Three years later, that rooster died.

He was the only one that had the right to a natural death. As for the others, we wrung their necks and they wound up in the pot.

'Voodoo Voodoo' came from a piano phrase written by Luciano Luisi, my keyboard player. That was the beginning. Then I went to New Orleans and visited the home of the Queen of Voodoo, a Creole woman who performed rituals with chicken feet, blood, and pins. I imagined I needed Voodoo to fuck this chick who I'd had my eye on. I start out singing, *"Lascia che il mio Voodoo lavori, eh! Funziona con tutte ma non con te!"* ("Let my Voodoo work, eh! It works on all the girls, but not on you!") And later on, *"Latte di letto, talismani e fiori. Comincio a fare il rito, un filtro speciale fatto apposta per te."* ("Milk in bed, talismans and flowers. I begin performing the ritual, a special filter made just for you.")

'Così Celeste' sounds like it could be dedicated to a woman, especially when I sing "She's my baby," but it's about faith. The lyrics go: *"Un altro sole, quando viene sera, sta colorando l'anima mia. Potrebbe essere di chi spera, ma nel mio cuore è solo mia."* ("When evening comes, another sun colors my spirit. It may be the color of someone who hopes, but in my heart, she's mine alone.") It was Pavarotti's favorite song of mine. He couldn't quite manage the chorus the way I do it, with a flip-flop in my voice, because there's a little swing to it. "Hey, how do you do that one?" he asked. Every time we saw each other he tried but still couldn't get it, and I would sing it again for him.

I'm somewhere in between the sacred and the profane, the Communist and the Church. I felt something in one place, then the same thing in the other. I grew up in the middle. To this day, I can't bring myself to believe in just one or the other. *"Solo una sana e consapevole libidine salva dallo stress e dall'azione cattolica."* ("Only a healthy and self-aware sex drive can save you from stress and Catholic Action.") I don't believe in the Pope. I don't believe in the bishops. I don't believe in the Church or any other institution. I've got more faith in the country priests who are forced to run their little churches on nickels and dimes. It's true, I'm attracted to churches. Wherever I go, all over the world, alone, when there are no services, I cross that threshold. I always visit the churches. I stay inside for ten minutes, smell the incense, light a candle, and it makes me feel good.

Back when I'd just finished refurbishing my place at Pontremoli, I remember it was summer and I'd brought my daughters there. There are some beautiful natural springs and a little waterfall in a village nearby. I like to go swimming in isolated streams and creeks where there are hardly any people—no one at all is even better. Alongside the springs stands an eleventh-century church, with its rectory, which is pretty much in ruins, although the church itself is basically intact. At one time, it was used as a hospital. While the girls were having a swim, I ducked beneath one of the poplars to take a nap or smoke a cigarette. I started staring at the church, at the huge closed door with its big lock and chain. There was never anyone around. I was curious. I wanted to see inside. I won't hide the fact that once I went there with this sort of picklock device and tried to jimmy the lock. It didn't work. Another time I tried to peer inside through the holes in the wall, but I couldn't see anything. One day I rode there on my Harley Davidson. By myself. I parked. Had my usual cigarette, meditating a bit, then I took off on my bike again. But I turned back. I took the gold-colored key from the Harley Davidson and tried to open the lock on the church door with it. It opened. I went in. Everything inside had been robbed. The altar was completely ruined. There was nothing left. I did manage to get in, but there was no meaning there, that's clear. But I ask myself: Why am I so attracted to churches? And why did I go back that time? And how could the key to my bike have opened that lock?

I remember one of the last times my father, who never went to church in his life, came to have lunch with us in Pontremoli. His illness was already at an advanced stage, and soon it would be Easter. Normally, when the priest came to bless the house, my father would bar him from entering and tell him to beat it. That day, however, when the priest came to give his Easter blessing, my dad let him in, and out of respect wanted to get up, but his illness prevented it. His eyes were glossy. For the first time in my life, I saw my dad cross himself. He understood now; he had been diagnosed. Here's what I sing in 'Papà Perché' ('Dad, Why?'): "*Papà perché il sangue non mi va in vino? Perché invece di sentire questo dolore non mi ubriaco? Perché papà, papà perché non ho uno spirito divino? Se fossi divino ti aiuterei. mi manchi tu e arranco lungo le strade così inutilmente. Ho sempre un po' di blues in fondo agli occhi, c'è sempre un po' di blu in questo cielo, ho sempre un po' di blues per te.*" ("Dad, why doesn't my blood turn to wine? Why don't I just get drunk instead of feeling this pain? Why, Dad, don't I have a divine spirit? If I were divine, I'd help you. I miss you and crawl uselessly down these streets. I've always had a little of the blues in the back of my eyes, there's always a little bit of blue in this sky, I've always got some blues for you.")

Dad, to you I dedicate the most important thing I've done in life: my blues. Divine spirit.

Then there was 'Il Volo' ('The Flight'). That was for my wife. "*Ho camminato per le strade col sole dei tuoi occhi…ci vuole un attimo per dirsi addio. Spara.*" ("I've walked the streets in the sunlight of your eyes…it takes a second to say goodbye. Fire!")

Angela shot me down alright.

I'd like to line up all the songs I ever dedicated to our love. And make her weep with emotion.

You Know a Guy Called Bono?

LUCIANO CALLED ME FOR THE SECOND EDITION OF *PAVAROTTI & FRIENDS* and said, "Do you know a guy called Bono? Bono Box? Vox? Do you know him personally?"

"Yes, I've worked with him. I can try to get in touch."

"Alright, then come on over to Pesaro tomorrow and we'll call him together."

Pesaro. The usual pasta feast.

"C'mon, let's call him. I've got his number. You talk first."

"Hi, Bono," I said. "This is Zucchero."

He was very cordial. "I realize the Maestro is insisting I come. But we're a rock band, and the band is against me doing these…basically…classical things. Even if personally I'd be into it. But I've got to answer to my band. There are four of us; if three say no, then it's no. I'm sorry, but unfortunately I can't come."

Luciano: "Lemme talk to him, lemme talk!"

"Bono," he said, "if you don't come, I'll tell everyone you refused to do a charity gig, a fundraiser for child victims of war."

He's crazy, I thought. This was Bono from U2. I was about to faint.

"Look, Bono, you've got to come. And if you don't, I'll tell everyone you don't practice what you preach."

Two days later, Pavarotti and his wife, Nicoletta, headed off to Dublin, cameraman in tow. He went to Bono's house, knocked on the door, and had their entire encounter filmed. I don't know how he did it, but he convinced him.

Bono came down, we had dinner: *tagliatelle*, as usual. Then they—not me—went for a swim in the pool. Bono jumped in with a lit cigar in his mouth. We were all feeling cheery.

Luciano made a habit of calling to ask for advice on rounding up guests for *Pavarotti & Friends*. "Well, now. What do you think about so-and-so?" One day he called and said, "You know this guy called Bov, Bovi, something like that."

"You mean David Bowie?"

"Yeah, that's the one. Is he any good?"

Ha!

"You want to call him?"

"Gee, maybe we could get him to come."

He never did come.

Sorry, Aretha

IN 1998, PAVAROTTI WAS NAMED MUSICARES PERSON OF THE YEAR. HE received that honor the night before he got his Grammy Legend Award. And the night before that, he invited me and Antonia, my Anglo-Brazilian assistant, to his Central Park South co-op for dinner. He did the cooking himself—he whipped out the *ciccioli*, salamis, boxes of spaghetti, and bottles of Lambrusco he had stowed in his suitcase.

While Luciano was cooking, Antonia went to the bathroom and came back with a couple dozen burnt corks. She was going to throw them away. But Nicoletta intervened.

"You're crazy. Those are makeup for tomorrow night's show."

The following evening, a great dinner was held in honor of the artists, attended by the upper crust of the music business. Pavarotti had invited his musician pals to sing a tribute to him. They included Sting, Stevie Wonder, even Aretha Franklin. There was a full-size orchestra.

At the afternoon rehearsal, I sang 'Va' Pensiero' and all went well. Last to sing was Aretha, the gospel, soul, and rhythm & blues legend. Pavarotti wanted me to keep him company while he got into the rehearsal. As for me, I couldn't wait to hear Aretha sing. She'd been an idol of mine ever since I was a kid. She's known as the Queen of Soul because she has the power to inject a dose of soul into anything she sings, not to mention her fantastic vocal skills. The State of Michigan declared her voice a natural resource. Now there I was, working with her. Another dream come true. I was happy, curious, thrilled—like any fan faced with his heroine. She'd always been my favorite singer. She started off with the aria 'Nessun Dorma'—her tribute to Pavarotti.

When she came to the finale, where she sings *vincerò*, she dragged out the "o" instead of the "e," which didn't jibe with the Maestro or the orchestra—they were perfect, but she hit the wrong accent. Then she got mad. She's got character, a real panther.

"I'm not singing tomorrow night if this is what it's gonna be. Forget it. I'm Aretha Franklin."

The Maestro was embarrassed, intimidated—but not at fault, and well aware that he'd sung his part exactly as it was written. They tried again. When they came to the finale, she threw her microphone down and screamed, "Fuck you!" to the entire world, the Maestro, the orchestra, and Phil Ramone, the organizer.

"The orchestra's fine. She's the one hitting the wrong accent," I said to Luciano.

"Go tell her that."

"I'd have to be crazy, feisty as she is."

Ramone spoke up: "I know her well. She's a true professional. She'll really appreciate it. She'll be grateful to you for the rest of her life."

He was taking the piss out of me.

"Go ahead, do it," said Luciano.

I went.

"Sorry, Aretha…" and I explained the problem of the accents to her.

Her two fiery eyes flashed out at me. "You do your job and I'll do mine."

She snubbed me during the session for the official group photo, just walked away from me and Pavarotti, who was beside me. Then she looked over and mouthed, "Fuck you" to me.

I told the story to Sting. He told me the night before he'd knocked on the door of Aretha Franklin's dressing room because his wife, Trudie, wanted to take a picture with her. Aretha showed the utmost cordiality and kindness toward Trudie, but barely even took notice of him. "Hi, I'm Sting," he said. And she was like, "Yeah, I've heard that name somewhere." Man, what a tigress.

Years earlier, just after *Rispetto* was released, I was with Rustici in producer Narada Michael Walden's studio. He told us how he convinced Aretha and James Brown to record a duet of his song 'Gimme Your Love.' They were both late for the recording session. Narada was losing his patience. He waited and waited, but neither showed up. The usual for artists. Prima donnas. He made a round of calls and found out they were already at the studio. But where exactly? *Outside*. Both of them. In their respective limousines. Neither one wanted to be the first to walk in, and each was waiting for the other to make the first move.

'Va' Pensiero' at the White House

SPIRITO DIVINO WAS RELEASED ON THE SAME DAY WORLDWIDE. A FEW OF the songs—'Così Celeste,' "Il Volo,' 'Pane e Sale,' and 'Papà Perché'— also had English and Spanish versions. 'Il Volo' was a Number One single in France; and even in Germany it sold really well. Then in Belgium, the Netherlands, and Switzerland. *Spirito DiVino* went platinum in Europe. In Italy, I had two Number One hits, first 'X Colpa di Chi,' followed by 'Il Volo.'

Vasco Rossi called me. He'd just put out his latest album. "Zucchero," he said to me, "I want you to be my manager. Fuckin' hell, man. How'd you get back to Number One when the record came out six months ago? I wanna know!"

For the first time, I did what was almost a full-blown world tour. Miles Copeland introduced me to an English agent, who used to work with Sting and now works with me, Phil Banfield. I played New Orleans, New York, Las Vegas, Boston, Washington, DC, Chicago, Los Angeles, San Francisco, San Diego, Miami. And throughout South America: Buenos Aires, Santiago, Venezuela, Brazil.

In Washington, I was welcomed by the Clintons for dinner at the White House, along with Italian-Americans who financed their party and election campaigns. Miles Copeland received the request for me to sing for our community. I was in Venezuela and had three days off. I took the first flight out of Caracas.

Forty-five minutes after takeoff, the pilot announces, "Ladies and gentlemen, we'll be returning to Caracas due to technical difficulties. I apologize for the inconvenience."

Fuckin' hell! I'm afraid of flying, too. It was night by the time we reached Caracas—ambulances on the runway, firemen. Fuck! The plane screeched as it landed, sparks flying, like one of those disaster movies. I did not want to take off on that plane again. I no longer trusted Venezuelan aircraft: I wanted an American plane. I boarded a flight, didn't sleep the whole night, and got to Washington just in time. Customs checks were thorough, all the guitars had to be checked. That took a while. The Italian minister of foreign affairs, Lamberto Dini, was there to lend me a hand. I didn't have time to change. Just slipped on a black jacket in one of the White House bathrooms. Bill was making his entrance with Hillary. I sang 'Va' Pensiero.'

I'd been wanting to do that song for quite a while. The idea had come to me one night at our friends' place in Reggio Emilia. They had a piano.

"Only I'm not doing it as a waltz, like Verdi wrote it—fuck that. I want to make a ballad out of it."

Mastroianni and Mickey Rourke

I WOULD HAVE LIKED TO HAVE HAD THE GREAT FILM ACTOR Marcello Mastroianni in the 'Papà Perché' video. He was supposed to make a brief guest appearance at the end of the song. We were going to have him come on, give me a hug, then just stand there talking to me. I'd imagined him dressed as my father, wearing a farmer's hat.

I tried to find a contact for him. A man named Franco Giusti turned up. He spoke perfect Romanesco, the slang and dialect of Rome.

"OK, we'll see you tomorrow in Milano, at the hotel where Marcello's staying. We'll have something to eat and talk about it."

Mastroianni was gracious and elegant, a true gentleman. He'd begun to succumb to his illness; his hands trembled. He said he'd love to play this little part and showered me with compliments.

"Talk to Giusti about the details. Seeing as I'm in Milano, I could even do it tomorrow morning."

"Hey, Zu, we're in there," said Giusti. "We'll do this thing and do it fast."

My record company contacted him, then informed me that, given how much they were asking for a brief appearance in a three-and-a-half-minute video, I could forget about it. It wasn't like the old days anymore. The recording industry had gone into recession.

"All the love in the world for Mastroianni, but he's asking way too much," they said. "We can't make that kind of investment."

I called Giusti.

"No discounts," he told me. "Maybe some other time."

Not long after, I flew to New York. A guy at Newark airport was waiting to pick me up. He was dark, curly-haired, and buff.

"Ah, Zu! Welcome! Right on time—don't bother lookin' at your watch, New York's always open, all night."

He spoke a funny mix of Romanesco and American English.

"Who are you?" I asked.

"Giusti sent me."

Giusti—so he mysteriously knew when I'd be arriving.

Then the guy said, "You wanna meet Mickey Rourke? He could be in your video."

"I already did the video."

"Well, you can meet him anyhow."

Mickey Rourke—now there's an actor I've always really liked. He was a person I was curious to meet, partly because of his turbulent off-screen life. So I agreed. He also happened to be Francesca's secret love. Ever since 9½ *Weeks*, she'd been crazy about him. Along with Sting, she considers him the sexiest man in the world.

"There are three men I'd cheat on you with. One is Mickey Rourke, one is Mick Hucknall from Simply Red, and the other is Sting."

Sting, of course. Like all the women.

"Hey, Zu, rest up for now and I'll see you later at Cipriani."

Rourke was expecting us. His face was already a bit beat-up. During a decadent period, he had gone on a boxing tour. He must have taken quite a few punches. He was waiting at the door with his Bellini. He started drinking at six p.m. and kept on till late that night. One Bellini after another. He said he'd heard my music; someone had told him about a couple of songs of mine whose names he couldn't remember. Then he started telling me about his problems. Besides his face, he'd also sculpted a character based on the role of the marginalized antihero with a loner's temperament. He was upset because he'd broken up with Carré Otis. He showed me his pinky with the missing joint and explained how in a moment of rage at Carré he had cut it off with a knife. He told me he was coming out of a period of decline, and how he went to church to pray and there was a priest who helped alleviate his suffering.

We were having dinner when this guy came in with no shirt on, brown-skinned with a pendant on his hairy chest. He apologized and took Mickey away with him. An hour later, Mickey came back.

"You know, these people have helped me a lot. I grew up with African Americans in Liberty City in Miami. Lots of cigarettes and gettin' my ass kicked at the boxing gym on Fifth Street in Miami

Beach. I won a lot of fights, but made one major mistake. These people, they're family members, they helped me out, and I owe them deference. When they call me, I go."

I was perplexed. But his bad-boy, rough-and-tumble stories fascinated me. He took me to a huge nightclub at the port in New York. There was an impressive parade of bottle service girls—at least 150 of them, and Mickey knew them all. He went there every night and stayed till the place closed at dawn. One by one he called them by name: "Maria, Alice, come on!" He had them dance for me. One came up and rubbed her tits against my nose, fondled me. Mickey slipped twenty bucks into her garter, then it was another's turn. Ten in a row, at least 20 tits rubbed up against my nose. I held up till four in the morning, while he kept pouring away. Then I left and went to bed while he stayed there, like he did every night. Later I happened to run into him again on a TV show, where we were both guests. He had just finished that awesome film *The Wrestler*, directed by Darren Aronofsky. He was wearing a white tank top with a big tomato sauce stain on it, and was holding a Chihuahua in his arms, desperately seeking a dog-sitter for his turn on the air. We hugged and I asked him to play a little prank on Francesca.

"Give her a call with your most sensual voice, like a real lady-killer."

Later, after the show, he called her.

"This is Mickey. I love you. I want to be there where you are, in your bed."

"Fuck off. Let me sleep, you shit."

"And to think, you said were in love with me."

Francesca, Blue, and *Bluesugar*

TWO OR THREE TIMES A MONTH. WE NEVER SAW EACH OTHER MORE than that. That was the kind of relationship Francesca and I had at first. We just let things happen. Although she was jealous of the other women. Once, when I was on my way home from Germany, I called her because I wanted to see her. We made a date for that evening. In the meantime, another friend of mine asked me out to dinner. I called Francesca back. "My flight's late. I won't make it back in time for dinner with you. We can get together tomorrow, Fra."

Francesca called Alitalia.

"I'd like some information on one of your passengers: Mr. Fornaciari."

"You must be joking. I can't give that information out."

"I'm not talking about Fornaciari the rock star. This Fornaciari is my husband. He works at the Dalmine knitting mill. I need to know whether he's on that plane. I have to speak to him. It's urgent."

"I'm sorry, but the only Mr. Fornaciari on that flight is the rock star."

When I got home, she was sitting in her car, parked next to my yard. Of course, she saw me arrive with my friend and the two little cuties he'd brought along. I came off as a total asshole. When the bell rang, I opened the door. She was nowhere in sight, but had left a book lying in front of the gate: *The Adventures of Pinocchio.*

There were lots of other similar episodes, and after a while she got fed up. She wanted nothing more to do with me. I think she suffered over it. Anyway, she knew I wasn't interested in having an exclusive relationship back then. I was just starting to get my shit together after stumbling around in the dark for so long, and I wanted to have fun. I took advantage of all the perks that fame had to offer. She went to New York on business. When she got back, I asked her to be my assistant. She's a skilled organizer, determined and intelligent. Speaks lots of languages. She agreed, but on one condition.

"We sleep in separate rooms. I don't want you getting any ideas."

We toured South and Central America, with her in charge of promotion and coordination. She was perfect. We played in Argentina, Chile, Brazil, Venezuela, Costa Rica, Mexico. Then we hit the States: Los Angeles, San Francisco, New York. Then onto Boston. After that show, I felt great. Had a bit to drink at dinner. My energy was pumping, I felt uninhibited. I went up to my room and Francesca followed. She saw how affected I was by the alcohol and wanted to make sure I got to bed alright. I threw myself down on the bed and lay still for a while. She pulled off my boots for me.

"Come here. Come on," I said.

"No, no. We said there'd be no…"

She didn't have time to finish the phrase and wound up in my arms.

The tour continued. We played Washington, DC, some dates in Canada, and then Paris. About 20 days had gone by since Boston, when Francesca said to me, "I'm going out to run some errands. You rest up." I always try to take a nap in the afternoon when I'm on tour, to make sure I'm refreshed and in good shape for the show that night. She woke me up when she got back.

"I don't know if this is going to…make you happy or not. But I just got the results: I'm pregnant."

Fuck. I felt a cold sweat coming on. What a blow. Like being woken up with a slap in the face. I felt a hammering inside my head. My thoughts whirled. Jarring, chaotic thoughts and images. Francesca, Angela, Alice, Irene, now this unforeseen development. New responsibilities. A new family. Once again, I'd have to answer to someone, just when I'd freed myself from my ghosts and regained my freedom. I could do as I pleased, come and go and get my kicks without anyone telling me what to do.

In retrospect, I understand what all my anxiety was about. I dreaded the possibility of suffering again. Unfortunately, I got it wrong, like someone who runs away rather than stay and face a situation. Overwhelmed by anxiety, I teetered and lost my head. Cold sweat. Panic. I knew it all too well.

I had no desire to sing anymore. I wanted to disappear. I wanted out. The hardest thing was forgetting myself. I thought I was dreaming. I didn't think I'd be up to the challenge, and feared it. There was no excuse for it, and today I can admit that. I wasn't ready. Back then, it seemed like a catastrophe.

"Don't take it so hard. You're stressed out. We'll talk about it when we get back to Italy."

Fra never loses control.

The days went by. I was rattled, assailed by doubts. We'd stopped seeing each other, and at first, she didn't even want to go on tour with me. Did she love me? Did she want my baby? Could I trust her? I was terrified at the idea of suffering all over again because of a woman.

Madrid. I was about to walk onstage.

"Hey, boss," someone said. "Your brother called. He said your father's in the hospital with aspiration pneumonia."

I knew what that meant. Food had gotten into his lungs and caused an infection. He wasn't going to pull through this time.

"Lauro, check to see if there are any flights. I'll catch the first one out."

My brother was desperate.

"The first one to Bologna's at seven tomorrow morning."

Fuck! What was I going to do?

"Just stay calm. Do your show and come tomorrow. Let's hope he's still with us."

Lauro was pretty choked up. It sounded like he had tears in his eyes. My voice was filled with anger like never before as I sang. I felt like shit. I hated the audience and they applauded.

I got to the hospital at noon. There was an old guy sitting next to my dad's bed, telling him a joke. My father looked like a skeleton. But he laughed.

He saw me and smiled. My mother cried.

They said to take him home; there was nothing more they could do. That night he closed his eyes forever.

My last concert of the season was in Naples, Piazza del Plebiscito. I was in a daze. No idea what was going on. If I could have, I would have got the fuck out of there, and fast. When I got back from the show, I went straight to Fra.

"I can feel it—it's already a baby. I can feel it inside. Two and a half months now. It's my child and I want to keep it. Nothing will ever separate us. Do whatever you want."

Do whatever you want. Her words echoed through my head. Whatever I want, whatever I want. But what did I want? We'd both been caught in a trap that mingled my fear of this new responsibility with an already apprehensive mother's tenderness. One day she said to me, "I'm going to the gynecologist for a sonogram. Come with me."

I went. I tried to keep my cool by joking with the doctor. "Measure his shin bone: I hope he's not short like his mother."

The doctor wasn't in the mood for jokes.

"It corresponds to the European average."

The sonogram images blew me away. The feeling was much different from all the anxiety I had felt before. Just the opposite, in fact. The sight of that tiny moving image inspired profound tenderness in me. I was confused and embarrassed. In any case, something changed inside me that day. That was my son. And already I loved him. Although not all my fears had disappeared. I still had to break the news to the enemy: my ex-wife. I was deathly afraid of how she would react.

"That's wonderful news," she said. "I'm very happy for you. It's a blessing from God."

Was she taking the piss out of me, as usual, or what?

"I already love this child," she said.

Was she serious? I wondered why.

"Because it's yours."

Incredible. Once again, Angela had floored me.

When the time came, Francesca checked into the Villa delle Rose Clinic in Reggio Emilia, where I was born. She's a woman of the world, cosmopolitan. My mother was thrilled and came to visit her every day. To avoid any risks, the doctor advised a C-section. And our baby was born. The obstetrician put him in my arms and asked, "What last name do we register him under?"

Fornaciari. Adelmo Blue Fornaciari. A kind of ancient yet post-modern name: Reggio Emilia meets the Far West. Blue was beautiful.

The hospital was crawling with paparazzi, so Fra and the baby left in an ambulance while I slipped out the back. I picked them up in Parma in the car, and we headed south on the Autostrada. Ten kilometers from Pontremoli, Fra, ever in command, asked nonchalantly, "So what do you want me to do? Go to my house or come with you?"

I drove past Pontremoli, still undecided. The decision of my life was waiting for me at the Sarzana interchange. This way was my house; that way was hers. She came to Avenza with me. We've lived together ever since.

I was still pretty freaked out. Everything happened so fast. I'd reacted instinctively, without reflecting, so many times. Now I needed to think and get things straight in my head. That's when I began work on a new record, which would become *Bluesugar*, which, naturally, was dedicated to my son.

C'è un Dondolo che Dondola—
There's a Rocking Chair Rocking

I'D GET HOME AT FOUR IN THE MORNING AND FRA WOULD BE THERE nursing Blue. Then she would lay him on my belly. The first song I dedicated to her was 'You Make Me Feel Loved': *"Chiara come un bel sole d'inverno, e trasparente stella all'imbrunire. Succhia questo bellissimo giorno e tutte quante insieme le mie paure. Dolce e cara domenica, dai tuoi solai io sento le campane."* ("Clear as a beautiful winter sun, transparent star at dusk. Suck up this beautiful day along with all my fears. Dear, sweet Sunday, I hear the bells from your rooftops.") (Back to Roncocesi, peace and serenity.) *"E sulla scia di un'elica, i miei ricordi di seghe, fossi e rane!"* ("On the wake of a propeller, my memories of masturbation, ditches and frogs!" (Jerking off with my friends in the sorghum field.) *"Che l'amore non ha niente da capire."* ("There's nothing to understand about love.") (I certainly haven't figured out a fucking thing, but that's love too.) *"Col mal di denti nel cuore sorrido a te."* ("With a toothache in my heart, I smile at you.")

Then there was 'Blu.' While I was recording in Dublin, I stopped by Bono's house. He'd already written the English lyrics to 'Miserere.' I was staying at the Clarence Hotel, which at that time was owned by U2. Bono lives in a beautiful home on the coast, but not the big gaudy mansion of a megastar. "Today I'm cooking for you," he said, and whipped up some penne with garlic, olive oil, and chili, which we enjoyed with a nice bottle of white wine. I gave him the music to 'Blu,' and a month later he called to let me know he'd finished the English lyrics. I wrote the lyrics in Italian. Bono didn't know I'd titled the song 'Blu,' yet when I saw his lyrics, there was the word "blue" staring me in the face. We were on the same wavelength, synchronized. "Stay, love. Stay tonight. These rainy skies tomorrow will be blue."

My song 'Arcord,' whose title is a word in dialect (like *Amarcord*, the Fellini film), which means "I remember," is dedicated to Augusto Daolio of the Nomads. At one point, the music stops and all you hear are waves and seagulls, and his voice sampled from the Nomads' version of 'La Canzone della Bambina Portoghese' by Francesco Guccini.

The legendary Steve Winwood—who played with the Spencer Davis Group, Traffic, and Jimi Hendrix, just to name a few—played

Hammond organ on *Bluesugar*. Wil Malone arranged the strings we recorded at Abbey Road Studios.

Then there's the song 'Puro Amore,' dedicated to my daughter Alice. She and her sister Irene helped me write the lyrics. "*Di te odio l'amore che forse non sai cos'è.*" ("I hate your love, and you probably don't even know what that is.") (We were in the middle of a conflict situation with my oldest daughter.) 'Donkey Tonkey' is dedicated to my donkey Camillo, the one who had such a hard time getting laid. "*Spero che fai l'asino sul serio per un po', e se fai il ballo dell'asino, io ci sto.*" ("I hope you're serious about being a donkey. If you do the donkey dance, I'm with you.") I like playing with stereotypes from other songs, referencing and mocking them. The pleasure of displeasing. All that linguistic weaving and sculpting with Pasquale Panella. He and I work so well together because he knows me better than anyone else. He's the kind of person who can describe you, who can come up with a faithful photograph of your soul. "Zucchero is a 'pre-singer'," he used to say. "He'll sing you the lyrics to a song before they've been written." Panella's got this trained, theatrical voice. The kind of guy who stays home all the time. I must have invited him to my place a thousand times, and he's only ever come once, with Michele Bovi, the only one who can get him up off his ass. When I first heard his voice over the phone, I imagined this huge man. In fact, he's short and stocky. A perennial hippie.

I've never met anyone with a better command of Italian. He writes weird stuff, rambles on and on. You can't use everything he writes, otherwise you'd get completely lost in his labyrinthine meanderings. Sometimes you have to get your feet back on solid ground. That's my role in our collaboration. We get together, kid around, then get serious and stick to the musical formats that have already been laid out. He creates such beautiful and amusing imagery, and puts lots of things together unexpectedly. Like the line "*Purezza e leccornia*" ("Purity and delight") from 'Blu.' Unbridled lust. "*C'è un dondolo che dondola. che belle scene di lei che viene. Da lune piene e si gongola.*"

("There's a rocking chair rocking. Pretty scenes of her coming. Like full moons. We rejoice.") One time I used a single line of his for one of my songs. "Don't you dare pay me royalties on that. Just hearing you sing that line is recompense enough." It was that typical Panella way of his: "Sometimes memories are more important than royalties."

The Golden Tapir

I WAS IN PARIS PROMOTING *BLUESUGAR*. I CAME BACK TO BOLOGNA to tape an episode of *Taratatà*, the TV program produced by Bibi Ballandi. It was the only TV show in Italy where bands played live. Afterward we had dinner with Andrea Bocelli, who also happened to be in Bologna. Torpedine was managing him now, too. We just wanted to hang loose and have some fun. We drank, told jokes, laughed. Wonderful atmosphere. Francesca was with me. Later, Bocelli headed home and Fra and I, along with Torpedine, went back to our hotel. I was feeling chipper, though tired from my trip. It must have been three in the morning. Suddenly out pops Valerio Staffelli from behind a column. He was a reporter for the satirical news program *Striscia la Notizia*. I had only ever seen it a couple of times, since I was always on tour abroad and really had no idea who he was. I thought he was a fan who wanted my autograph, a picture together with him and his wife. Instead, he pulled out a recorder, pressed play, and said, "Signor Fornaciari, do you recognize this song?"

I listened.

"Sure. It's 'Era Lei' by Michele Pecora."

"There you go. Poor Pecora. Why would a great musician like you go and copy a song by poor Pecora? What's in a name? Poor guy." *Pecora* is Italian for sheep.

"First of all, I didn't copy anybody's song. Second, who the hell are you?"

"Ah! I'm Staffelli!"

"Like I said, I didn't copy anything. Besides, Pecora's a friend of mine. I even wrote a hit song for him, 'Te ne Vai,' after he made it to the big time with 'Era Lei.' And I certainly don't need to go copying anything from anybody."

"Pecora claims you copied it."

A while back I'd heard from Pecora. He was looking for new songs, but I had no time. He hadn't said a word about any of this. But now apparently, he was claiming that 'Blu' had a line in it lifted from 'Era Lei': "*Poesie d'estate dimenticate*" ("Forgotten poetry of summer"). Those lyrics were written by Panella. Pasquale Panella! A guy who lives in his own world. With all due respect to Panella, he probably didn't even know who Pecora was.

The lyrics are beautiful. The story of two people fucking. Some of the words were mine; others, Panella's—the way we usually worked. "*Ti sento amore mio, sento già il frullio di una notte Blu. Gira in aria un feeling che sale su, mi ricordo, siamo bambini, siamo sempre noi, lassù. Sere d'estate dimenticate.*" ("I can feel you, my love. I can already feel the coming of this blue night. There's a feeling, spinning as it rises. I remember. Up there we're children, yet still ourselves. Summer nights forgotten.")

"Summer nights forgotten" instead of "summer poetry... forgotten."

Lovely. I had nearly become a veterinarian, and now I was dealing in comparative linguistics and semantics. Pecora's lyrics went like this: "*Era lei poesie d'estate / Era lei dimenticate*" ("She was summer poetry / You forget that was her") with respect to Panella's "Summer nights forgotten."

Listen to the words of Maestro Panella, grand wizard of wordplay. Listen to their great cheer: "*C'è un dondolo che dondola...che belle scene di lei che viene...da lune piene e si gongola. Cammino e penso a te, ai grilli e le cicale, a quelle strane suore... Respiro, respiro te, purezza e leccornia.*" ("There's a rocking chair rocking. Pretty scenes of her coming. Like full moons. We rejoice. I walk and think of you, of cicadas and crickets too, of those strange nuns …I breathe and breathe you in, purity and delight.") That's Panella at his best! Linguistic fireworks. "*Fuoco della sera. siamo destini.*" ("Fire in the night. We are destinies.") That's Panella alright. "*Siamo sempre noi…ma più vicini. Stretti e supini, è lui, siamo sempre noi, lassù. sere d'estate dimenticate, c'è un dondolo…che dondola…da lune…lei che viene…si gongola…sale su il ricordo, siamo destini, siamo sempre noi…sere d'estate dimenticate…c'è un dondolo…c'è un ciondolo che ciondola…e poi…che belle scene di lei che viene, io di bocche piene che fan pendant!*" ("We're still ourselves… only closer. Side by side on our backs, that's us up there. Summer nights forgotten. There's a rocking chair rocking. Pretty scenes of her coming. Like full moons. We rejoice…There's a pendant dangling… matching mouthfuls for me.")

The only thing the same was the rhyme of "*estate*" ("summer") and "*dimenticate*" ("forgotten"). Completely by chance. There's no connection whatsoever between the two songs—they're about two entirely different things.

Staffelli tried to hand me one of his Golden Tapirs, which he awards to entertainers, politicians, and others in the public eye when they commit some kind of gaffe. It fell to the ground and smashed to pieces.

"Oops! What a piece of junk! Maybe I should be giving it to you!" But he kept on.

"Look, cut the shit. It's late. I'm going to bed!"

As I was saying all this, I spied a smiling Franco popping out from behind another column. He was a cameraman from Bologna who had worked on all my videos. Good guy. I thought it was all a joke. More like *Candid Camera* than *Striscia la Notizia*.

"I didn't copy anybody," I objected.

"Poor Pecora. From Bologna, Valerio Staffelli: *Striscia la Notizia*."

That was Staffelli's sign-off. Then he said, "Zucchero, now that we're off the air, tell me the truth. Did you or did you not copy that song?"

He came up close to me, very close. He was wearing a microphone around his neck. I was tired, in a daze, and maybe a little drunk. Franco laid his camera on a table; the show was over. But the camera was still on.

"Listen," I said to him. "If you wanna come out and drink a beer with me, fine. Otherwise I'm going to bed. But if you keep this shit up, I'll spit in your mouth."

Maybe I should have said, "I'll spit in your face." Which in itself wasn't such a grand thing to say. But the guy was breathing down my neck with that microphone—"I'll spit in your mouth" is just what came out. That's the way I am. Sometimes I lose it and start saying stupid shit. Francesca saw how riled up I was and took me by the arm. She knows me. I was raving, and she dragged me away. As for Torpedine, he never budged. He just stood there watching the show. On the video I looked like some fucked-up, drunken ogre attacking Staffelli, who came off as the victim. When my ex-wife, friends, and even my daughters saw it, they asked if I was on drugs that night. They took me for someone else.

Pecora sued me for copyright infringement. And lost. From a musical perspective, he never had a chance. A sworn expert testified that research on descending and ascending scales indicated that there were at least 2,000 songs that might resemble this one. The charge regarding the rhymes fell apart soon enough as well. But all this never appeared in the press, except for a short article in *Corriere della Sera*. Of course, the news never appeared on *Striscia la Notizia*. In exchange, at one of my shows I saw a banner with the words: "Thief! Go Home! Copycat!"

A boost for my image!

One night I was out with Dori Ghezzi, who's a friend of Staffelli's. We ran into Antonio Ricci and cleared things up.

"Why did you treat me like shit?!"

"Chill out, man. That was nothing."

That's *Striscia la Notizia* for you.

The incident was a stumbling block in my career. It conditioned me psychologically. For some time after, whenever I sat down to write new music and lyrics, I was afraid one note might sound like some other note, one word might rhyme like some other. I was roasting over hot coals. No longer free. Free to create. Somewhere I read that good artists copy and great artists steal. Picasso. That helped.

"I Lay Down with an Angel"

IN 1999 I DID A EUROPEAN TOUR AND THEN WENT BACK TO AMERICA. When it was all over, I found a surprise waiting for me: We'd overrun the budget. I'd busted my ass for a whole year touring the world, and it ended up costing me money. I called Henry Padovani and Miles Copeland to go over the accounts with my accountant and my lawyer. We'd overspent. Miles had been in Los Angeles and didn't know. He'd started out so well, got me the gig at Woodstock. My *Greatest Hits* album sold four million copies and we toured the world. But for *Bluesugar* he'd done practically nothing, as I saw it. I fired them both.

Roger Forrester managed Eric Clapton, and was more like a big brother or father figure to him. He was well regarded in the music business, highly respected. He became one of our family, too. He and his wife, Annette, were Blue's godparents when we had him baptized at the Church of San Ilario, in the hills of Pontremoli. He even opened a bank account for Blue in England. We spent a lot of time together in Pontremoli.

Eric Clapton had been attending A.A. meetings and was back in shape. One night I met him at the Hotel Baglioni in Bologna and we had dinner. I was about to pour him some wine when he stopped me.

He was steadfast and unswerving. After some pretty dark years, he was finally getting his life back together. He told me he'd lost control for so long. I found it all very disturbing. When Eric let Roger go, Roger came to me.

"The time has come: I'll manage you, if you want. I'm no longer working for Eric, so I'll have the time to dedicate to you."

In an attempt to patch things up before our working relationship finally came to an end, Miles Copeland arranged for me to appear on the soundtrack for a movie starring Sharon Stone. I was to sing the rhythm & blues classic 'Let the Good Times Roll' together with the legendary B.B. King. Wow! I couldn't wait. We recorded it in New York with Pino Palladino on bass, Steve Jordan on drums—a couple of legends in their own right—and B.B. on guitar. I was supposed to be at the studio by midnight but didn't manage to get there until two. The great B.B. King was crashed out on a grubby old sofa in his stocking feet. The blues oozed from his every pore. He woke up as soon as I got there, put his shoes on, and started wailing. Singing with such great musicians was so inspirational, a truly priceless experience. We rehearsed the song just once, then recorded it. And what a recording it was.

I had bought a small property in Marina di Carrara and turned it into offices for Roger Forrester Management, represented by Roger Forrester. He only spent about one week a month there, and then he was off again. He probably just came for fun.

I spent the winter writing material for my next album, *Shake*. Corrado Rustici and I decided we'd record it in Calistoga, north of San Francisco. Once Indian country, the wide, open spaces of the Napa Valley are now famous for their wines. Francis Ford Coppola's winery is nearby.

Shake is an album steeped in soul. I took inspiration from Moby's *Play* and all the electronic sampling. I used lots of crudely recorded stuff from old vinyl. But there's nothing like the sound of those bluesmen, it's simply beautiful. I sampled Ray Charles, Barry

White, Blind Teddy Darby, Big Bill Broonzy, Al Green, and Muddy Waters. Some gospel choirs too. My aim was to use their old voices like instruments to create a new sound. Of course, they all received royalties. I cowrote 'Sento la Campane' with Isaac Hayes. I had John Lee Hooker come into the studio for 'Ali d'Oro.' He was perfect for it, with his archaic voice—the most erotic voice with the most sensual phrasing. A hypnotic voice that travels through time and can stop your heart from beating.

I had always dreamed of playing with John Lee Hooker, the great old bluesman. Extraordinary voice. Savage temperament. We had some trouble finding him—he had no fixed abode. The old blues warrior was by now in his eighties. I called Eric Clapton: "How can I find John Lee Hooker?"

"Forget about him, man. I've been trying for years. He'll say yes, then he never shows up. He's tough to pin down. He's pretty old now, too. I dunno."

I came up with a contact for John Lee's guitarist, Roy Rogers, and invited him to the studio for a jam session. I told him how I dreamed of playing with John Lee Hooker. "Gimme the song," he said, "and I'll bring it to him. Your chances of playing with him are slim, but we can give it a shot."

A few days went by, and still no news from John Lee Hooker. Not that I ever seriously thought he would come anyway. But then Rogers called: "If it's alright with you, I'll bring you John Lee Hooker tomorrow at twelve noon. He likes your song."

I was so stunned the Virgin Mary could have appeared before my eyes and I wouldn't have noticed.

Long black limousine. John Lee Hooker stepped out. Dressed in mother-of-pearl gray. Matching hat. Sounded like Barry White when he spoke. With two amazing chicks in tow. Not young, they must have been at least 50. But they were two gorgeous, buxom American beauties with big thighs. Dressed to kill. They took care of him, pampered him with caresses and pecks on the cheek. He could barely walk, dragging his physical decay around like a heavy suitcase. Thin as a rail. But he enthralled me with his intellectual energy. He told me the blues was born a long, long time ago. "You know when?" he challenged me, and without waiting for an answer, said, "When God banished Adam and Eve from earthly paradise. That's when pain was born, and the blues right along with it."

Then he grew quiet and said no more.

He made a triumphant entrance into the recording studio and sat down, with the two hot chicks at his side.

"Don't ask him anything. Just loop the music and you'll see something happen," said one of the ladies.

He took off on his own, improvising. "Yeah...oh, yeah...all right." Then came the Mississippi Delta guitar. Then he'd sing a little more, making up the words as he went. "I lay down...oh, yeah...I lay down." I was loving it! His voice filled the studio, and my bones quaked with the blues. "I lay down with an angel, 'cause she treat me kind sometimes." After a couple of hours, he was tired. We used those recordings for the song 'Ali d'Oro.' It gave me the goosebumps. The phone rang while I was mixing the piece. John Lee Hooker was dead. They found him lying lifeless in his bed. He knew he had an appointment with an angel that he couldn't miss. His last.

He left me his spiritual testament.

Ho Visto Nina Volare—I Saw Nina Fly

ON MARCH 12, 2000, I SANG 'HO VISTO NINA VOLARE' ('I SAW NINA FLY'), by the legendary Italian singer-songwriters Fabrizio De André and Ivano Fossati, at the Carlo Felice Theater in Genoa. The occasion was a tribute concert to De André, called "Faber: Amico Fragile"— "Fabrizio: Our Fragile Friend."

Songs need time to rise to the surface. The more I listened to 'Ho Visto Nina Volare,' the more enthusiastic I was. His wife, Dori Ghezzi, felt the same. So why not do a cover? Interpreting De André is no easy task; it's very risky. Fabrizio was a very personal musician. Melodically speaking, his approach ran along different lines than mine. And his lyrics can be burdensome. His music may not require technically great singers, but it cries out for skilled interpreters. Dori chose that song for me to do at the show, and I think she hit the nail on the head.

Bingo!

I HAD TWO SONGS AT SANREMO IN 2001. ONE I WROTE FOR GIORGIA, THE other for Elisa. Caterina Caselli wanted Elisa to take part in the festival, but Elisa wanted to sing in English. And that isn't allowed at Sanremo.

Caselli said she'd thought of me because I was the only one in Italy who could write lyrics in Italian with an English sound.

"Sorry, but I'm busy with my next album. I don't have time."

At that point, however, she convinced Francesca, and that was it.

It was a great song. I wrote the lyrics in two hours.

"I like it, but I don't want to go to Sanremo. Caselli's the one who's insisting on it."

Elisa was skeptical.

While all this was happening, Giorgia's manager asked me for a song for her to sing at Sanremo. I had one on the shelf, that I'd written with Mino Vergnaghi and Matteo Saggese. She had her doubts at first, but it was perfect: "Di Sole e d'Azzurro." Elisa got her song too: "Luce."

Then came the announcement: "Second prize goes to a song written by Zucchero Fornaciari, 'Di Sole e d'Azzurro,' performed by

Giorgia." Wow! I was watching on TV in Sausalito, California, with my guitarist, Corrado Rustici. He'd done a splendid arrangement for Elisa. The host, Raffaella Carrà, was blaring out the news. "First prize: another song by Zucchero, 'Luce,' performed by Elisa!" Bingo! Who would have thought?! Fucking bull's-eye! I wrote those songs in 10 minutes. And neither Elisa nor Giorgia wanted to perform at Sanremo that year.

Più Badili e Meno Chitarre— More Shovels, Less Guitars

'SENTO LE CAMPANE' IS A SLEAZY ROMP. I IMAGINED SOME SCUMBAG AT a bar, drinking to forget. He insults the bartender affectionately, like they're old friends. Then he goes out looking for a whore. It's a world of outcasts, prostitutes, and dives. A world teeming with emotions, but no lyricism. "*Quando vedo te, sento le campane. Mi scappa la pipì dall'emozione.*" ("When I see you, I hear bells. I'm so thrilled I have to pee.") The story of a guy who goes with a whore. It's the most he can hope for. But in her he sees a flower and he gets all choked up. The song ends on a note of lighthearted sarcasm, wrapping up the sleaze: "*Mi scappa solo la pipì su questo mondo infame.*" ("All I do is piss on this wretched world.")

The first three songs come out blasting. 'Music in Me' opens with a black chorus and a driving rhythm. At the time, I was writing a column for a fanzine, and one day I laid into some inexperienced DJs and musicians who were very fashionable and being heavily pro-moted on TV. "Guys," I wrote, "you should be out tilling the fields! More shovels, less guitars." That went on to become the line "*Più badili e meno divi*" ("More shovels, less superstars") in 'Music in Me.' I want music, not charlatans. "*Voglio l'uva e voglio l'Eva.*" ("I want grapes, I want Eve.")

'Porca l'Oca' is set in a discotheque. An *oca*, or "goose," is basically a slut with a taste for DJs. "*Lei è la più figa laggiù, ma nella penombra e nei giochi di luce della discoteca io non la vedo abbastanza bene. Fammi vedere la verità, fatti vedere adesso! c'ho il pane e c'ho il salame e la Fra' che mi fa gola.*" ("She's the hottest chick out there, but in the shadows and shimmering lights of the disco, I can hardly make her out. Show me the truth; I want to see you now! I've got bread, I've got salami, and Fra' driving me wild.") Fra' is, of course, Francesca. "*Ma la foca no.*" ("But not the seal.") Which turns out to be a transvestite. "*Dai, fammi vedere come si fa.*" ("Come on, show me what you can do.")

Then there's 'Baila,' which was a huge hit. Here's how that song was born: One day Roberto Zanetti, a friend of mine from Marina di Massa, showed up with a tape. I hadn't seen him in years. He played with me in a group called Taxi, one of the bands I played in when I was working my way up. In the 1980s and 1990s, he got into disco and sold tons of records all over the world. He made a lot of money and bought himself a beautiful villa on the coast. I put on the tape and listened: "*Baila morena, sotto questa luna piena…under the moonlight.*" Just piano and vocals. We sat down and worked on it. After 10 minutes we had the music, verses, and bridge. A few days later we made a demo. I wrote the lyrics, which by the way contain a quote from *Thus Spoke Zarathustra*: "*Che devi avere un caos dentro di te, per far fiorire una stella che balla.*" ("One must have chaos within oneself to give birth to a dancing star.") Now what do you say, Nietzsche? Maybe he's dancing. With Morena.

'Baila' was a big hit in continental Europe, Number One in many countries. I happened to meet up with Manà, a Mexican band with a huge following in the Hispanic community in the United States and beyond. They did 'Corazón Espinado' with Carlos Santana, which was a big hit. An impresario in Ibiza told me I should have a jam session with them, but I had no idea who they were. I contacted them. They were psyched about bringing their music to Europe. I proposed Manà to Luciano and Nicoletta for *Pavarotti & Friends*, and they were glad to have them. We performed 'Baila' together, and the song went on to become a hit all over South America.

A dear friend of mine invited me to Cuba. Another world, I fell in love with the place as soon as I got there. Someday I'd like to play in Plaza de la Revolucion in Havana, and bring in local musicians to play with my band. Cuba is famous for its skilled percussionists and horn players. Maybe we could invite Santana, Jean Luis Guerra, and Fito Paez.

'Scintille,' along with 'Dune Mosse,' is one of my favorite songs, even if it was never a single. A Christmas-y ballad. *"Scende giù la neve, come viene lieve. Sto pensando a te, in questa notte che fa scintille. E non è il tempo, sai, che ci manca. E non è il vento, sai, che ci stanca. Non è il tempo che ci cambierà. Amore mio, dov'è che ti manco? Perché tu manchi a me, sulla mia pelle."* ("The snow is falling softly. I'm thinking of you on this sparkling night. It's not time we're missing. It's not the wind that drags us down. It's not time that will change us. My love, where do you miss me? I miss you on my skin.")

I wrote 'Dindondio' with Panella, but the title is mine. *"Campane di domenica e non io, che resto muto nel cigolio."* ("Sunday bells ring out, and with their groans my silence.") He'd hit upon the sound of Sunday, described it. Classic Panella.

When I think back on all the songs I've written—maybe 250— and the music that inspired them, the bells theme keeps coming back again and again. It harkens back to my roots, and my love for the village I grew up in, and all the places I knew as a child. All that comes out loud and clear in this song.

Spirit

"DREAMWORKS IS BIG ON THIS." I WAS TOLD. "THEY WANT YOU TO DO the Italian version of the soundtrack."

The original soundtrack for *Spirit: Stallion of the Cimarron* was by Bryan Adams. I was supposed to adapt the songs to sing them in Italian. I was somewhat perplexed. I didn't think I had the touch this thing required. It would have been better for someone much younger, who could watch the cartoon and let his or her imagination run wild. My daughter Irene came to mind. She was very much into horses at the time. She had a beautiful Arabian called Gastone that lived in Pontremoli. She used to ride him around. Then, unfortunately, he died. She was 16 when they asked me to do the *Spirit* soundtrack. The two of us went into the garden and together we did the Italian version. She was super psyched. The next foal born on the farm was, of course, called Spirit.

Sixteen-year-old Irene had her first big project as a songwriter under her belt. I could see she had talent.

And kids still stop me on the street, and call me Spirit.

Succhiando l'Uva—Sucking the Grape

"*Farei l'amore nelle vigne. M'inchino a te. Mi dono a te... succhiando l'uva.*" ("I'd make love in the vineyard. Kneeling down to you. Giving myself to you. Sucking the grape.")

In 2002, the great Italian singer Mina agreed to record one of my songs, 'Succhiando l'Uva.' She came out with a fantastic single. I was on tour, in Alicante, Spain. One blazing-hot afternoon inspired the lyrics in me. I was heat-laden with poetry. "*Io sono il mito. Non sono mica burro che ci rimane il dito.*" ("I am legend. Not butter sticking on your fingers.") It was like saying she was in a hot room in Alicante and wanted to fuck (she being me, that is). Ritual. Fantasy. Hearts torn to pieces. "*Mi in-canto a te...*" ("I'm enchanted by you...")

"Zucchero, your lyrics are wonderful, but they aren't suitable for a 60-year-old lady like me," she told me over the phone.

"Mina, you're the sexiest woman in the world. You open your mouth, and you're tremendously sexy."

That convinced her.

She sang the song and it was divine.

Zu & Company

THE ALBUM *ZU & CO.* WAS RELEASED IN 2004. IT WAS A PECULIAR greatest-hits record, with a lot of remixes and rearrangements of songs I'd done with international artists. An anthology of duets with friends, combinations of different styles, cultures, and voices. It took strength and patience for me to create another dream. Twenty million copies sold throughout the world.

For the first time, I was working with my new manager, Stewart Young, who had managed Emerson, Lake and Palmer, and AC/DC. Laura Vergani was also on board—she's been a precious collaborator ever since. And what a lineup: Miles Davis, a great soul. On the job, he came off as a tough guy, but he was awfully sweet in his interpersonal relationships. Sting, who always signs his letters to me, "your brother, Sting." Vanessa Carlton, very composed. A beautiful *Maestra* of the piano. Mousse T. A wizard. He knows the ins and outs of sound. Macy Gray, stupendous. If I were a woman, I'd want her voice. Manà, *cinfoncissimo*—which is to say, perfect. It's a Mexican expression. John Lee Hooker, the old blues great. An icon. What more can you say? Sheryl Crow, pure sensuality—that's the idea she gives me. Dolores O'Riordan, ultramodern. Her voice reaches all the way to the bottom of your soul. Eric Clapton, inimitable. He's the musician I love most in the world. Tom Jones, the one-take wonder. His performances are good right off the bat; technically he's in his own class. B.B. King, a founding father—the kind of musician that everything descends from. Ronan Keating, an Irish gentleman. Cheb Mami, a nightingale, whose voice flies so very high. Solomon Burke, the King. When he stepped onstage with his scepter he was the Lord Master of soul. Paul Young, a great artist. He assured me that one day I'd make it too. Brian May. What a player, what style, a true gentleman. Luciano Pavarotti and Andrea Bocelli—they helped me discover a new love: the melody of Puccini.

Fifteen years had passed since I first met Miles Davis in New York, since Eric Clapton invited me to play with him in London at the Royal Albert Hall. In all those years, I'd had the good fortune to meet and play with so many great artists onstage and in the recording studio. I'd kept our recordings, those pearls, in the drawer. It was going to be like tasting a fine wine that's been aged just right. A megaconcert, a celebration at the Royal Albert Hall, together with all my friends. Although it was a party rife with suspense. Eric Clapton had fallen ill and cancelled at the last minute. But during 'Hey Man' he pretty much sneaked into the theater, which was something of a home for him. Luciano called in sick as well. But good friend that he was, he had the loveliest surprise for me. Donning his cap and multicolor shawl, he showed up and sang a version of 'Miserere' that I'll never forget. The crowd at London's Royal Albert Hall went wild. That was May 6, 2004.

Merde Merde, Putain Putain

A DUET THAT DIDN'T MAKE IT ON TO *ZU & CO* THOUGH, WAS 'UN Piccolo Aiuto.' The road to the recording had begun in France in 1996, when we toured the whole country, from Normandy to the Riviera. I rode with a crazy but nice French driver, Serge. He peppered his phrases with "*Merde, merde. Putain, putain. Couillon, couillon.*" I saw all of France. That was the first time that I took Francesca with me on the road.

Great memories. We went to Le Château de Tigné, two hours outside Paris, in search of Gérard Depardieu. He wasn't there. But I did visit his wine cellar and tasted the wines he produced. The Cyrano was very good. The caretaker told us, "He doesn't live in the castle. When he comes here he stays in this hut." I liked that. The place was messy, though. Muddy boots, tools, work clothes strewn all over the place. I suppose I would have done the same.

When we finally met, he knew I'd been to his place. "Shit, man, we could have done something together. I like to sing."

"I didn't know you were a singer," I said.

He did a great job on 'Un Piccolo Aiuto,' I must say. The song was open to various interpretations. It didn't call for anything outrageous, but still, he was amazing. The French version is titled 'Une Petite Coupe de Main.'

Depardieu, Bob Dylan, and the Pope

I WAS WITH DEPARDIEU WHEN I BOTCHED IT AGAIN WITH THE press. I'M a horrible communicator. I always say what I think, and oftentimes I'll just think up some bullshit and say it. In 1997, I was at the Venice Film Festival with Depardieu, who'd become a great friend. He's a down-to-earth kind of guy, and I like that. We even strolled down the red carpet together, and Francesca was with me, too. I ran into Bibi Ballandi, the manager from Bologna, who was organizing the concert for the Jubilee, the one where Bob Dylan and Adriano Celentano sang for the Pope.

"You must make an appearance. It's going to be an extraordinary event. The Pope's going to meet with young people and admit that rock isn't the devil's music."

"There you go. Then I'll come and sing 'Solo una Sana e Consapevole Libidine,'" I said jokingly.

Ballandi, a priest by nature, took me seriously and grew dark.

"No way, man. If you're going to come and bust people's balls ..."

I hadn't realized we were standing in the middle of a group of journalists—movie reporters, not music writers, and I didn't know them.

"You're wrong. Even Bob Dylan received his redemption on the road to Damascus."

"No, my dear Bibi. Bob Dylan was redeemed alright—for 450,000 dollars."

That was his fee for singing for the Pope, as far as I knew.

The next day the headlines in all the Italian dailies read, "Bob Dylan Redeems Himself for 450,000: Zucchero."

Once again, I'd made a fool of myself. But basically, it was true.

Dustino

STING AND TRUDIE CELEBRATED THEIR TWENTIETH WEDDING ANNIVERsary at Lake House, their Elizabethan manor in Wiltshire, England in 2002. It was a grand affair of course. I was already seeing a lot of Francesca, though we weren't yet a steady couple, and she came with me. The whole world was there, all of Sting's friends: Madonna; Tom Hanks; Peter Gabriel; Eric Clapton; Father John, the Irish priest who was Sting's spiritual guide; as well as Stewart Copeland and Andy Summers of the Police—at the end of the party they even played together, their first reunion since breaking up. Sting came riding up on a white horse with Trudie. I was the least well known among this stellar crowd, and at first kept off to the side with Francesca and the Irish priest, who enjoyed talking to me.

Then Dustin Hoffman came over and asked, "Are you Zucchero?"

"Yes."

He kneeled down before me, right there in front of everybody, and started screaming, "Zuccheroooo! Zuccheroooo! You're the best!"

Then he started singing, "*Ho bisogno d'amore perdio …un'overdose d'amore!*" He was crazy. I figured he was taking the piss out of me. I'm a skeptical country boy. You never know. He kept yelling in front of all those people, practically the world's whole star system. Everyone turned to look. Why was he making this ridiculous scene over me and making me look like shit? We'd already had cocktails, maybe he was drunk. I'm shy. I must have turned a thousand shades of red.

"Dustin, please. Stop. Quit teasing me. I'm a big fan of yours."

His wife stepped in. "He's not joking," she explained. "He has all your records."

I couldn't believe it. He went on singing and hugging me. We sat across from each other at the table all night. Every so often he'd look at me, give me the thumbs-up, and shout, "Number one!"

Meanwhile Peter Gabriel joined Eric Clapton onstage. The Police played too.

Then it was time to go.

A year or so later, I was in Capri, getting some work done and sleeping in the guest room at Capri Studio. I was taking no calls, except for Francesca and my ex-wife. Yet a phone call from someone else woke me at seven one morning.

"*Ciao, sono Dustino.*"

Deep voice.

"What?!"

"*Sono Dustino. Mamma mi scappa cacca.*"

Very deep voice.

"*Vaffanculo!*" I said.

"Hey, this is Dustin. Dustin Hoffman," he said, carefully enouncing his name with that booming voice of his.

I was a bit confused.

"Hey, I'm in Sorrento, on a boat with friends. My wife and kids are here, too. All they listen to all day long is classical music—it's a real drag, man. So, I sent someone to pick me up *Best of Zucchero*. That's a lot more fun. I read in *La Repubblica* that you're recording in Capri. We're due in the port at Capri tomorrow at five p.m. Send someone to pick me up."

Alice and Irene were with me. We took a cab to the port and got out at the top of the little square. Dustin Hoffman, his wife, and their three kids disembarked. It was August, and Capri was mobbed. We're in the shit, I thought. We were alone. He looked at me and muttered, "No bodyguard, no security."

He took his kids' hands and walked through the crowd, my daughters and I trailing after. He was totally cool and restrained as he waved to the crazed throng. He reminded me of Moses. We made our way on foot to the studio, located under the ancient ruins of Villa Jovis. That afternoon I was supposed to record Bono's version of 'Blue' (for *Zu & Co*). I asked Dustin to wait in the mixing booth while I gave it a shot. By that point, however, I'd lost my concentration and just started laughing. Dustin came over and asked if we could sing a duet together. The thing is, he can't sing. He put on the headphones. We sang into the same mike. I sang Bono's lyrics. He stuffed a pillow under his shirt to make it look like he had a belly like mine, and tried to bleat out a countermelody. Completely out of tune.

"I love jazz! I love blues!" he said.

Then he sat down at the piano and played a song he wrote. Kind of a fifties swing.

Later we went to Ciro's for pizza. Irene was sensitive about her weight back then. He told her a story. He was holding auditions for his latest film and all these super-skinny, super-foxy model-type chicks showed up. Instead, he chose a girl who was pretty, yes, but also a little on the chubby side.

"Her face was so interesting, though. You shouldn't worry about your figure. What's more important is the twinkle in your eye and the feelings you transmit to others, your aura."

Irene listened, enraptured. Dustin gave her lots of confidence.

After that, she plastered the walls of her room with posters from *The Graduate*.

After we'd finished our pizza, I had a guitar brought over and sang 'Everybody's Talkin',' which Harry Nilsson performed on the *Midnight Cowboy* soundtrack. Dustin invited an old lady from another table to dance while I sang and played. Kindness, genuineness, harmony, humility—distinctive features of the greats.

How Can We Fly with Eagles When We're Surrounded by Turkeys?

YOU DIAL A WRONG NUMBER AND THE PERSON WHO ANSWERS STARTS insulting you, even if you apologize. If you hesitate while driving, people behind you start honking their horns. Those are the turkeys. It's the turkeys that keep us from flying. They're intolerant, arrogant, and ignorant. And everyone's got his or her own turkeys to deal with. Turkeys in every city and town. That's why my album *Fly* is subtitled *How Can We Fly with Eagles When We're Surrounded by Turkeys?* In the song "Quanti Anni Ho" ("How Old Am I"), I long for a calmer, less conflict-ridden world, one similar to that explored by Bernardo Bertolucci in his film *1900*, which recounts a bit of the history of my land—the land I love.

In my song 'Occhi' ('Eyes'), I write: "*Ho visto gli occhi suoi, come il grano in mano al vento.*" ("I've seen her eyes, like wheat in your hands in the wind.") It had been years since I sat beneath a fig tree. With a guitar by my side and the melody born impulsively out of a farmer's soul, a man of the earth. They say that back in the days of the earliest poets, if an artist sat beneath a tree, the wind would go elsewhere to sing so as not to disturb his music, and the birds would all sing together, to help his fingers seek out the right harmonies. I wonder if it was really like that. At any rate, it's true, that record harks back to my roots—a longing for skies and the meaning of the land, the taste of life's basic pleasures, the dreams that help us take off in flight. And the relaxing color of blue: the color of the sky and the sea. It's also my son's name: Blue, to whom I dedicated a song. The album is energized by "that blue poetry" I talk about in 'Pronto' ('Hello'), in the conviction that the disaffected age in which we live is coming to an end. There's a verse in it that says, "I'm afraid of Americans, the British and Italians, Muslims and Christians too." True: In this ongoing conflict I fear all of them, along with many others not listed in the song. They're fears we all have, the product of globalization.

For *Fly* I changed producers. This time we had Don Was on board, himself a rock legend who's produced other rock legends, from the Rolling Stones to Bob Dylan. He's someone who stresses feeling as opposed to technique, and he had me play lots of different instruments. There were musicians in the studio who played way better than I do, but Don understood my music: the flavors of "fat" Emilia, the sound of the Hammond, my nondenominational altar—I first tinkled it with my fingers back when I served Mass with Don Tajadela. I would hang out at the parish just to be able to practice on the organ. That was my first concrete relationship with music. I called in another legend, Brian Auger, to play it on *Fly*. I worked with Jovanotti on the song 'Troppa Fedeltà' ('Too Much Faithfulness'), and with Ivano Fossati, another great songwriting poet, on 'È Delicato' ('It's Delicate').

The album contains all my familiar elements—including some lyrics in English and Spanish, for their phonetic quality; pagan religiousness, with plenty of Hail Mary's, fired-up sensuality, bread, wine, sky, Lucky Strike tobacco; and tenderness for my son Blue (on 'Quanti Anni Ho').

With good old Brian Auger on keyboards, Pino Palladino on bass, Michael Landau on guitar, and Ahmir Khalib Thompson (Questlove), the drummer from the Roots, there's a requiem for various scenes:

269

Down with San Francisco, where the flower children's utopia once existed. On the flipside, it's long live Cuba, marijuana, lasagna, blue skies, and gin & tonics. Basically, in my maturity I have a predilection for earthly weaknesses.

Why were the records of the past so much better than those of today? Not that I wanted to do a vintage album—I also wanted a share of young lions in the lineup. But I played a lot of the instrumental tracks myself, since it wasn't virtuosity we were after, but feeling.

The album also contains 'Let It Shine,' dedicated to New Orleans and the tragedy of Hurricane Katrina. There was a recording studio there that was like a second home to me—destroyed by the storm's wrath. I wondered if someday, when I went back, whether I'd find the same extraordinary humanity I once knew.

'Occhi' is pure romanticism, an intense ballad that recalls the styles of the 1970s, dedicated to the kind of woman who allures you in the blink of an eye. 'È Delicato' is another moving ballad, an anthem to absolute love.

That record was my little white cloud of love amid the rain of disharmony all around us. There's plenty of love in it, alright, but there's also a song that never went over too well with feminists: 'Troppa Fedeltà.' It so happened that while I was recording the album, Jovanotti paid me a visit. He wanted to meet Don Was. I already had the music for 'Troppa Fedeltà,' but the words weren't coming. So together we worked on the lyrics. The starting point was that I've never been overly faithful in love, but now I've decided to not even try to exhibit any self-control on that front. If I'm going to cheat, I'm going to do it in the open. At this point, I'm too old to be sneaking around.

The song 'Cuba Libre' was born just before Castro took ill. A coincidence. I didn't hold any particular liking for the man, but he meant a lot to Cuba and to Cubans. I wrote it at a time when America (in the role of protagonist and planetary leader), and the state of California in particular, by slapping bans left and right on smoking and eating various kinds of meat in a health craze gone berserk, became way too invasive, as far as I was concerned.

The album also included a cover of 'Salty Dog,' the Procol Harum classic, with lyrics in Italian by Pasquale Panella, re-titled 'Nel Così Blu' ('Into the Blue').

Melody—a distinctive attribute of Italian music—abounds on *Fly*. It's a sound that doesn't need a string section or high-tech wizardry. All it takes is three chords and genuine emotion. Team that up with the raucous, rough-and-tumble rhythms of black music, and that's me, my reflection in the mirror.

You Sideshow Freak!

INTERNATIONAL STARS HAVE ALWAYS PLAYED AT CALA DI VOLPE, IN Sardinia's Porto Cervo. Joe Cocker, Barry White, Ray Charles. There's always a huge celebration there in August for the Feast of the Assumption. We were on the Fly World Tour in 2007 and on our way to play at the Roman Amphitheater in Cagliari. We had three days off. The offer came to play at Cala di Volpe. When you're on tour, these kinds of offers are key—they help balance the budget.

But while there a few years earlier, I'd caused a bit of trouble. Among the guests were Lamberto Dini and the Spanish dancer Joaquin Cortés, who really got into it, and I had the ladies dancing. We had a ball. And these are people who normally stay seated, with their thousand-euro dinners, wine not included.

Then I started yelling.

"I wanna see you peglegs get up! You bunch of rich, fat-bellied derelicts! Work off some of that sadness and come down here in front of the stage and dance! Dive in the pool! You're all dead!"

All it took was Cortés and his erotic dance moves to get the hags and plastic surgery addicts out of their seats and fired up.

That year we were on our way to Malta when the same offer came in. When we got to Cala di Volpe, we were greeted, one by one, by a life-size (or bigger) margarine statue of Zucchero. Nice idea. I was all greasy.

I repeated exactly what I'd done at Cala di Volpe five years earlier. Same words, same somewhat sarcastic flavor for an evening that was supposed to be fun. The first time nothing happened. The morning after, I ran into Lamberto Dini at the airport. Oh, God, I wonder how he took it? But he just said, "Fornaciari, a stupendous evening, bravo! I really enjoyed myself."

My job is to entertain people; I like it when everyone dances. At a super-luxury hotel, poolside, with people who maybe don't exactly love rock or the blues, and know nothing about any of it, you need a different approach from when you play a stadium or big arena. I work a lot with sarcasm, with humor. I say bad words. I'm not a nightclub entertainer, I'm not a crooner or intimate singer—I've got a hot-blooded temperament. Half the people there that night figured this out no problem. They appreciated the show, danced, and applauded at the end.

In short, I'm a guy from the fields, from the streets. I come from a working-class background; everybody knows that. When I'm with friends, we use foul language with fondness, bad words are compliments: "Come here, you piece of shit!" "What're you doin', you slut?!" So, you can imagine that, for us, playing and singing while people are eating their dinner isn't what you'd call an ideal situation. It was natural for me to ratchet up the tone and the rhythm: "Get off your asses and dance!" That's my style, like it or not. My fans like it. I normally have a good relationship with audiences that don't give me any flak. And it certainly would have been easier to just do a regular show. "Good night, ladies and gentlemen. Thank you for the applause. See you next summer."

I walked onstage after being introduced and immediately saw a lady sending text messages. She didn't even look at me, just went on typing away and playing with her cell phone. At one point, I got totally fed up with her and said so. There was a table of 21 Russians in front of the stage. None of them looked at me either, amid a crowd of plastic surgery addicts and neo-yuppies escaped from the 1980s. I started singing and nobody moved. The plastified hag kept crassly working her phone. By the time we got to 'Baila,' the audience was interacting. But the Russian lady kept on doing her own thing, chatting away, sending text messages, not paying the least attention or showing the slightest interest. She'd come with that ridiculous thousand-euro ticket in her pocket to purposely not listen. The only time she turned toward me was to give me the finger. That's right. Fuck you. By that point I was pretty worked up, and said the first thing that popped into my head. If Beppe Grillo had said it, everyone probably would've laughed. Instead, her date, a huge Russian, jumped up and threw a lemon at me, or a bottle—I don't remember the succession of objects he threw. I replied. The whole tableful of Russians rose up in rage. Some tried to get onstage to exact justice then and there, but they were stopped by security. I thought, *they're paying, they might as well listen.* Otherwise, why pay? A thousand euros and up, just for dinner?

It was then that I exploded. I'm basically shy but impulsive, and I lost it.

"Why'd you get a table in the front row, just to act like a stuck-up little bitch? What lovely people in Cala di Volpe tonight! You sideshow freak! Trash bin! Super slut!" And on and on.

The agreement was that all telephones were to be turned off during the show, to avoid any unauthorized audio or video recordings. But I didn't realize the whole scene was being recorded by the Italian satire website Dagospia.

Meanwhile my Russian friend was trying to get onstage again, but security kept him at bay. He threw a few more lemons, which I dodged. It was great entertainment. I was super pissed off as we went into 'Diavolo in Me,' because I had noticed there was an open bottle of Gatorade on the stage—which, with all the cables and wires around, was dangerous. So, I gave it a kick, and wouldn't you know, it made a splash landing right smack on the Russians' table. At which point they all left in a great huff. The upshot was that I immediately received an advertising offer from the management at Gatorade.

The situation degenerated even further during the encore. I introduced 'Indaco dagli Occhi del Cielo,' saying it was a cover of a song by a group from Glasgow, the Korgis.

"You're paid to sing, not talk!" I heard someone yell.

It was Daniela Santanchè. An Italian politician of the far right.

I didn't take the bait.

The next day, thanks to Dagospia, news of the show hit all the Italian papers and TV shows. Santanchè advised women to boycott my records, because in her opinion they were offensive.

Before leaving, I went to say goodbye to the hotel director, just so he wouldn't take me for a bum.

"My dear Fornaciari, we certainly enjoyed ourselves last night, didn't we?"

I thought he was being facetious.

"Well, sir, I'm sorry there was a bit of confusion…"

"My dear Fornaciari, you must be joking! A little rowdiness to shake things up was exactly what we needed around here!"

"So, Fornaciari," he continued, "tell me: Are you a Communist?"

What did that have to do with anything and why should he care?

"Because," he insisted, "here we're all very much right-wingers."

And he gave me the Roman salute.

Go take a shit, dude.

I didn't sleep that night because I was afraid the scandal of the summer had broken out. For hours on end, I got calls from the editors of newspapers who wanted to come interview me in Pontremoli. I flat-out refused.

I read a beautiful article that appeared on the front page of *La Repubblica*. I wasn't familiar with Edmondo Berselli's writing before, but this episode gave me the opportunity. I called him right away to thank him for explaining that a little bit of anarchy and outrageousness was appropriate to ridicule that bunch of rich louts. Then there was Francesco Merlo, who wrote an article headlined "What If Zucchero Was Right?"

I quote: "When it comes down to it, calling a boor a boor is not an insult. The singer Zucchero deserves our understanding for feeling the need to denounce the boorishness of an audience that nibbled on his blues while nibbling on caviar."

Too graceful. Here's more: "Zucchero at Porto Cervo wasn't a frustrated revolutionary with an axe to grind. It's more like he earned his degree in music anthropology. He's the first singer-ethnologist. And just as Petronius depicted Trimalchio in *Satyricon*, at Cala di Volpe Zucchero dug summertime Sardinia out of its oyster, its Champagne and its 43-meter-long yachts. He did a better job than we journalists and sociologists have done—the latter having created a false image of Italian excellence based on the boorish Sardinia of the tourists, and not the natives."

After that episode, I was afraid I'd get booed at my next show. There was a celebration in my town, so I figured I'd go test the waters.

"*Te fatbein a dirghel!*"—"You did good to let 'em have it!" they yelled.

I lucked out.

On the beach, someone put up a banner that READ TRASH bin in big block letters.

I got a message from Silvio Sircana, the spokesman for Romano Prodi: "If you want to start up a Party of the Plastic Surgery Addicts, call me!"

Romano Prodi, who hails from Emilia Romagna like me, called too.

"No damage done, don't worry. It's the funniest thing all summer! You're really going to have some concerts now, you'll see!"

To hell with the spirit of the times, the spirit of plastic surgery addicts.

In this absurd, surreal contest between a musician of plebian origins, possessed of a hot-blooded temperament, and the rich louts of the Emerald Coast, we put it all on the line.

Chocabeck

AUTUMN COMES TO PONTREMOLI IN LATE SEPTEMBER, THE SEASON when we eat mushrooms and *testaroli* with pesto. It was around that time in 2009 that I began writing material for *Chocabeck*. I'm a musician: I'm all too glad to open my toolbox for you. This time I began with the vocals. I wanted something raw and rough. Something that would stand out, something different. A new sound with respect to what I had done up to then.

We'd gone through some dark years in Italy, not only for music but for creativity in general. The Middle Ages all over again, kind of like the 1980s. Back then, at least there was still disco—something decent in a sea of commercial trash. I hadn't heard anything new that I liked in a long time, anything that impressed me, that gave me goosebumps. Except for an album by Johnny Cash, the famed American singer-songwriter known for his country-folk tunes and talking blues, *American VI: Ain't No Grave*. The album was put together posthumously, from recordings he'd made shortly before his death. It's more country-western-folk than blues. With his big, raspy, 70-year-old voice, you can hear the saliva smacking when he sings. His vocals are in the foreground, and what little instrumentation there is accompanying him is in the background—heartrending arrangements.

Blues, soul, rhythm & blues—those are the sounds I adore, my first loves, which I used to forge my own music. I still listen to those sounds, and they're constantly running through my mind.

Anyway, that record by Johnny Cash really impressed and inspired me. I wanted to strip down and go it alone. Just my voice, a guitar, and not much else. *Chocabeck* features minimal percussion. No complete drum kit, just various percussive elements, like the bass drum that sounds more like something out of a marching band. There's no electric or double bass—the bass sounds were created with a Hammond organ, an instrument I've always loved (my non-denominational altar), and the low notes of a piano put through a compressor. By dispensing with two basic components of the rhythm section, it instantly changed the sound of the album. I wanted to hear sounds that remained suspended in midair.

I used lots of acoustic guitars and arpeggios, a little like the singer-songwriters of the 1970s: James Taylor, the Byrds; 12-string guitars, mandolins, guitars with Nashville tuning, which is an octave higher than standard tuning, for a sound almost like a harpsichord, light and bubbly on the high notes. The dominant sound, though, comes from the church organ—the sound of my childhood, the sound of Sunday, just like I played at Don Tajadela's church.

It was all very simple, really. As far as instrumentation goes, the church organ is upfront; there are lots of guitars, limited percussion, and a piano. For rhythmic counterpoint, we used a combination of electric and traditional string instruments for a chipper, lively, syncopated sound, as opposed to that of a classical orchestra. As I said, the sounds and atmospheres are suspended in midair—colors, dust, shooting stars, magic spells. They open up the soundscape, but you can't really tell what the sound is. They're not synthesizers. They're keyboards. Brian Eno's a master at this. I replaced the traditional rhythm & blues horn section—saxophone, trumpet, and trombone—with French horn, bassoon, oboe, bass tuba, and English horn. Very warm sounds.

When I wrote the first song, with all these ingredients, I realized I'd found the sound of Sunday, the one I was looking for to evoke the atmospheres of that time. Sounds, colors, visions, love, affection. The memory of a link with a place and relationships that were a fundamental part of my life, which I now miss enormously. That song was 'Un Soffio Caldo' ('A Warm Breath of Air'). As usual, I didn't have lyrics yet, and I sang it in what I call *maccheronico*, that is, fake English, which inspires the sounds of the actual words to come. As soon as I heard the arpeggios, the flutes, the piccolos, the English horns, the sound of the bells—lots of bells—I heard the sound of Sunday. The color of the countryside. I could smell the hay and the barns. More recollections; the intermittence of memory. The church in Roncocesi, the organ, Marzia, me serving Mass, the dairy cooperative, the river, the bridge, the school, the valley, the old men with hats playing cards and drinking Lambrusco, the diatribes of the priest and my Communist uncle, children running and shouting in the churchyard, the chair-o-plane ride in the square at the Feast of Saint Biagio, Popsicles and *fruttini* (fruit-flavored ice cream), the good taste of our neighbor's *prosciutto* and *coppa*, two slices of *gnocco fritto* (fried dough) dripping grease and melting the fat of the *prosciutto* in one corner, the smell of *lesso* or *bollito* (boiled beef)—I'm still crazy about it, with the fragrance that wafts through the kitchen like gusts of goodness bedazzling and enrapturing you—green sauce, red sauce, *la giardiniera*, or mixed pickled vegetables, which my mother would add a hard-boiled egg to for good measure—with seed oil, since there was no olive oil where we lived.

In the suspended, fable-like life of Sundays in the village, on the wave of my memories, an intimate flow of memory, so very personal—I abandoned myself to it. In my village, wheat was still yellow. A pretty, pure, authentic village. My roots. Emilian roots. Farmers' roots. Today Roncocesi is a suburb, a nondescript outlying district swallowed up by Reggio Emilia, a strip of hinterland marked off by traffic circles.

Every Monday, when I was growing up, my father and I would go to Correggio to buy cold cuts directly from the producers; there was no superhighway. You had to board a train with your car at the Pontremoli station, which passed through Fornovo, shortening the trip by a couple of hours. It was weird, putting the car on a train, like something out of a vintage Western epic. Through the window, I could watch the scenery transform at such high speed it looked like the land was moving and vibrating. I thoroughly enjoyed those cheese-and-*prosciutto* journeys with my dad. It was always an adventure. Traveling the frontier, crossing borders, along the river, up the mountains. When, years later, I had to decide where to put down roots, I was torn apart. The family I adored was in Reggio, while my beloved daughters were in Forte dei Marmi. I chose a place in the middle, equidistant—my sentimental geography. In Pontremoli, I rebuilt that old farm where we eat only what we produce ourselves—from the flour we grind in the mill to make our bread, the milk, fruit, vegetables, and meat—pigs, rabbits, and lamb. It's a genuine lifestyle.

The world has gone to pot. There's no solidarity among people; wars rage. There's no tolerance, only worship of money and success; collective narcissism and egoism instead of friendship; noisy self-propaganda, vulgar self-exhibition, with everyone thinking only of themselves; everyone's alone, people spend their Sundays surfing the Web. I perceive a generalized malaise. I crave authenticity, only it's not about getting back to "the way we were." It's about values. Healthy, simple, ancient values. Values for people who know how to roll up their sleeves and get to work. Food, home, instinctive solidarity. Tastes, colors, smells, shapes. The rhythms of the seasons, the rhythms of songs, the rhythms of words. There, living was living. It meant surrendering yourself to the rhythms of man and nature. Neither suffering and distressed, nor celebrating it—you simply accepted those rhythms for what they were.

For me Sunday was magic—peace all around. I could hear the

sounds, smell the smells, experience emotions and sensations I didn't notice on other days because I was too busy.

Now I no longer hear the sound of Sundays. Everything stopped, in a time suspended and rarified—the sound of children running and playing, bells ringing, plates on the table, utensils, the ladle pouring out the broth, the spoon clanging in a dish. We were a patriarchal family, 12 of us—14 for Sunday dinner.

Around Christmas time, Sunday dinner would feature *cappelletti in brodo*, my mom's homemade *capltón* (green pasta stuffed with herbs), and tomato sauce cooked in lard. Then came *cotechino* (a spicy boiled pork sausage) with various sauces, small, marinated eels (*stortino* in dialect; the poor folks' *capitone*, a large eel). Followed by fried pork rinds, coppa, salami, boiled hen, rabbit. And plenty of Lambrusco.

Fish, never. The men in our family didn't fish. The people from the cooperative used to go fishing in the river and return triumphantly: "I caught a catfish!" Or a tench, or a carp.

The sole exception was when my mom breaded and fried up pieces of cod. They were delicious, and my dad really loved them.

My mom and aunt did the cooking, and it was mostly based on pork. The pig slaughter was a big event. There'd be *sanguinaccio* (blood sausage), *frittelle di sangue* (fried blood cakes), *ciccioli* (fried pork rinds), *cotenne* (pork skin)—we'd eat the whole pig. We survived the winters on pork. Grandma Diamante was already quite old and had to take care of my grandfather, who never recovered after the death of their son. He had cold sweats. He was melancholic. He was afraid of dying, and not a day went by that he didn't go into his mantra-like litany around evening time, "Old lady, I'm dying." To which my grandmother would reply, "What do you mean dying, Cannella?!" He had panic attacks, but back then, especially in the countryside, no one really knew what they were.

"I'm all sweaty, I'm dying," my grandfather would say to my grandmother Diamante.

"No, Cannella, what are you talking about?"

Patiently she would sit him down in the *cadrega* wicker chair, take off his pullover the color of old-time undershirts, and dry off his sweat with a towel. She'd make up some hot broth and have him drink it, and then he'd smoke his cigar—I remember the spittoon beneath the *cadrega*—after which he would lay down in bed.

When I started having panic attacks, my symptoms were the same as Grandpa Cannella's. Cold sweats. The first sign of a panic attack. In the beginning, when you don't know what's happening and haven't learned to live with them, you might think panic attacks are a form of congestion. You get short of breath, your heart starts racing, you feel like you can't move, you don't care about anything else, you think you're dying. When the specialist Professor Cassano of the University of Pisa examined me at San Rossore, he asked whether anyone else in my family had ever suffered the same symptoms, explaining that there could be a genetic factor involved. I talked to Aunt Faustina about it, and we recalled Canella's illness. Unfortunately, it was a family trait. My grandfather's panic attacks had begun one evening at dusk toward the end of the war, after he got the news that his son had been killed. A messenger showed up and without much ado came straight out with it: "Cannella, your son is dead." From that fateful moment on, every evening at Vespers, Cannella would shut himself up in the attic, where the bundles of long sticks were kept, and only come out again two hours later, after the bells of Vespers stopped ringing. For him, the sound of the bells that signaled prayer time was also the announcement of his son's death. And every evening, at that same time, he would have a panic attack, triggered by that sound. The sound of death.

On Sundays in my youth, the ice cream man would come by with his cart. I would scrape together 50 lire for a cone with two flavors. Otherwise I'd get a *bif* (Popsicle) at the Cooperative bar. If I opted for ice cream, that meant no Popsicle.

There was space, lots of open space. Green meadows, fields of wheat and corn, where I walked hand in hand with my grandmother as she told me her stories and fairy tales with infinite sweetness. She wasn't an authoritarian, like the ones who always tell you to change your shirt and not to sweat or get dirty. That stuff didn't matter to her. What counted most was just being together. And loving each other. And talking. Always in dialect.

Then there were afternoons with my uncle—when I helped him build a guitar for me, or we'd tend to the chickens and rabbits. The air I breathed was serene.

In winter, we did our homework in the barn. It was the warmest place, since the only time the adults lit the cheap stove inside the house was to make dinner. At nighttime, when it got cold again, we'd go to bed with our "priests" and "nuns," as we called the bed warming pans. It was deathly cold. But snuggled up under the covers, it was nice and warm.

The vegetable man had his megaphone. The mattress man, his wool.

"Ladies, the knife grinder is here!"

I'd just completed the longest tour of my life, played and sung all over the world. Big cities, world capitals. Maybe it was my anxiety and fear of globalization that made me crave a whole new mindset. Fuck it, I said to myself, I need to get back to my roots. The real ones. The authentic ones. Why not make a record where I describe with words, but mostly with music—because music talks, it immediately takes you to a place, it conjures up an atmosphere, a situation—what Sundays were like in the village?

With a laugh I challenged Leopardi, and I did it. The village from morning to night. My Recanati was Roncocesi, the place I want to bring along inside me when I go traveling around the world, when I want to feel good and think of things genuine and healthy, and fall asleep with those moments running through my head. It's not nostalgia. I'd been feeling good lately, in the present, in my own age. It's remembrance. It's the book of my love and affection. I wanted to leave Zucchero aside for a while and go back to being Adelmo. The boy inside me isn't dead or dormant—a teacher of mine wrote me that in a sweet and delicate note she sent after seeing me on TV at Sanremo. In fact, sometimes I'm still capable of the same boyish pranks my teenaged son used to pull. And saying naïve, childish things. That's a part of me I've always wanted to protect and keep safe. God bless the child in me.

What Does Sunday Sound Like for You?

WHEN I MET LEGENDARY SINGER-SONGWRITER FRANCESCO GUCCINI TO ask him to write the lyrics to 'Un Soffio Caldo,' these were the ideas I was trying to convey, the themes I wanted to explore on my album. Like me, Francesco is an Emilian and lives in a mountain town: Pàvana, in Tuscany. He captured the spirit of the sound of Sunday to perfection.

"*L'alba ai granai, filtra di qua dal monte. un respiro d'aria nuova. Chiudo gli occhi e sento di già che la stagione mia s'innova. I sogni, sai, non dormono mai. Sento pace nell'aurora, un soffio caldo di libertà.*" ("Dawn at the granaries, filtering in from over the mountains. A breath of fresh air. I close my eyes and feel my season anew. Dreams, you know, never sleep. I feel peace in the aurora, a warm breath of freedom.")

The magnificent words of Francesco. The song is about the lack of freedom today, about the false sense of freedom we have been granted. It begins with a description of the light of dawn filtering down from the mountains to start the day; it lights up the river and crosses the bridge. This warm breath is what you need. You seek it out in order to feel better, to warm your dreams. But sometimes dreams are broken. You have to be careful; there are lots of dogs, lots of masters. They tell you what to do, fill you up with obligations, and restrict your freedom. But each day the light returns, crossing the bridge, bringing hope, passion, and enthusiasm.

I've known Francesco for years. I grew up with his music. One day I asked him to write some song lyrics for me. "Sure," he said, "but if they're no good, just throw them away."

'Soldati Nella Mia Città' ('Soldiers in My City') captures the postwar atmosphere of Grandma Diamante, and this song is dedicated to her—I loved her so very much that I asked a true poet of the modern Italian song, Francesco De Gregori, to write it for me. It's the story of soldiers leaving my city, and the days of sunlight to come, along with the rain that cleanses everything, and fear as well.

"*È un peccato morir*"—"It's a shame to die"—is an expression used by old folks where I'm from. What the fuck, Zucchero, you're talking about death? Not at all, just the opposite. I'm talking about life.

"*Aio magnéun salam cle un pchè murir.*" ("I ate salami because it's a shame to die.") "*Aio vest ona acsè bela cle un pchè murir.*" ("I saw a beautiful girl, what a shame it is to die.") "*Inco a staj propria bein, le un pchè murir.*" ("Today I feel great, what a shame it is to die.")

A song in praise of life, which I wrote with Pasquale Panella, full of the double entendre we're known for when we write together. I truly enjoy writing songs with him. Pasquale and I have written lines like "*Se fossi un lago dilagherei*" ("If I were a lake, I'd overflow"), for the song 'Rossa Mela della Sera' ('Apple-Red Evening'); and these lines, from 'È un Peccato Morir': "*Ai piatti pieni a tavola / alla gente nostrana senza boria né buriana*" ("To the full plates on the table / to our people who put on no airs or uproar") and "*Almeno prima di fare centouno*" ("At least before turning a hundred and one"), another expression our old folks use—turning a hundred and one means dying—and "*Come sarà l'altra vita da suino?*" ("How will our next life be as pigs?"). I don't believe in reincarnation, though if it does happen, I'd choose to be an old pig—the pig being the totem animal of my land. A prayer singing the praises of life: birds that sing, the sun, good food and the flavors of home, the longing to live long enough to relive everything.

Then there's 'Vedo Nero' ('I See Black'), featuring the scene with Vittorina, a girl from my hometown. There was a refrain Mimmo Cavallo had written, a demo he'd sent me a while back, and I still had it but didn't know what to do with it. It went: *"Come disse la marchesa camminando sugli specchi: me la vedo nera"* ("As the marchioness said while walking on the mirrors. It looks black to me")—a cute little romp, perfect in this kind of context. The song was inspired by one of my greatest muses, Vittorina, and extols the pleasures of the flesh. The drama of eros was, of course, another powerful force from my roots. I remember seeing my aunt naked in the washtub; jerk-off contests with my friends in the sorghum fields as our hormones were bubbling up, on the verge of exploding; the toothless calves with their warm, juicy, welcoming mouths in Tagliavini's barn, where we went to do our homework in winter; and the eruption of sex from Vittorina's hairy cunt.

I'd seized on a key moment from my adolescence. It was all about discovery, vision, the explosion of desire. The erotic tempest. Boys, teenagers would stop me in the street and say, "Hey, Zucchero, I see black too!" One night at dinner, a nephew asked, "Uncle, what does 'I see black' mean? What were you trying to say?"

"Come on," I said, "I think you can guess." At which his cheeks flamed red, he was all embarrassed. I've got a lot of fans among kids—they're quick to pick up on figures of speech, wordplays, having fun with language. Whether it's explicit or mischievous.

"Pippo, che cazzo fai?" ("Pippo, what the fuck are you doing?" from the song 'Pippo'). *"Funky Gallo, chicchirichi"* ("Funky rooster, cock-a-doodle-doo," from the song 'X Colpa di Chi'). *"Il tuo cervello non pesa un chilo"* ("Your brain weighs less than one kilo," from the song 'Un Kilo'). Now it was time for 'Vedo Nero': *"E non c'è pace per me"* ("And

there's no peace for me"). *"Come disse il pesce infarinato: sono fritto"* ("Like the flour-dusted fish said: I'm fried.")

'Oltre le Rive' ('Beyond the Shores') is a ballad with a line that goes *"Io sarò sempre qua. E tu arriverai senza fare rumore. Oltre le rive"* ("I'll be here always. And you'll come without a sound. Beyond the shores.").

The Modolena Creek flows through Roncocesi about 300 meters past the church. I spent a lot of time there with friends when I was young. We caught fish with our hands. It was there that I cut my finger on a shard of glass, a pretty deep gash, while going after a fish in the mud. Beyond the banks of that creek was another world. It wasn't a river like the Po, but it was still fairly big. On the other side stood another village, Villa Cella—and the people there were no longer us; they were them. *"Io starò sempre qua e ti aspetterò. oltre le rive, al di là del confine. Tra la vita e la morte"* ("I'll be here always, waiting for you. Beyond the shores, across the border. Between life and death.").

In 'Un Uovo Sodo' ('A Hard-Boiled Egg'), double entente abounds. *"E intanto un mirto ai mirti colli già sale"* ("Meanwhile a myrtle rises upon myrtle hills"). This goes back to when I was rejected by Marzia, a girl from the village who I was in love with. I was crazy about her. She was my girlfriend, only she didn't know it. She chose Tagliavini instead. He was fat, with pimples. *"Sono qui che ti aspetto, steso al sole che asciugo il dolore, mi sento un uovo sodo senza te perché non c'è più posto per me, se non c'è posto dentro al tuo cuore"* ("I'm here waiting for you, lying in the sun, drying of my pain. I feel like a hard-boiled egg without you. There's no place for me anywhere if there's no room in your heart for me.").

It's a sunny day kind of song, upbeat, like 'Vedo Nero.' I didn't want to make an album featuring only ballads. Memory is melancholy, but it's also good cheer. Vitality, feeling carefree, exploding with the energy of life.

When you're feeling embarrassed and she doesn't want you but you're there waiting for her, looking for her, and she won't give you the time of day, you feel gawky, deflated; you're not flying anymore. Well, what's gawkier than a hard-boiled egg? *"Un uovo sodo, senza te."* ("A hard-boiled egg, without you.")

'Chocabeck' is a portrait of me as a child. I wrote the lyrics with Pasquale Panella. I'd written the music years earlier, in the 1970s, but hadn't done anything with it. Back then I called it 'Anni Sessanta' ('The Sixties'), and recorded it on two tracks. I found it among my piles of cassettes. It started out the same way, with a chorus going "uh uh uh uh." I'd forgotten all about it. Just one voice singing in fake English, and a piano. So I updated the sounds—I already knew what I wanted—and I arranged it like the rest of the stuff on the album.

"Ecco io, laggiù laggiù, da ragazzino ne sapevo di più. di più, di più. l'amore fu un calcinculo e tante stelle lassù. adesso che non so chi sei, che sette, otto, nove, dieci sarai"—of course, that part was by Panella—*"mi manca sai il chocabeck"* ("There I am, down there. I never knew much more when I was a kid. Love was a kick in the ass and a starry sky overhead. Now that I no longer know who you are, seven, eight, nine, ten you'll be. I really miss chockabeck, you know").

Today I'm a lucky man. I can have six, seven, even ten of anything I want—but I'll always miss 'chocabeck,' that dialect expression my father used. I just anglicized the spelling to globalize the term. Just as all my work reflects a global outlook. The choruses on this song are great, featuring the magic of Brian Wilson, legendary leader of the Beach Boys. His contribution did a lot to improve the music I'd written.

Younger fans may not realize there was a time when the Beach Boys were even bigger than the Beatles. The Beatles were inspired by the Beach Boys, and took plenty of cues from them in their trajectory from pupils to masters. As for Brian Wilson, he spent years in isolation, before finding a way to start working again. I was lucky that he happened to be working in the same studio in Los Angeles as me; and the great Don Was, my producer—who'd worked with the Rolling Stones and Johnny Cash, among others—knew Brian well.

The hottest producer of the moment, Grammy Award–winning Brendan O'Brien, co-produced the record. He produced acts like Pearl Jam and the Red Hot Chili Peppers. Even though he was super-busy, with tons of commitments, he agreed to work with me on *Chocabeck* because he fell in love with the material. It did pretty well in the UK and the United States, probably because it sounded so much more American than my previous albums.

I'd finished recording the music and had begun mixing tracks at EastWest Studios in Hollywood, when I started wondering about the lyrics in English for 'Il Suono della Domenica' ('The Sound of Sunday'). Who was going to write them? I figured that if anyone could capture the meaning and atmosphere, it would be Bono Vox. I called him and sent him the song. He said he liked it and since he wasn't touring, he would try to come up with something. Bono is very frank and direct, he's good to work with—he's always willing and able to provide a host of different solutions without showing off.

"I'll give it a shot," he said, "and if you don't like it, no problem. You can do what you like and use whatever you want. If this one's no good, let me know and I'll write something else."

That's the right approach to working together. There's nothing presumptuous about Bono—the way a lot of artists are, the ones who write lyrics for you, then come out with a menacing "Take it or leave it."

A month went by. I started thinking, he hasn't come up with a fuckin' thing; this is going nowhere. Then one Saturday morning, in the studio in Avenza where I do my writing, concentrating on the Italian lyrics, I get a call from Bono.

"Hey, man! I'm working for you. I've got a concept in mind that I'm still chipping away at. I'm definitely into it. Check this out." And he starts reading: "The wine is pressed and despite the rain it's been a good year. To walk these fields again in the chapel of our youth, we bowed down to beauty and truth."

I was struck by the images. They were perfectly in synch with what I was working on for the Italian lyrics. Bono soon sent me the finished version. I speak English well, but speaking is one thing—singing is a whole other ballgame. So I asked him to send me a rough cut with his voice over the base I'd laid down. I somehow doubted he'd go for it. But the very next day he sent me an MP3. What a thrill it was when I heard his voice singing to my music. I was with Francesca at the time, and even she was captivated and moved. And when I sang those words of Bono's, I got goosebumps. He sent me this text message, which I've kept to this day: "I'm proud of having done this song with you."

Bono's version is titled 'Someone Else's Tears.' There's a verse that goes, "Why can't I stop crying? And nothing is as it appears. I can't stop crying, but I'm crying someone else's tears." I never asked him what he meant by that, but I think it refers to his father, with whom he'd always had a very conflicted relationship. He had passed away recently, and I had the feeling Bono hadn't been able to work things out between them. The song starts out, "You feel familiar, but I'm not sure I know your name." Bono laid his insecurity about his own identity and his feelings of guilt on the line.

I recorded it. Before the record went into print, Bono was in Rome for a concert at the Olympic Stadium. He hadn't heard my version in English yet. I went with Francesca to pay him a little visit and give him a listen—most of all to see if he approved of my English. In his dressing room, before going on, he put on a pair of headphones and gave it a go. He held his hands on his head and was really concentrating on it. I was sitting there feeling pretty tense, worried about whether, or not, he'd like it. When the song was over he opened his eyes, looked at me and said, "You've given me a great gift." He had tears in his eyes. When he got up on stage he cried out, "Zucchero, I love you."

Iggy Pop also worked on the project. He came up with English versions of 'Chocabeck' and 'È un Peccato Morir.' We worked via email since he was on tour while I was recording. I asked him to rewrite some stuff. I wanted his words in my mouth and I wanted to feel they were wholly my own when I sang them. He proposed chatting online. I must admit, I have my issues with high-tech. Go ahead and try to download a *tortellino* from the Internet.

Roland Orzabal of Tears for Fears penned the English version of 'Un Soffio Caldo,' titled 'Live.'

As I said, Francesco Guccini wrote the lyrics to 'Un Soffio Caldo.' I had never worked with him before. His mother, who was from Carpi, had said to me many times, *"Delmo, fa bein quel con Francesco"* ("Delmo, be nice to Francesco."). Around the same time that I sent the music to Bono for what would become 'Someone Else's Tears,' I called up Francesco. He's my idol, I'm a huge fan of his, and have been since I was little, back in the days when the Nomads sang his songs. This music is perfect for him, I thought. It gave him the opportunity to use lots of words, the way he usually does—he's a great narrator of song. He's also one of the slowest men in the world, and always puts everything off.

"When are you coming back from Los Angeles?"

"In four weeks."

He went on the defensive, which was par for the course.

"I'll give it a try, but no guarantees. I'm an old man. I hope I'll have something for you."

I called him when I got back. Fuck! The guy had written just four lines. It was the opening of the song and they were beautiful. But at this rate, we would never finish.

"Francesco," I said, "I'll come over to your place in Pàvana tomorrow. We'll hang out a while, I'll give you a little push."

I got there.

Francesco: "First let's eat."

We set to work in the afternoon, together with his cats. I sang to him in fake English, and he would turn out lines in Italian, very pretty words. But they weren't broken up the way I did them in English, because Italian is less syncopated, it has fewer truncated words. I said to him, "Francesco, instead of saying it this way, can't we say it in such and such a way, just to shorten the words?"

"No way, eh. No, no. That's a whole 'nother story."

He wouldn't budge. "You can't shrink *my season is renewing to my season is newing*." That is, one syllable less. "No way! There's no such word as *newing* in Italian!" He's the professorial type. Still, we managed to finish most of the lyrics by evening. Over the next few days, I worked out the rest at home. My son Blue adores Francesco and his music, and can even do a perfect imitation of him, including his characteristic French pronunciation of *r* when he sings "Amerigo"—Blue knows it by heart. "He was old now, he wore a holster and a gun."

We filmed the video at the Guccini family's old mill, which originally belonged to his great-grandfather, Chicòn: walking along the river of Francesco's childhood adventures; sitting in front of the cracked fireplace; Francesco writing the lyrics with a pen nib in an old notebook. Afterward he came to Pontremoli with his wife Raffaella. We ate and stayed up till five in the morning, while he sang us Argentinian songs his guitarist Flaco had taught him. We spent some beautiful moments together.

'Alla Fine' ('In the End') is the second song I wrote for *Chocabeck*. I composed both music and words together, which is rare for me—though that's also how I wrote 'Overdose d'Amore' and 'Diavolo in Me.' There's a line in it—"*Che alla fine, mi manchi addosso*" ("How in the end, I miss you all over")—I came up with when thinking of a friend of mine. Roberto. Nicknamed Belìn. Not an old friend. A recent friend, from Rapallo, who hooked up with me and my pals three years earlier. I have a group of friends in Pontremoli: Eddy, Oriella, Bugelli, the minstrel from Lunigiana, Armanetti the diviner,

Oddo and Anna—the same crowd for the past 20 years. We hang out on Saturdays and Sundays. Roberto was a man who loved the sea, captain of his yacht, handsome fellow, a youthful 60-year-old, endowed with spirit. An exquisite human being. We got along tremendously.

"I really feel good when I'm with you, Belìn."

True friendship, shared by men. I never talked about music with him. He used to bring me *focaccia di Recco*. White pizza with a little cheese in it. He was a gentleman, gallant with the ladies, somewhat 1950s style. And how he loved to dance!

It had been a while since I'd last seen him, and he looked much thinner.

He said, "I eat like I used to, but I'm losing weight. I dunno, maybe it's the heartburn."

A month later he was even skinnier. He had a tumor in his pancreas. Deadly. I felt like shit when I heard the news. I thought of him when I wrote this song. To tell him how I felt. And to remember him always.

I played it for our friends, who told his wife about it. His wife told him. And he wanted to hear it. I went to his home. He was in bed, skinny, emaciated, suffering. Hollow eyes.

"*Caro mio dolce amico, siamo caduti bucando il cielo, che alla fine mi manchi addosso oramai, che alla fine manchi anche adesso.*" ("My dear, sweet friend, we made holes in the sky as we fell, and in the end, I miss you all over, in the end I miss you now.")

"*Spicinfrìn*" is another expression in Lower Reggiano dialect that my grandmother Diamante and my mother would use. That's what my mom would call me—she was sweet, affectionate, loving. "*Vin ché spicinfrìn!*" ("Come here, you naughty little boy!") A beautiful sound. It sounds American: "Spicinfrìn Boy." Which is me. "*Flying angel in the sky, mia madre, vedo un Pino tra i rosai, nel tramonto bello assai, e un bambino che ha gli occhi suoi.*" ("Fly angel in the sky, my mother, I see Pino among the roses in the beautiful sunset, and a boy with his eyes.") That's me. *"Ancora non ti ho persa, stai soltanto dormendo nella mia testa. Passa un treno che va via, di un colore nostalgia."* ("I still haven't lost you, you're just sleeping in my head. A nostalgia-colored train passes by and goes on its way.") Referencing Guccini's memorable nostalgia-colored dishes in his magnificent hit from the early 1970s, 'Incontro' ('Encounter').

"E pasciuto di sciupio, sono già più vicino a dio." ("And well-fed on waste, now I'm closer to God.") Mamma mia! *"Non ti ho mai perduto amore, stai soltanto dormendo in fondo al mio cuore."* ("I haven't lost you, love, you're just sleeping deep within my heart.")

Closing out the album is a blues tune, 'God Bless the Child'—a blues ditty featuring the town band and violins off the staff—the way I imagine Stravinsky might have been played in 1930s Louisiana. Dissonant horns and gritty vocals. I'd originally intended it for just vocals and piano. Sooner or later, almost every musician in the world winds up an album with a vocals-and-piano piece, or vocals and guitar. I was looking for another idea. Max Marcolini, my longtime collaborator (he studied at the conservatory, works as a producer, and plays guitar in my daughter Irene's band), worked out these sounds together with me on the computer in my studio. Daring. Without following any specific guidelines. Not knowing where we'd wind up.

I presented the album in public for the first time in Brescello, the town in the Lower Reggiano area where the author Giovannino Guareschi set his extraordinary bickering between Communist mayor Peppone and the priest Don Camillo. In the piazza, the chair-o-plane ride blared the songs from *Chocabeck*.

Truman Capote once said, if you could put all the scents and sensations of childhood into a bottle and seal it tight, it would be a great comfort in later life, when at last your days are numbered, to open that bottle back up. I have held onto that bottle, and when I turned

56 on September 25, 2011, I opened it up and transformed its contents into the 11 songs that recount my life and my roots.

Now the sound of Sunday is gone, except for its echoes in the fantastical village lost in memory.

Moral of the Story

IN MY COUNTRY—ITALY—CULTURE HAS BECOME FOR THE FEW. THAT'S called moral decay. I'm Italian, I feel good at home, I enjoy the story of my origins, of those around me, and especially of those I don't know. Because when it comes down to it, music feeds off history. It's nourished by stories.

But I can't be proud of my country today. Traveling the world has often meant witnessing a solidarity among men that we don't have in Italy. If you're an artist or an author, you have to be a kind of peeping Tom. You've got to mix yourself up with others and live inside them. This is the sensibility of those who create art. And learning to see, hear, touch something different from myself has always shown me a human reality that can't even be imagined here in Italy. I suffer a little from this: Working with all your passion and energy, and realizing you're surrounded by malaise, arrogance. It's almost no longer civilization at all.

When I'm abroad, I can see in the eyes of the people who interview me a mixture of contempt and compassion, a gaze that doesn't completely understand the drama of living in a country that paralyzes and deadens culture. Why can't we change things?

I'm not the sanctimonious type. My religion is transgression. I'm anarchic, irreverent. And I believe the only channel for youthful, creative expression is art. Art needs to be nourished, because so long as there's art, there's freedom.

Epilogue

I'VE BEEN THROUGH THE MEAT GRINDER OF DEPRESSION AND PANIC attacks. I didn't think anything had any sense anymore. I let myself go.

I love life. When I'm here at Lunisiana Soul, this place that I've built in my own likeness, that fits me like a glove, I feel fine.

Blue's wild; he's got my coloring, I see a lot of myself in him. He's Emilian, he was born in Reggio Emilia. He's got a positive attitude. He's exuberant about life. Doesn't say too much; he's taciturn. He's lively, full of life, and introverted. Funny, sharp, sarcastic. He teases me. He can be a bit of a son of a bitch, like me.

He adores Emilian cooking, its fat-soaked flavors, its delectable smells. He's a kid who loves running across the fields barefoot, his curls in the wind, like I used to do when I was little.

Alice has the complex character of her mother. She's a free spirit, independent, anarchic. Can't stand authority. She's a stylist. She's worked with Mariella Burani, Cavalli, but she hightailed it as soon as she could, because she can't stand working under a boss, and set out on her own. She preferred being an artist-craftswoman to having a career in the fashion business. She designs clothes and jewelry, and sells them in her store in Sarzana.

Irene is combative, tenacious; she never gives up. She wants to do what I do, even though she knows first-hand all the difficulties involved. She loves to sing. She never thought she'd be doing this when she was younger, but she's doing it now, facing up to the challenge with all her strength. And no help from me.

I feel very close to all three of my children, and in each of them I see something of myself, renewed and transformed into their individual identities. In their energy, in their youth. The two girls call me *Babbo*—they're Tuscan and that's Tuscan for "Dad." They scold and berate me when, say, at dinner, I go off on some foul-mouthed rant, or when I tease my partner Francesca, Blue's mother, with some innocent obscenity. Blue, on the other hand, is Emilian and calls me *Papà*. He's a big fan of cuss words too.

It was on the *Chocabeck* tour that for the first time we played with 11 musicians on stage—12, counting me. Besides the quintet I've been playing with for years, I added a string section—young kids, first-rate—with a viola, a violin, and a cello, plus a horn section.

I like to experiment, to floor audiences. I've got lots of material that hasn't appeared on my albums. I don't like it when records have too many songs. If it were up to me, I'd do it the old way and make records with eight songs. The music business and the radio stations want songs that last no more than three minutes. I didn't give a fuck—'Un Soffio Caldo' lasts seven minutes. The way songs used to be. Times have changed. Now songs are a format, all-alike. Designed to work on the radio. But *Chocabeck* is a record to be listened to in its entirety. It's not like going into a deli where you pick and choose—a quarter pound of *mortadella* and a quarter pound of salami. I can allow myself to be free.

My mission as a musician is to write in complete freedom.

When I came in next to last at Sanremo, I thought I was a goner. If 'Donne' hadn't worked, that would have been my last chance; I would have given up and found a regular job. When the results were announced, the people from my record company ran for it. If they'd had their way, they wouldn't even have taken me out for pizza after the show. They were embarrassed. I saw my demise in their eyes. All they cared about was the rankings. But I didn't, even though I could see my fate written all over their faces. Sliding doors. I passed 35 exams in veterinary school at the University of Pisa. I knew how to deliver a calf. I would have gone back to school and taken up where I'd left off. I'd dropped out because I needed money and tried to earn it by playing music. Sliding doors. 'Donne' was a hit on the radio. They played "*Du-du-du*" over, and over again. Fans still ask me to play it today, and

I must say, I feel a little embarrassed singing "*Du-du-du.*"

I'm exhausted. Writing a book is a grueling endeavor. The most beautiful finale of all is in *Martin Eden*, when Jack London writes, "And at the instant he knew, he ceased to know." Now I know. I've never undertaken such a hard and honest introspection, a journey inside myself. Never before have I seen so clearly, now that I see nothing more.

Zucchero
Lunisiana Soul, Summer–Fall, 2011

Lightning Source UK Ltd.
Milton Keynes UK
UKOW03f0647240417
299766UK00004B/324/P